LAHORE
1947

Compiled & Edited
by
AHMAD SALIM

SANG-E-MEEL PUBLICATIONS
25, SHAHRAH-E-PAKISTAN (LOWER MALL) LAHORE.

954.9143 Salim, Ahmad

      Lahore 1947 / Ahmad Salim.-Lahore:
Sang-e-Meel Publications, 2003.
    307p.
    Bibliography : p. 305 - 307.
1. History - Lahore. 2. History - Pakistan.
I. Title.

2003
Published by
Niaz Ahmad
Sang-e-Meel Publications,
Lahore.

ISBN 969-35-1421-1

SANG-E-MEEL PUBLICATIONS
Chowk Urdu Bazar Lahore. Pakistan. Phone 7667970
Phones: 7220100 - 7228143 **Fax:** 7245101
http://www.sang-e-meel.com e-mail: smp@sang-e-meel.com
25 Shahrah-e-Pakistan (Lower Mall), P.O. Box 997 Lahore-54000 PAKISTAN
PRINTED AT: ZAHID BASHIR PRINTER, LAHORE.

To,
Ashis Nandy
and
CSDS Friends!

Contents

EDITOR'S NOTE

This work is the result of my continuing study in the Partition stories of diverse dimensions. Fortunately, I got an opportunity to have in-depth interviews with a number of Muslim, Hindu and Sikh refugees in Pakistan, India, Bangladesh and England. I also went through several memoirs and autobiographical accounts on the tragedies of Partition in Urdu, Punjabi, Sindhi and English anthologies. This work is a compilation of such accounts published in India and Pakistan.

Let me admit that this is not a book on the history of Partition that implies a certain scholarship, a running theme on which new knowledge is imparted and so on. Frankly, the pages to follow are a collection of memories for interested readers and students of Partition history.

I would like to express my gratitude to a number of people from whom I have received generous help and encouragement in my research for this anthology. First of all, I must thank Ian Talbot, whose thoughtful introduction is apart a of this book. I am grateful to the late and living authors, portions of whose works are included in this publication. They are: Amrita Pritam; Alys Faiz; B.C. Sanyal; Khushwant Singh; Satish Gujral; Parkash Tandon; Ibrahim Jalees; Gopal Mittal; Fikr Taunsvi; Mian Amiruddin; Jahanara Shahnawaz and others.

I am also indebted to Dr. Mushirul Hasan, Anees Jillani, Najam Sethi and other editors/publishers who allowed me to use excerpts from their publications for this book. Mr Anuj Bahri and India Research Press were the real spirit behind the compilation, completion and production of the first edition. Thanks are also due to Mr Niaz Ahmad and Mr. Afzaal of Sang-e-Meel Publications for bringing out the present Pakistani edition.

Thanks to Hafizur Rahman for his translation from Urdu publications in this book.

July 2002   Ahmad Salim

INTRODUCTION

The 1947 Partition remains the defining moment in the modern history of the Indian subcontinent. Contemporary communal and national stereotypes draw sustenance from the climacteric events which accompanied the British decision to divide and quit. Partition permanently altered the demographic, socio-economic and cultural landscapes of such major cities as Karachi, Lahore, Delhi and Calcutta. Their huge refugee populations have also profoundly impacted upon these conurbations' political life. The continuing effects of Partition at political, cultural and psychological levels extend far beyond the focus on Kashmir which has sometimes been dubbed 'the unfinished business' of Partition. They point to the fact that Partition should be regarded as a process rather than a single historical event confined to August 1947.

The emotional intensity of the Partition process has resulted in a vast cultural outpouring on both sides of the Wagah border. Some of the greatest works of Urdu literature[1] have been produced in response to the trauma. Saadat Hassan Manto's short story, *Toba Tek Singh* has become a symbol of the confused and torn identities arising from separation from one's ancestral home. Rajinder Singh Bedi's *Lajwanti* sensitively uncovers the agonies engendered by the abduction and recovery of women who were Partition's 'greatest sufferers'. The humanist approach to the communal violence has been expressed in the works of Krishan Chander and other progressive writers. Some of the best known Indian writings in English have been produced on the Partition theme by such luminaries as

Bapsi Sidhwa, Khushwant Singh and Chaman Nahal. A number of these works have been made into films. Doordarshan in 1988 serialised Bhisham Sahni's moving Hindi novel *Tamas* which is set in the Partition period.

Partition has until recently fitted less easily into historical discourses than popular culture. Academic history concentrated on the 'high politics' of the British departure from India, rather than on the human dimension of its impact. The work of Anita Inder Singh, *The Origins of the Partition of India, 1936-1947* (Delhi, 1987) and R. J. Moore, *Escape from Empire: The Attlee Government and the Indian Problem* (Oxford, 1982) exemplify this concern with causes rather than consequences. They revealed how the British came to accept the idea of Partition as the only solution to the communal problem which imperilled a speedy and smooth transfer of power. Moore provided the first authoritative examination of Labour Party strategies and policies towards the transfer of power. Singh argued forcefully that the British short-term aims of encouraging the Muslim League as a counterweight to the non-co-operating Congress during the Second World War undermined their long term commitment to a United India.

For many years, Indian and Pakistani nationalist historical discourses reduced Partition to a mere footnote as they dwelt on the triumph of independence rather than its costs. The field was thus left open for communalist writings which for their own purposes emphasised violence, always with the aim to attribute blame to the 'other' party. It was in fact not until almost the Golden Jubilee of Independence that historians began to construct a historical discourse on Partition 'from beneath.'

This enterprise required new sources. Such writers as Mushirul Hasan[2] began to turn to fictional representations

10

to uncover human feelings and emotions. Much of the most exciting work on the 'new' history of Partition has relied on the oral accounts of previously silenced and marginalised social groups. A gendered dimension to Partition has emerged powerfully, for example, from the works of Ritu Menon, Kamla Bhasin[3] and Urvashi Butalia[4]. The extent to which Partition evoked cross-community co-operation as well as brutality and violence is beginning to be uncovered in a major research project by the leading academic and intellectual figure Ashis Nandy. He too is relying extensively on interviews conducted by research teams in both India and Pakistan.

Alongside the concern to recover authentic voices, there has been the realisation that conventional histories which end in August 1947, limit our understanding of Partition's continuing impact. The important issues of refugee rehabilitation and resettlement were at the centre of official and semi-official studies in the 1950s, as exemplified by M.S. Randhawa's work, *Out of the Ashes*,[5] but they have been largely neglected since. Growing concern with the aftermath of the subcontinent's division has placed the locality at the forefront of study. Historians have realised that province-wise generalisations concerning patterns of violence, migration and resettlement cannot account for the considerable variety of refugee experiences. The locality provides the locus for studying how different economic and social groups experienced the complex realities of the Partition process. In many instances these are seen to be interrogating the stylised and stereotypical portrayals of nationalist and communalist discourses. In their recent edition, *The Aftermath of Partition in South Asia*, Tai Yong Tan and Gyanesh Kudaisya begin to examine the experiences of different localities through a consideration of the imprint of Partition on South Asian capital cities.[6]

Lahore provides an important localised context for this new approach to Partition's impact. It was the pre-eminent educational, commercial and administrative centre of the Punjab, the region most affected by India's division. The fact that it was inhabited by around 240,000 Hindus and Sikhs who at the time of the 1941 Census accounted for a third of its total population.[7] Further increases its value as a case study. Much of the city's wealth derived from the commercial activities of its minority communities. Virtually all of the shops in the famous Anarkali Bazaar which stretched for a mile outside of the walled city from Lohari Gate to Nila Gumbad were in their hands. Older established commercial centres in the walled city such as the area around Shah 'Almi Gate and Chuna Mandi were also non-Muslim.

In all, Hindus and Sikhs owned two thirds of the city's shops, four fifths of its factories and paid seven tenths of its urban taxes. In addition to the dominant Hindu and Sikh localities with their distinctive architectural styles, economic and ritual life, non-Muslims conspicuously occupied the new schools and colleges, banks, offices and courts established by the British. Despite the Mughal splendours of Shah Jehan's Shalimar Gardens, Akbar's imposing Fort and Aurangzeb's massive Badshahi Mosque, Lahore was not an Islamic city, but rather possessed a cosmopolitan feel. This still shines through in the nostalgia of such works by former Hindu residents as Pran Nevile's *Lahore. A Sentimental Journey*[8] and Som Anand's, *Lahore. Portrait of a Lost City*.[9] Unsurprisingly, the city was at the centre of conflicting claims, when the boundary commission chaired by Sir Cyril Radcliffe went through its deliberations in July 1947.

Ultimately, numbers not wealth counted in the judgement on which side of the new international boundary Lahore

12

would lie. Within the Lahore district, Muslims accounted for three fifths of the total population. In the city of Lahore itself, the proportion of Muslims was slightly higher, although Hindu politicians claimed that this was the product of boundary changes which had 'gerrymandered' the inclusion of Muslim outlying villages in the city boundaries. The award of Lahore to Pakistan was only made public the day after independence. By that stage, extensive areas of the city which had been inhabited by Hindus and Sikhs were in ruins[10] following weeks of what has been termed a 'communal war of succession' in the city. The cosmopolitan 'Paris of the East' was a distant and poignant memory.

Most studies refer to Lahore only in passing when talking about the Punjab's Partition. Muslim violence against Hindus and Sikhs in the West Punjab was chronicled albeit in a partisan manner in works by Talib and Khosla.[11] Counterpart studies have been produced in Pakistan including such titles as *The Sikhs in Action, Note on the Sikh Plan* and *RSSS in Punjab*[12] designed to show that Muslim attacks in such localities as Lahore were in retaliation for the earlier genocide of Muslims in the Indian East Punjab. The most detailed account of developments within the city has been compiled by the Pakistan Government in a work entitled, *Disturbances in the Punjab 1947.*[13] The work draws on a range of official and party documents, including Lahore Special Branch reports to chronicle the violence from its beginnings on 3 March 1947 through to the aftermath of Partition.

This edited volume brings together writings in English and Urdu translation which shed light on Lahore's five month descent to chaos from March 1947. Some of the pieces are well-known autobiographical accounts of such prominent non-Muslim intellectuals as Khushwant Singh and Som

Anand who worked and lived in the city on the eve of the British departure. Pran Nevile whose book, *Lahore. A Sentimental Journey* has served as a landmark in both India and Pakistan provides a brief personal account of his journey to Delhi in the wake of the violence which followed the resignation of Khizr Tiwana's Unionist led coalition government early in March.

Well-known contributions by former Hindu and Sikh residents are balanced by the accounts from less famous Muslim inhabitants. The piece in Urdu translation by Mian Amiruddin, the Mayor of Lahore on 'Memories of Partition' represents a fresh contribution which is of considerable interest to the historian. It lays bear the conflicting and ambiguous emotions at the time. On the one hand, individuals like Amiruddin could save the lives of members of other communities at considerable personal risk. Simultaneously they could gloat at the removal of their "enemies'" symbolic and physical presence. The bleak sadistic brutality of the Partition era, emerges in a number of the contributions. It is in part uplifted in Satish Gujral's contribution which points to refugee columns not only supplying each other with water and other necessities when their paths crossed, 'but more significantly with profound emotional understanding.'

What emerges from the edition is both the sense of helplessness and the belief that despite the spiralling violence, non-Muslim residents who fled the West Punjab would one day return. In the poignant words of Prakash Tandon, 'the thought that this was a going away for ever, never crossed anybody's mind.' These sentiments are mirrored in interviews conducted with their Muslim counterparts who were driven from their ancestral homes in East Punjab.

The edition points up the anticipatory flight of non-Muslims from Lahore before the demarcation of the boundary. The destruction of the Hindu stronghold of Shah 'Almi marked a crucial turning point in this respect. It also reveals, especially in the piece from Fikr Taunsvi, the psychological effects of Lahore's curfew ridden 'war of communal succession.' 'The air was full of suspicion and terror' Taunsvi noted in his diary, 'that made you think that everyone had a dagger or a bomb hidden on their person.'

The selections provide clues as to why communal harmony broke down in the Punjab. The arrival of refugees with tales of atrocities supported by the gruesome evidence of trainloads of corpses encouraged revenge attacks on minority communities. In the longer term, Lahore and more generally Punjab can be seen as a victim of political uncertainties and communal polarisation elsewhere in India. Contributions also hint at the fact that relations between communities had been correct, but lacked warmth. Social distance, as vividly brought out in B.C. Sanyal's account arose in part because of high caste Hindu concerns about pollution and inter dining. Such attitudes rather than the non-Muslim domination of Lahore's wealth and commerce provided the undercurrent for the politicisation of identities during the Pakistan movement. The Muslim League's claims that Muslims could only live in dignity in their own homeland were not just rhetorical slogans, but struck a popular chord.

From the minorities' perspective, it was not just the circumstances of the 1946 elections and the subsequent bitter campaign against the Tiwana government which prevented their acceptance of a future within Pakistan. But the sense both of superiority which is hinted at in some of these extracts and the fact that a neo-Hindu and Sikh identity had been constructed since the late nineteenth

15

century around hostility to the Muslim 'other' based in part on a selective reading of the 'oppression' of Mughal rule.

Ahmad Salim is well equipped for the task of producing a collection which casts different lights on the Partition experience. A well known poet and Urdu journalist, he has been collecting and compiling stories of Partition for a number of years. He acted as my able research assistant both in advance and during a visit to Lahore in September 2000 which gathered oral histories of migration and refugee resettlement as part of a wider comparative project. He has also established his own Partition-related archive dedicated to the preservation of primary material. While most of his work has been focused on the Pakistan experience, he has visited India on a number of occasions both to attend conferences and to gather further material.

This compilation thus emerges out of a sustained personal and academic engagement with the complexities surrounding the human dimension of Partition. More work is required not only on developments in Lahore, but across North India, before our understanding is complete. Nevertheless, such steps along the way as represented by this volume should be applauded. They contribute not only to scholarship, but to the breaking down of the stereotypes of communal hatred which continue to afflict the subcontinent.

Ian Talbot
Centre for South Asian Studies
Coventry University

References

For a useful introduction to fictional representations of the 1947 Partition see:

[1] John A. Hanson, "Historical Perspectives in the Urdu Novel", in M. U. Memon, (ed), *Studies in the Urdu Gazal and Prose Fiction* (Madison, 1979), pp. 257-84;
M. U. Memon: "Partition Literature: A Study of Intizar Husain",(Modern Asian Studies, 14, 3 (1980), pp. 377-410).
[2] M.Hasan (ed) *India Partitioned: The Other face of Freedom*, vols.1 and 2 (New Delhi, 1995).
[3] R. Menon & K. Bhasin: *Borders and Boundaries, Women in India's Partition* (Delhi, 1998)
[4] U. Butalia: *The Other Side of Silence. Voices from the Partition of India* (New Delhi, 1998)
[5] M.S. Randhawa: *Out of the Ashes.: An Account of the Rehabilitation of Refugees from West Pakistan in Rural Areas of East Punjab* (Bombay, 1954).
[6] See Chapter Seven of Tan Tai Yong and Gyanesh Kudaisya: *The Aftermath of Partition in South Asia* (London, 2000)
[7] The 1941 Census enumerated the Muslim population at 433,170 and the non-Muslim at 238,489.
[8] P. Nevile: *Lahore. A Sentimental Journey* (New Delhi, 1993)
[9] S. Anand: *Lahore. Portrait of a Lost City* (Lahore, 1998)
[10] By mid-July 1947 over 700 Hindu and Sikh houses had been burnt down.
[11] S. Gurbachan Singh Talib: *Muslim League Attack on Sikhs and Hindus in the Punjab 1947* (Allahabad, 1950); G. D. Khosla: *Stern Reckoning. A Survey of Events leading up to and Following the Partition of India* (New Delhi, 1989)
[12] West Punjab Government: *The Sikhs in Action* (Lahore, 1948); West Punjab Government: *Note on the Sikh Plan* (Lahore 1948); West Punjab Government: *RSSS in the Punjab* (Lahore, 1948)
[13] Government of Pakistan: *Disturbances in the Punjab 1947. A Compilation of Official Documents* (Islamabad, 1995)

1

The Sixth River

NINETEEN FORTY SEVEN

AMRITA PRITAM

The most gruesome accounts of marauding invaders in all mythologies and chronicles put together will not, I believe, compare with the blood-curdling horrors of this historic year. Tale after tale, each more hair-raising than the last, would take a whole lifetime to retell. Uprooted from Lahore, I had rehabilitated myself at Dehradun for a while, but later went to Delhi for work and a place to live in. On my return journey. I could not get a wink of sleep on the train. The pitch-black darkness of the night was like a sign of the times. So piercing were the sighs the winds carried and echoed, it seemed we were back in mourning over this Watershed of History. The trees loomed larger and larger like sentinels of sorrow. There were patches of stark aridity in between like the mounds of massive graves. The words of Waris Shah, "How'll the dead and departed meet again?" surged back and forth through my mind. I thought, a great poet like him alone could bewail the loss a *Heer* once had to bear. But who could lament the plight of millions of *Heers* today? I could think of no one greater than Wāris Shah to chant my invocation to. In the moving train, my trembling fingers moved on to describe the pangs I went through.

From the depths of your grave,

Wāris Shah,

Add a new page to your saga of love

Once when a daughter of Punjab wept

Your pen unleashed a million cries,

A million daughters weep today, their eyes turned

To you, Wāris Shah.

The published poem found its way to Pakistan.
Later still, Ahmed Nadeem Kasmi disclosed in his
foreword to a book by Faiz Ahmed Faiz that he had read
the poem in jail. On his release, he recounts having seen
copies of it with common men who would weep when they
read it.

At a BBC interview in London (1972), I was
introduced to Sahāb Kizilbash, the Pakistani poetess, who
exclaimed: "Arre! So this is Amrita...the writer of those
lines! I ought to be embracing her. . . ! " At Surinder-
Kochhar's an evening later, Sahāb and other Pakistani
poets, Saki Farruqui, Fahmida Riaz, Abdullah Hussain, the
famous author of *Udas Naslain*, Nizakat Ali, and Salamat
Ali had assembled. The cultural life of London that night
was enriched by much reciting of poetry. When it was
Nizakat Ali's turn, someone pointed out that he had never
recited without some instrumental accompaniment. Yet, for
one who had written on Wāris Shah, he was chivalrous
enough to consent and his superb voice enriched the airs
afloat that memorable night.

In 1975, Mashkoor Sabri, a famous poet from
Multan came to Delhi for an 'Urs recital. He told us of the
Wāris Shah annual celebration at which a folk-art
exhibition is held, folk-dances are performed, and folk-
songs are sung. The climax of this cultural evening is a

20

Poets' Symposium. This multifaceted programme ends with a half-hour recital of *Heer Ranjha*. The grand stage (100' by 80') on which the *Heer Ranjha* sets form the darkened background, gradually lights up showing Wāris Shah arising from his grave. The sets then continue to change with the shifting light, to synchronise with the lines of the poem. The reverberating sound effects of the finale acclaim a new dawn awakening a new spirit of love.

It was ironically the same poem that a quarter of a century earlier had evoked so much censure and disapprobation, with the Sikhs holding me guilty of not having addressed my invocation to Guru Nanak, and the communists, to Lenin or Stalin. Many a poet conspired to rant against the poem itself....

In the totality of myself as a writer, the woman in me has had only a secondary role to play. So often have I nudged myself into an awareness of the woman in me. The writer's role is obvious. But the existence of that other being have I increasingly discovered through my creative works.

(Excerpt from her autobiography *Raseedi Ticket*)

THE SIXTH RIVER — A DIARY OF 1947

by

Fikr Taunsvi

9 August:

Last evening a bomb exploded in a cinema house in Bhati Gate.

They say the bomb was of British manufacture. That is why fifty persons of Indian origin were killed by it. All the dead were Muslims, so indisputably the man who threw the bomb must have been a Hindu, who, inspired by the British way of thinking, fulfilled the important duty of deciding to destroy the unclean through a British-made bomb. The bodies of the unclean were being conveyed to hospital in *tongas*. Some had half a leg blown away, others had open skulls, and the intestines of still others had been exposed. People were running about, hither and thither. The bazaars were shut and the roads deserted.

Arif and I could not have our evening tea in Nizam Hotel. We couldn't hold our learned converse on politics and literature, nor could we swallow ideas about people's art and about science and philosophy with hot sips of tea. Today the hooligans of Lahore dispelled the notion hidden in the feminine bangles sent to them from Amritsar. After all, how could the brave *thugs* of Lahore tolerate the insulting taunt of the brave *thugs* of Amritsar --- "You women! Put on these bangles and sit at home. This work is not for the likes of you!"

After this the brave could not sit at home, and taking out their daggers and fuses of dynamite and their bombs, pistols and swords, came out on the roads and bazaars. The result was that within an hour of the bomb explosion about a hundred and fifty cowards had been murdered and fifty houses burned to ashes. Since the bazaars were deserted, the police had been posted to watch the beautiful sight of burning houses, and in order to bring empty roads to life again, noisy trucks carrying policemen and the military were roaming all over the place. And then, at night, the musical strains of *Allah-o-Akbar* and *Sat Siri Akal* were dispelling the sadness that pervaded the atmosphere, while crimson red flames and flying sparks from torched houses helped to illuminate the darkness.

So the bombs continued to explode, bullets were being fired all the time, people went on dying in the streets and the curfew was on. The police went on patrolling the streets so that no one dare break the law. The beauteous beloved of religion was being protected in the shade of mosques and temples. Industrialists and feudal lords opened up their cash boxes so that anyone who eyed this beloved with a sinful gaze should be shot at once. One bullet, one dead, fifty rupees! One dagger, one stabbing, sixty rupees! And the one who threw a bomb could get two hundred and fifty rupees. This was the price placed on the life of a heretic, an unclean dissenter. Human bodies were going cheap in the market. Everyone was satisfied --- the rich and the poor, the rulers and the ruled.

This morning I could not get out of the house till ten o'clock. Spent the morning listening to the radio and trying to forget myself in the melodious songs of Shamshad Begum and Sehgal's ghazals. But my mind had become inert. I could find no peace in anything. Ghalib's *Diwan* stood on the table, staring at me. Einstein's theory of relativity lay dozing. Faiz's *Naqsh-e-Faryadi* screamed to be picked up and then lay silent. The Buddha's bust gazed at me like a dumb picture. Art, literature, philosophy, science, were all mute, all in mourning. But their grief was different from that of the washerman who lived on the ground floor and who had become the father of a tiny baby at three in the morning, and who was worried that the bazaars were shut. The sweet-seller who sold milk had locked his shop from inside and was hiding there. He had received no supply today because all milk-vendors are Muslims, and this being a Hindu locality, they couldn't step into it. Hospitals were not functioning, neither were doctors and nurses and medicines, and both the mother and the infant were crying. The children were asking, "Will the curfew never be lifted? Shall we never get milk?"

Desperate with tension and anxiety, the washerman walked into my room. I looked towards Einstein and the Buddha and Ghalib and Iqbal. "Come on. Speak up," I said to them, "What reply have you for this man? What can you do to save his little one? If you can't get the curfew lifted, if you can't bring the nurse to this washerman's house, then why did you give us all this philosophy and literature and culture and knowledge? It were better if one of you had been a Muslim *gujjar* who could walk boldly into a Hindu locality with his milk I wish you had the strength to ask great brains like Jawaharlal Nehru and Jinnah and other statesmen and *maulvis* to wear the guise of this unlettered washerman for a moment. Then you may go and request the British to give you freedom. Then demand Pakistan and Hindustan. Then you will have permission to hold conferences with Labour leader Cripps and Lord Mountbatten, and inform them that we despise each other, that we shall wring one another's necks. We can do without freedom, but we cannot tolerate that there should be two

24

swords in one scabbard, that two civilizations should co-exist in one country. Tell them to draw a line between us and proclaim that we are unconnected and no longer one. Beyond the line the Hindu will rule, this side the Muslim will prevail. Divide our rivers, cut our mountains into two, and also cleave our Punjab into two. Divide our Ravi and Beas, divide our heroines *Heer* and *Sohni*. Otherwise --- otherwise we shall suffer to be cut into pieces but not let ourselves be free. Never!"

But the Mahatma Buddha and Iqbal stared back at me, mute and dumb. The washerman wept while Shamshad sang, "Oh, the lovely rain!"

11 August

As the curfew lifted this morning after 24 oppressive and soul-searing hours I went out. Life was making itself felt again, though in a half-hearted and dampened manner. The fear and tension of the past day still infected the atmosphere, and people stepped out of their houses with care and caution. The air was full of suspicion and terror that made you think that everyone had a dagger or a bomb hidden on their person which they would use any moment against the enemy. People would pause to look behind them, as if all others who walked the streets were not their co-citizens but their enemies. Hundreds of the enemy, each one of them frightened within himself, had emerged from their homes. They were nobody's friends.

After roaming around for a while I got on to the road in the purely Muslim locality that led to my office and where a bomb had exploded three days before. I went this way out of habit, a habit that was embedded in my personal culture. What else could I do? Taking a safer way would be unacceptable to my nature and would amount to mental torture. At one point I was surrounded by flames and smoke as a magnificent building near my office burned with a loud crackling noise. A large crowd was gathered to watch it. It was a strange crowd, consisting of both Hindus and Muslims, and all of them trying to put out the fire. For a moment the conflagration united the two cultures, the two religions. I welcome such a fire, I bow before it with respect, and I am ready to sacrifice at its altar all the world's ideals of philosophy, literature and knowledge for blessing the Hindus and Muslims with a common grief on this eleventh of August.

The upper storey of the structure bore its name: Bishan Das Building. About the ground floor it was stated that it was occupied by a firm of book-binders where scores of workers were employed to bind printed copies of the Holy Quran. Both were on fire: the building of the Hindu and the Quran of the Muslim. On the upper floor some people were trying to extricate the body of a boy of seven or eight from under a heavy girder. So, up above Bishan Das's son was burning while below Muhammad's Quran was in flames. God's law was in flames. And Hindus and Muslims were jointly trying to extinguish the fire. Two swords in one scabbard!

I began to enjoy the spectacle. I had never seen in history anything to match this. We were writing a new kind of history. I walked away. At about ten paces I saw a withered old man lying in a corner with his mouth open. Blood was oozing out of his mouth and his chest. His sightless eyes gazed at the sky, while a policeman brandishing a stick guarded his body. In the square ahead the corpse of a thirty-year old young man rested tranquilly under the caring protection of a sub-inspector of police and five of his men. By his side lay a cloth packet from which wheat flour had burst out. The killer had run away because

26

he was in a hurry. Maybe he had to dispose of a few more heretics before he went home for the day. He didn't even wait for the policemen, one of whom was muttering, "These people have been warned so many times not to go through localities where there is danger, but they don't listen." The torn packet of flour was unable to say anything to this.

After locating Arif I went with him to a Muslim's restaurant to have lunch. The place was more noisy than usual. Most of the people talked in whispers while a few were shouting in a loud voice.

"We'll tear these Sikhs to pieces!"

"We'll drink the blood of these Hindus!"

"We'll not let any of their children go alive!"

This storm of anger and passion was enough to create panic. We were told that the morning had seen the arrival from Amritsar of lorries full of harassed policemen and screaming Muslims. The policemen had been let loose by their officers for they had achieved Pakistan. Maybe the officers thought they no longer needed to work under Hindus in a kind of bondage. They had been disarmed and had fled for their lives. In Lahore they spread all over the city and the volcano of blood and fire had again erupted. A man with a short beard was shouting, "God save us! Have you heard? Nearly 120 people have been murdered since the morning. This city is in for a terrible time."

Arif was in a panic. He was worried about my safety. Suddenly the restaurant began to be closed and everyone rushed out. A crowd shouting slogans was passing on the road while a vehicle hurtled by with the announcement, "From 12 noon curfew has again been imposed, curfew for 90 hours!" I said to Arif that the number of curfew hours had been increased because figures of serious crimes were going up. Crime and curfew were inter-connected. I don't know from where the packet of flour crops up in all this to disturb the mind.

I proceeded towards Anarkali. I didn't want to become curfew-bound at home. As I crossed The Mall the leading literary figures of India emerged from the coffee house. Their art and their writings were not more sacred than the curfew, so, in a frenzy of alarm, they were hurrying home --- Bari, Salahuddin, Yusuf, Mittal. In his typical style Mittal said to me, "Well Fikr, what about going away to India? I'm leaving." I counselled him, "Friend, the curfew will start soon. Go home. In any case you won't be able to leave this country of free people before 90 hours. Better go home now." All the time I was thinking, "Where is this progressive writer off to?"

My head was about to burst. To me it seemed as if I was not in my senses. As I passed by Rahbar's house I remembered that Comrade Rahbar had left the city a few days ago. His parting words were still ringing in my ears, "I'm going but I'll come back. I'll come back. I'll surely come back." There was sound of guilt in his repeated affirmation. Bored by this I had retorted, "Go, comrade, go away." Then, instead of going home I went towards Jagdish's place.

I felt a hammering on my brain. My nerves were on edge, as if they would explode and destroy my body. The continuous sharp chain of the morning's turmoil enveloped me in its tight embrace. Jagdish was not at home, but his servant was busy packing up and putting his things in a heap in the courtyard. Jagdish had gone to find a truck. So, he was also going. That lover of Iqbal, the votary of Islam, the poet of Urdu, was also running away. Mittal was on his way to India. Rahbar had already left. Kapoor was off. And I was being hounded by sleep. Sleep, oblivious of exploding bombs, impervious to the rat-tat-tat of bullets, not caring a hoot for fleeing poets and writers, sleep was overtaking me. I'm going to sleep!

12 August

I ran away from Jagdish's house. He was overwhelmed with worry and frustration which he expressed in loud, literary and intellectual terms. I was getting afraid for him. He was saying, " Brother Fikr, it is no longer possible for me to live here. I have loved this city all my life. But now it is like a mad dog. Today many lorries full of dead and wounded Muslims arrived here from Amritsar and they have stoked the fire of vengeance in the city. Go and see, all the Hindus of Lahore are being slaughtered like goats and sheep and are running to the refugee camps to save themselves. No one will live here now. Neither I nor you. No one. Where will you go? Let's go away to India. Are you ready?"

I told him I was going to Multan.

"Multan!" he exclaimed with astonishment. "You'll go to Multan? Idiot. Multan is now in Pakistan. Have you gone mad? Are you in your senses? The railway station presents the scene of a holocaust. Hundreds have been killed there since the morning, and you are talking of going to Multan. All right. Tell me. Will you buy my radio set, this bed, this wardrobe? What will you give for them. Let me have a hundred rupees and take everything. Okay?"

I ran from Jagdish's house, like a mouse getting out of the paws of a cat. He had set up shop. Tell me, tell me, what will you buy? Do you want Lahore? The waves of the Ravi? Eight annas for every wave. Ranjit Singh's mausoleum? Ten annas for a brick. Sitla Mandir? Six annas

29

for every idol. The Mall itself? I'll take a rupee for every furlong. Speak up. What do you want to buy?

What am I to do! I cannot live in this maddening atmosphere. On the streets of Santnagar people were running in groups, loaded with their goods. I shut my eyes to them; put my fingers in my ears. Some Hindu boys had broken open the shop of a Muslim vegetable-seller and were throwing his wares --- bananas and guavas and oranges --- into the gutter and were laughing away and singing at their achievement. They were drunk with fun and pleasure. I hung my head and walked away, going on and on. Slowly. Maybe I was going towards my house, or was I aiming at the refugee camp? Perhaps it was to The Mall to have a cup of coffee in the coffee house.

The coffee house was shut. Today Lahore's writers and poets and politicians and philosophers and historians had not been able to come out. Miraculously, as if filling a vacuum, an omnibus of Route No.4 drove up. I jumped into it, without thinking where it would take me, and when. It stopped at the Regal Cinema, for beyond that was the danger area.

14 August

What an extraordinary day! It invaded my brain the whole night.

That slim, diminutive short story writer clung to the sides of my brain like a lizard. I don't want to fling him away because I find him absorbing. I am interested by his vague tangled talk. When he speaks it is as if a Plato is hiding in his soul. His apparently imprecise conversation confuses me, My boredom takes the form of irritation. Even so I enjoy this boredom, this irritation, because he

30

admits defeat at every step. Though despite this admission his Plato does not succeed in attaining *nirvana*. Actually he is not easy to describe, like the gloaming between night and day.

And yesterday, in the gathering dusk, when I was roaming most foolishly, and with a kind of bravado, on the lonely, uninhabited road full of unpredictable dangers, he could not reconcile himself to my presence there. Peering at me closely he was trying to find out why this slim, diminutive man who could lose his senses at the sound of a challenge from a Muslim street-killer, whose spirituality, art, and poetry, and more especially his religion, could be done to death with the point of a dagger --- why is he going about with such mindless courage on this perilous road in the raging hurricane of blood and fire, as if his death is not necessary to sustain Islam? Why?

Death with all its horrors awaited the unwary on Lahore's roads and bazaars, at street corners, on closed shop-fronts. It peeped out of the eyes of Hindus and Muslims and Sikhs. Only its satanic gaze did not seem to fall on this slim diminutive poet. Or maybe death is intimidated by his manner, his readiness to approach it with open eyes. You man, it says, who are you? Don't come like this towards me. You don't even know how to walk into the valley of death? Go away. Away! Get out of my sight, you idiot! Go and roam the roads and alleys. I have not been able to understand you. What's your name? What's your religion? People with a faith like yours are not fit to be victims of these times of barbarity, of terror, of blood-thirsty animal instincts. Who are you looking for, by the way? You wish to meet Mumtaz? Do you trust him? That Muslim? You think there is no Islamic spirit and passion left in him that he can't even spare a dagger thrust for you? Don't you know that one dagger can kill twenty, thirty, forty people? It can show the road to eternal peace and

31

salvation to two hundred and forty million deities. It can deal a death blow to the awakened spirit of Islam in seventy million Muslims. Just one dagger . . What kind of a man are you?

Yes. Looking at the strange sight that I presented, with my eyes towards the sky, every hair on Mumtaz's body became tense. Like the sharp edges of a sword lines of sweat formed deep furrows on his face. "Is that really you?"

"Yes," I replied, trying to look worried.

"Where are you going? Don't go. That road passes through the locality where firing went on the whole night. Don't go, in this darkness . . ." He gave me this advice instinctively, without thinking, but somewhat fearfully.

I said to him, "The fact is, *yaar*, I can't live in Santnagar now. I feel that I shall die there and for no good reason. My brain will burst. I am not going anywhere, I have come to stay. I shall stay with you, as long as you do not forget the courtesy of refuge, of protection. There, in Santnagar, I feel stifled among my co-religionists, my Hindu brothers. They are all minor gods, and now the gods are fleeing. They are fleeing from their homes, their courtyards, their streets, their loves, their hates, their habits and their feelings. In fact they are running away from themselves. Why? Why are they running away, Mumtaz? Will this quench the flames of these burning buildings? Will the exploding bombs run away too, along with blood-drenched human beings and these ear-splitting slogans of Bhagwan and Allah? Will these too run away? Tell me, Mumtaz, tell me. I don't know what to do. Should I too run away? But where? I don't know the etiquette of fleeing. If I try to flee I won't know how to find my way out in these numerous ways. Does this way go to your house? You, who were born in a Muslim household, and take this path every day, and are never afraid for a moment; and I who have forgotten the way home and take the way to your house, and am not afraid for a moment, is this the wrong road for me? Do you know where this road ends, Mumtaz? Do you?"

I kept on making this purposeless and meaningless speech, trying to overawe his mind. He took me inside to his sitting room, and threw cigarettes and matches before me. With my head resting on the back of the chair and my feet planted on a bed in the room, I began to smoke. He went inside to get tea for me, but I'm sure he was saying to himself, "What foolishness! But then, what else can he do except be foolish, and terrified." Then he addressed me. "You are safe here. Don't worry about anything. No one will look at you with a threatening eye here." And, as he served tea, he continued to console me. And as I drank his tea I listened to him. At last I asked him, "What do you think of the philosophy of Confucius?"

What a day it was! I can't get it out of my mind.

15 August

The whole night the radio screamed "Freedom! Freedom!"

Today we are free of white imprialism. Mumtaz is happy that our politics has at last found a stable conclusion. Early in the morning I went into his room with an agonized face. Do you know, Mumtaz, that at one minute past midnight we were free, and there was firing the whole night. What has not been freed are *Allah-o-Akbar!* and *Har Har Mahadev!* and *Sat Sri Akal!*. The whole night they were shouting in protest at the top of their voice what

33

sounded like "We don't want to be liberated. We want to remain alive. Freedom will be our death."

I don't know what was wrong with me this morning. I felt as if I had been dipped in a pool of poison during the night. Sparks of hate, irony and savagery flared out of my body, and I was murmuring to myself the verse: "O life, what is this place where you have stopped?"

Mumtaz said, "Are you unhappy at getting freedom?" But I continued to sing that verse to myself. Then he added, "Come, let us celebrate to welcome freedom."

"Yes, Mumtaz, you are right. We should welcome this fairy. We'll greet it with the piles of dead bodies of Hindus and Sikhs and Muslims, with burning buildings and murderous bombs. Haven't you heard? Delhi and Karachi were decorated like brides last night and were celebrating their weddings with music and dance and noisy carousel. It was their night of love. And what did we do in the Punjab, in Lahore? In this night of love the earthen pot of *Sohni*, the bangles of *Heer*, the waving fields of corn, gave the final sacrifice of their innocent children, their young virgins, their greying old people and their manly youths."

Disgusted with my emotional harangue, Mumtaz asked if I would like some tea. His eyes betrayed his thoughts: "From where has this man got so much poison within him? Why is he trying to hide stark reality behind a façade of sentiment? What we are facing today is reality, the truth. His tears cannot wash away that truth."

Maybe Mumtaz was thinking that I hate the rapture that the young man derived from fixing the Star & Crescent atop the secretariat building. No, no, he cannot hate that happiness. Then what? Perhaps, perhaps . . . His senses were again confused. Why can't he analyze the hatred in my soul? He is a psychologist, an expert in probing the human mind. Why is he unable to understand me? He was getting more and more certain that I'm an idiot.

"Yes, an idiot, Mumtaz. The whole of India is dancing with happiness to the tunes of joyful music. But why don't these waves of rejoicing find an echo in me? Mumtaz, tell me the reason for the death of their echo." I went on saying this with my gaze fixed on the ceiling. But where within me lay hidden the secret of their death?

Yesterday while we were talking I had told Mumtaz about the spine-chilling sight I had seen on the Ichhra road. An angry crowd, armed with staves, was gathered in front of a place of worship. The charred dead bodies of the worshippers were being loaded on to a military truck. The sturdy army *jawans* had come in the morning to save these corpses and, extracting them from the burnt-out building, were throwing them into the truck, like sacks of putrefying grain.

The two of us didn't go out of the house the whole day. On this day of freedom we remained imprisoned indoors. Something would try to come out of me and stick in my throat. We had innumerable cups of tea. Many times Mumtaz asked me to go out with him and see the flag of freedom waving on the buildings, instead of the Union Jack. People must be going mad with joy at becoming independent, he said. But I couldn't move. It was as if my feet had forgotten how to walk. I could not bear the thought of witnessing the expression of wild happiness. What sort of joy was this that it contained no rapture? What kind of wine was it that it did not inebriate? What form of music was this that it was emerging in the shape of tears? Shut off this music! Throw away this harp! And go to sleep, go to sleep. Shut your eyes. Let the Joint Defence Council be on the watch. Let the Boundary Commission keep vigil. So that when you open your eyes you may see nine million people soaked in their own blood. Your awakening will be greeted by destroyed habitations, cities razed to the ground, shriveled harvests and dried up rivers. By that time the protectors and guardians will have left. And in any case, what need will there be for protection after that?

Sounds of wailing and weeping were coming from the ground floor of the building. Mumtaz told me that a family had arrived there from Amritsar. Out of a household of fifteen what had survived was just two five-year olds, a girl of seventeen and an old man. Oh my God!

17 August

There has been most horrendous news during the last two days. Contrary to all expectations we have not been able to remain in peace after winning our freedom. Lahore and Amritsar have spread the flames of their fires to East and West. Twelve of the Punjab's districts have been declared riot-affected areas and handed over to a British army officer, because the representatives of sovereign governments have no time from festivity. They have no doubt about the integrity of the British, because the bona fides of a nation which can withdraw from the gold mine of India can only be suspected by a madman. The British officer is loth to see the joint culture of the Punjab being destroyed. That is why he has posted Muslim army units in areas where Hindus and Sikhs are in a majority, and deputed Hindu and Sikh soldiers in Muslim districts, so the free army of this free country may do its duty unhindered. However, despite this obviously sincere measure, heart-rending reports are pouring in.

Reports continue to come in. So do dead bodies. There are hordes of the wounded and the maimed; people wailing and weeping. Why is all this? Why these wounded and their cries? It is said that the military is decimating the

36

killers and murderers, but one doesn't see any killers among the wounded, among the dead. The Muslims think it is Hindu and Sikh villains who are going on with barbarous acts, while the Hindus and Sikhs maintain that it is due to Muslim scoundrels. The only result is increase of responsibility for both sides, with a corresponding increase in the number of the dead. We have gone back to the Stone Age. Apparently British politicians and statesmen think that unless we recede to the Stone Age we cannot attain *nirvana* and the true taste of freedom.

Even today, neither in the morning bulletin nor in the afternoon, did the radio broadcast that great news for which the entire Punjab has been fighting itself and cutting one another to pieces. The Radcliffe Award is still reserved. In this award is that line hidden, that snake lies concealed, which will insinuate its thin poisonous self into the dramas of Kalidas, the "self" of Iqbal, the *Heer* of Warris Shah, the Gitanjali of Tagore and the *ghazals* of Meer and Ghalib, and tell them to turn their faces away. "Look," it will say to them, "you starving values, there lies your share of the meat. Yours and yours. Recognize it, snatch it and dig your teeth into it." But the hungry are still waiting and the snake still lies coiled in Radcliffe's basket. Where has this snake come from? Do you know, Mumtaz?

Did you listen to the speech that Churchill made in the dance hall of jugglers when Britain threw two pieces of meat at us in the form of India's freedom? He said, "This will be written down in history in golden letters." It made Churchill's past open up before me. Darkness! Darkness! Atlantic Charter! And I was pleased with Churchill at this darkness. My leaders were pleased at it too, while Gandhi sat in Calcutta begging for peace and amity. But those who had this gift to give him had spread themselves all over the Punjab, in every city and every village. They were making demented slaves aware of freedom by piercing them with bayonets, by setting fire to their hovels, by turning them out of their homes and their fields.

In sheer ennui Mumtaz and I went out. The green crescent waved over houses and shops, but the flags seemed to be appealing to the heavens. Their fluttering did not carry the sound of happiness. There was no spontaneous triumph in them that we used to see in the Union Jack. People stood about in small groups talking in a low voice, with defeat, sadness and fatigue on their faces, as if they were saying, "What is the use? What use is all this?" Little children were selling small flags. "One *anna, babuji*, only one *anna*." They gathered around us, each insisting that his flag was the best. Mumtaz bought one, but when I said, "What for?" his answer was, "Otherwise we'll become conspicuous. Now we are bona fide Muslims. No murderous rascal will suspect us." Okay, I muttered, Okay. The boy took the *anna* and leapt towards a cigarette shop to smoke a *beedi*; the free son of a free country. One flag, one *beedi*. The flag bearing the authoritative seal of Islam. Was this flag the proof of Islam?

I lovingly stroked the flag on Mumtaz's bicycle and said, "Mumtaz, I shall be a loyal citizen of Pakistan. But have you heard? The tricolour was not allowed to be hoisted on the district courts in Amritsar, because that would have been an insult to Guru Nanak. The Guru of Mardana and Bala. Only the flag of the Guru should be flown in the city of the Guru. And this tricolour? What is it but the pennant of Hindus and Muslims and Sikhs and Christians and Achhuts and God knows how many other riff raff! The Guru's flag is higher than it. Now its the flag of religion, the flag of faith, the Hindus' flag, the Sikhs' flag, the Muslims' flag."

Anarkali felt like a corpse, and lay there as if it was a lifeless body. Sad and grieving. One of the buildings was still smouldering. They say it contained goods worth millions and was owned by a big Hindu merchant. Just opposite to it the magnificent shop of a Muslim merchant had been reduced to ashes. This merchant too had made millions through the black market during the war. Pasted on a half-burnt wall of this shop were the words "This is now the property of Pakistan." At a *paan* kiosk a miscreant wearing a cap at a rakish angle looked at us with suspicion. Mumtaz went up to the *paan-wallah*, salaamed and asked for a paan. The rakish cap seemed disappointed and went its way. So did we. The clock in Anarkali chowk stood still at five minutes past seven. Time had stopped. Its feet had refused to march. The pendulum did not move. Maybe it was thinking, "What is all this? The handcuffs worn by the convicts for centuries have snapped open. Free again, they were madly whirling in the dance of death and fire." Time was surprised: how could this happen? Maybe it couldn't keep its balance and had gone ahead.

A huge stately temple near the chowk was on fire. Openly and shamelessly, and nobody had the nerve to stop it from burning itself. The cloud of smoke was thick and intense. Scores of gods and deities had been imprisoned in this temple ---Krishna, Rama, Shivji, Parvati, Hanuman --- all were consumed by the fire. So were the laws of *Manu*, the *Rig Veda*, the *Ramayana* and the *Shastras*. Their souls had left their bodies and they were now free of the material world, The head priest had run away, along with his female companions.

A mammoth idol of Hanuman lay in pieces in the courtyard. What a hero he was! It is said that once he fell from a flying object and crashed against a boulder with not a scratch to show for his mishap. He was lion-hearted, a fearless son. And now he was lying in pieces in the temple. The smoke also carried the scent of sandalwood and incense. Today, in the *yagna* of human beings it was the gods who were performing the sacrifice of fire. I asked a policeman who was dozing at the gateway of the temple, "I say, will the priest of this temple ever come back?" The man's mouth was agape with astonishment. "For God's sake, *babuji*, what a joke!" So, invoking the Almighty, Mumtaz and I lighted our cigarettes.

Just ahead of the temple a long line of houses was dancing in the blaze. It was as if houses had acquired the habit of getting burnt and it was a daily occurrence for them now. "Mumtaz, haven't we stopped feeling sorry at these burning houses? If they must get burnt, let it be once a week, or every two or three days. But this daily fire, getting burnt every day without fail, loses its charm." Mumtaz got hold of my hand and dragged me away. Maybe he had noticed the poisonous tears within me and was anxious to protect me. He thought if this poison continued to devour me then one day, one day. . . .

On our way back he bought another little flag for an *anna*. Its good to be careful.

19 August

Radcliffe has announced his award. The culture of Bengal, its art and music and dance have been divided. The green fields of the Punjab, its songs and its romance have been torn apart. One strange feature of this partition was that both the Hindus and the Muslims are dissatisfied. But to what purpose this dissatisfaction? This was a verdict of fate, and fate lay in the hands of Radcliffe. Serious observers were terming this dissatisfaction as sentimental nonsensical in view of the fact that political leaders on both sides had committed themselves to accepting Radcliffe's verdict, whatever it turned out to be. Mumtaz had bought a map of the Punjab, and as the details of the new boundary were given out over the radio he accordingly went on drawing the line on it with a pencil. He was making the snake, a thousand-mile long snake. When he saw that the snake had thrown his hometown, Batala, to India, his face grew red with anger. I could imagine millions of other faces growing similarly red with anger and indignation. They must be screaming, "Why wasn't our home included in Pakistan?" "Our place of birth should have gone to India!"

Millions of faces were wreathed in torture, disappointed, frustrated. But what was the remedy? The snake had been sent by Fate, and Fate was neither concerned with Mumtaz nor with Batala. It had only to follow divine orders. Mumtaz's throat was choked with tears. "This is an evil conspiracy," he was saying. In a loud protesting voice he was telling the result of the award to other neighbours, other *babus* like him, in the street. Writhing within himself he was thinking, "Ninety per cent of Batala city is Muslim. How can it go to India? This is rank injustice, an atrocity. No, it cannot be like this." His veins stood out with anger. As I looked at him I was frightened by his condition. How could I calm him, give him solace? I wanted to lift him out of this small world and throw him into the wide international world.

"Look, Mumtaz," I wanted to say, "Just come out of your Batala shell. This is a collective tragedy and not yours alone. You believe in individuality as a writer, but who is bothered about individuality today. The world is fast getting divided into two fronts. In the process of its rotation and revolution our planet has come to a crossroads. Those who understand it as a planet are waiting to see what it does now, what the partition of India and Pakistan presages. Their new birth is but a small part of the planet's orbit. What are you? What is your Islam? What is my Hinduism? Nothing at all. We are just pawns, my dear. Wherever the chess player wants us to go he places us there. He places Batala in India, and sends Nankana Sahib to Pakistan. The other pawns are shouting ---we won't allow this game to go on, this is cruelty, injustice. But the play goes on, Mumtaz. And it will go on till it ends. Look at that bright light, that spark turned into fire, which is giving the same light to the Himalayas, to Arabia, to Batala, to Nankana Sahib. The same heat, the same passion. Look, look at its effulgence, half hidden in darkness. The darkness that is violating us, robbing us of our dreams."

But Mumtaz had gone downstairs. His state of mind, his pain, his grief were about to shatter his brain. I called after him, "Mumtaz, Mumtaz, have a cold bath otherwise you'll go mad. These are days of madness. Madness, barbarity and torture have spread their wings in the atmosphere. I know that your darling Achha, your dear mother and all your other relations are in Batala, and Batala is caught in India's net. And if today Sikhs and vandals and ferocious animals are rampant in India, what can you do? My wife and my daughter are here in Pakistan. What can I do? But then, look at me. I am sitting calmly here, reading Iqbal and studying Goethe, although my skull seems about to burst. My nerves are on fire. But I am satisfied. I don't see any deceit in the Radcliffe Award. Your lovely son, your Achha, will come to you. If you have faith in your love and its sacredness, your Achha must come to you. Yes, Mumtaz, he will come."

But Mumtaz was nowhere and I was addressing empty air. His servant told me he had gone to look for a lorry. "God knows what will happen now *babuji*. Mumtaz Sahib seems to be losing his mind."

It is evening now and Mumtaz is not back. I am getting increasingly worried. Sometimes I laugh, sometimes I smile and sometimes I become silent. In this ocean of silence I swim far and wide but I do not espy the shore. All that I can see everywhere is distrubance, storms and fighting. Blood and fire, blood and fire. This fire has spread all over. From the cities it has erupted in the villages, in the shed where village people sit together, in the fields, in thatch cottages. Its flames can be seen leaping everywhere. The whole of the Punjab is on fire. A flame is touching the face of Achha in Batala. In Taunsa the veil of my wife's *saree* is being singed by it. In my imagination I have got to my village. My little daughter, busy playing, goes into Ali Muhammad Butt's house. Ali Muhammad picks her up and smashes her body against the ground. Her bones have become powder.

Ali Muhammad is my childhood friend. We used to play together in the street. Now he is a big landowner and occasionally writes me letters full of affection. He has brought my daughter's dead body to my house and says, "Forgive me, friend, I didn't break off this branch. It was a sharp and violent gust of wind. It just fell in my courtyard." He is crying. There is noise of wailing in the village. Maybe the Mahsud tribe has again attacked, and the Hindus and Muslims are jointly resisting them. Maybe the Hindu and Sikh military has started killing Muslims. Maybe the Muslims have begun to murder the Hindus. My little one is lying dead on the ground. Ali Muhammad hands over his six-year old son Rasheed to me. "Smash him on the ground, brother, so that my sin is expiated, so that I am punished, so that peace comes to my heart. Smash him, my friend." I hug that little flower of a Rasheed to my bosom. "Go away, Ali Muhammad, you dog. You are mad, mad. Why don't you get yourself treated. No, I will not hand over Rasheed to you. He's my son, my son."

During the last four or five days I have felt as if I am hanging in mid-air, as if living in a dream. Bitter, violent realities confront me on all sides and are enough to shake me out of my coma but I can't get rid of my sleep. I haven't seen Mumtaz all these days. I am groping in the dark. He too must be groping in the dark The universe is rotating like a whirlwind in the all-embracing darkness. I try my hardest to make my mind concentrate on one thing, one point of view, but it slips out of my grasp. I can't get my grip on anything. If I had aeroplanes I would have bombed out of existence those scoundrels who are killing people in the trains which, soaked in the blood of Muslims, then arrive in Lahore. Dead bodies pile up on the platforms. So that the railway platforms of Amritsar, Ludhiana and Jullundhur should be equally washed with blood, groups of Muslim *mujahids* fall upon the trains carrying Hindus and Sikhs out of Pakistan, so that the people of India should not think of them as shameless cowards. What madness!

O God, why don't I come out of my sleep? Why doesn't Mumtaz wake up? Why don't Jinnah and Nehru blink their eyes. Now that independent governments have been formed in India and Pakistan, and the people want them to function and are behind their leaders, ready to give their lives at their behest, why is the public getting itself butchered without orders from them? The leaders have not asked them to die fighting, to burn down whole habitations, to turn out the Hindu from Pakistan and the Muslim from India. Where has this new form of hatred come from. Its lines are not familiar, we never saw it before. What do these people want? Just to fight? To fight without a cause? Freedom came to us nearly ten days ago, but the fighting goes on. It is beyond understanding, this haze-filled flood of hatred which is carrying all of us on its crest. It is an ocean of blood which attacks us and then passes over our heads.

Mumtaz goes out every morning. He is in search of a lorry that can bring his darling Achha and his mother and sisters and other relations from Batala. Every evening he comes back disappointed, for the Pathan lorry-owner wants a thousand rupees for the trip. Mumtaz doesn't have that much money. Meantime Achha waits for him; Achha, the souvenir of his old love. But now love has become a marketable commodity, and the dealers are making thousands because of love and selling it in the bazaar. Mumtaz goes every day to this market. His love is imprisoned in that Pathan owner's lorry, and the Pathan wants his price to release Achha. All that Mumtaz has is his collection of short stories, books on the psychoanalysis of Freud and Adler, theories about art for art's sake and art for life's sake. For the Pathan these are not legal tender. He wants hard cash.

I keep on looking at a haggard and weak old woman on the opposite roof. From the distance between us she looks like a statue. This statue is placed their every morning and till evening stares at space and the sky. Mumtaz tells me that this statue was alive till a week ago, it breathed, spoke, laughed and walked about. But then, they say, a star fell from the sky and dazzled her sight, stopping her breath. The old woman thinks the star was her son, but for a killer he was a Muslim and therefore deserving of death. The killer has turned her into a statue that glares at the sky with lifeless eyes from dawn to dusk, trying to see her son in the fallen star.

Oh Mumtaz, what shall I do? Stop commenting on the news about the riots. I can no longer bear to listen. There is a vacuum in these reports, and that vacuum can only be filled by Achha. I know your Achha will come back to you, though you say I am trying to console you

45

with assurances that have no basis. My friend, you are changing, and changing remarkably. The Plato inside you is dead, and you are like a bit of mercury for which there is no calm. You have no confidence in yourself, no control over yourself. You are bored with my emotional outbursts. You will make me mad too, and I don't want to go mad. Shall I go away?

This evening I went to Qateel's. There was no trace of worry on his face. His curly hair carried a new sheen and his visage shone as if it had been washed by the waves of a new life. He told me he had got married to a friend of his, a Hindu actress. The *maulvi* of his street had solemnized the marriage for five rupees, and asked him to inform him at once if the girl feels threatened by any rogue or vagabond. "I will set the man right for she has recited the *kalima* in his presence." I said to Qateel, "No one will harm her and the *maulvi*'s help will not be needed, because by spending five rupees you have saved a human life. For me this is the greatest happiness. But tell me, Qateel, how come this new spark of liveliness in your face?"

Qateel let off whirls of cigarette smoke towards the sky and said, "It is the culmination of romance." He is looking for a new house now, because his neighbours say he cannot be allowed to live there with a Hindu girl.

29 August

I couldn't sit still. In a fit of disquiet I went out. The state of inaction continued in the city's life, although something akin to a little liveliness had impregnated it, though there was a kind of fatigue and helplessness in it. The Walton Training School had been converted into a refugee camp. This served to provide a new kind of movement to the people. People were coming and going.

46

Lorries full of dead bodies passed before me. Soaked in blood they had been sent by those in Hindustan as a gift for Pakistan. Those who had the duty to receive this gift bore a determined look, as if they were saying to themselves, "We shall send a bigger gift across the border."

I walked on, looking at everything, and trying to re-acquaint my eyes with the ways of my beloved Lahore. These buildings, of which city are they? Where have these roads been brought from? From where have all these people infiltrated into my city? I felt like stopping at a crossing and shouting at the top of my voice, "Brothers! O you savages! Get out of my city and go to the wilds of your ancestors. Who asked you to come here? Go away, wherever you came from, for you have not yet been blessed with human traits."

But I couldn't shout at any crossing. People were saying that now no Hindu and Sikh can live in Lahore. But why? I felt as if someone had struck me in the brain. Why, why can't I live here? I who have roamed these streets, I who have left the sounds of my songs on its roads. These tall buildings hide the gleam of my tears, the echoes of my laughter, the buds of my smiles. Who can stop me from living here? No, I will not go away. You idiots, I understand my responsibility to this new state better than you. I have developed my mind here. I have painted the walls of this city with my colours. This is my city. How can you know what it means to have a city of one's own? Go and ask Jawaharlal and Jinnah. Have they ever felt the touch of this city's roads and bricks and fed their glances on its angles and turnings? If not then they have no right to ask me to leave.

At a street corner on The Mall I asked a *tonga-wallah* if he would take me to the railway station. He was a Muslim. But if he was a Muslim why didn't he plunge a dagger into me? No, he couldn't be a Muslim. Drowned in

47

these thoughts I got into the *tonga*, on the road to the station. It was the same road, the same crossings and turnings, but not a Hindu or Sikh was in sight. Where had they all gone to. They say there were four lakh Hindus and Sikhs in Lahore. What had happned to them? The *tonga-wallah* assured me with authority and confidence that all the unbelievers had gone into the camps.

The station, the magnificent railway station of Lahore was silent, as if it had been strangled. Absolutely silent. There was the noise of thousands of people, but this noise could not dispel the building's stillness. Barbed wire had been put up all around the station, overseen by the military, and people were bringing the wounded from the platforms. The wailing and crying of relatives had turned the place into a house of mourning. A relief camp had been set up, and the wounded and the dead were being loaded on to lorries for being taken away.

I shook my head violently, as if getting the dust out of it. Then assuming a normal demeanour, I went to the booking office where a soldier was on duty. I asked for a ticket to Multan. The man gave me a surprised stare and replied, "No trains are going anywhere." I returned to The Mall. The Coffee House was closed, so was Cheney's Lunch Home. Just opposite these two was the road that led to Santnagar where I lived. For a moment the road looked strange to me. Getting hold over myself I walked over to it. The whole of Santnagar was deserted, and there was not a soul in sight. All the house-doors were adorned with locks but I still knocked at a few of them. The only response I got was the caw-cawing of crows and the screams of hungry birds. Everyone had gone. How cruel of them to leave the stillness of death behind!

This was the *paan-wallah's* kiosk; here was a hospital; here sat the old woman with her spinning wheel; at this point an aged cobbler repaired and polished shoes.

All of them were gone. Water taps were still running at places. They seemed to ask me, "O Poet, will our clear pure water go to waste? Where have all the thirsty folk gone?" Military soldiers stood at crossings. Cows and buffaloes, their udders bursting, roamed about with no one to accept the offer of their sweet and beautiful milk. The atmosphere had been orphaned, paradise had been lost and no one knew where Adam and Eve had gone.

I wanted to laugh violently --- violently enough the blow off the roofs of the houses and make the taps squirt their water on the clouds. I should then open my eyes to an eerie landscape in which I should be alone, left to give birth to a new life, with everything fresh . . . But my laughter was stifled, because when I opened my eyes I was in the refugee camp for Hindus and Sikhs. These people had left heaven and come to this hell, and were happy that their faith had been saved. There was bustle and noise everywhere with goods and chattels being loaded on to lorries in an overwhelming mood of despondency.

"Where are you off to, my friends, you progeny of *rishis* and *munis*, where are you headed for?" On every face was a vague triumphant smile. "We are going to Hindustan, to our country, our homeland." And I left the camp of my compatriots or go back to a foreign land. Mumtaz was not back. Maybe he has not been able to get his love released by the Pathan lorry-owner.

31 August

Today I met Arif after 22 days. His eyes shone on seeing me; I found the glow in his eyes familiar, as if I was looking into a mirror. I felt as if I had been wandering for centuries in search of this radiance. "I say, Arif, where were you hiding this light so far? Let me bathe in it to my

49

heart's content." But the light began to fade, as if it was being overtaken by the shadow of some grief. I could sense the shadow, for today life is composed of this shadow all around me. Arif told me his family had at last reached the camp from Amritsar, barely escaping with their lives. He was going to the camp to meet them. A young sister was still missing. Arif's father had insisted on staying on in Amritsar and Arif didn't know what to do. His worry had a bitter-sweet quality in it. The old man's resolution made him proud, but he knew what that stubbornness would lead to, and that left him in a trauma.

"Comrade Fikr, where have you been. I was greatly concerned on your account. Come, my friend, let me embrace you." "Before you do that," I said, "go and meet your family. That is more important. I'll see you tomorrow. But I must say your father's persistence has had a strange effect on me. OK, we'll talk about it tomorrow. But I may tell you that I don't want to live in Ichhra any more. I don't see this light in the eyes there."

I roamed about with Qateel who seemed to spend his time smoking *beedies*. His film company had failed as the proprietor had run away, and now he was starving. He was also looking for a house. There was no shortage of vacant houses in Lahore now, for their occupants had left and these houses were shouting for new occupants. Our search took us to a grand building in Paisa Akhbar owned by a Hindu businessman. We took possession of it, Qateel, Arif and I. Tomorrow we shall move into it. This locality is famed for its killer-vandals who have given a good account of their bravado during the riots. This was the place where a miscreant had promised to provide safety to a widow and her two daughters and taken 5,000 rupees from her as protection money. He disposed of his charges by throwing them into a burning house next door. For this act of bravery the headman of the locality had permitted him to ransack

50

and burn down three other houses. He was now living the life of a decent gentleman.

Tomorrow I shall be leaving Ichhra. The outlines of Mumtaz's face are no longer clear to me, and his Platonic thought is caught in a whirlpool. Sitting under the tap he bathes in cold water five times a day and smokes his *hookah* incessantly. He seems to be hiding something from me, but he does it in a way that is not incomprehensible to me. He is in some kind of agony but refuses to recognize it as such. I wish I could share his troubles with him. But it is not easy to share thoughts with this strange man. He sees only the dark side of everything new that he comes across, and then seems to say, "That's all, you are to think no more about it."

I have been thinking the whole day about an intriguing piece of news from across the border. The Maharajah of Patiala has announced that a large body of men from the state forces has deserted along with their weapons. It is said that the *Maharajah* is greatly perturbed at this. But what could he do? The men didn't take permission from him before deserting. What I fail to understand is where this large body of deserters has gone? Unless this can be found out what conjectures can one make? But then why make conjectures? I'm sure the *Maharajah* couldn't have stooped so low as to purposely allow his men to take part in the prevailing plunder and murder.

2 September

Why all this? Why are things happening like this? I have spread out my alms cloth in the darkness, but the strong winds of this darkness are tearing it to shreds. I can

51

here it being torn. Kapur was right when he said that we the self-styled representatives of knowledge, literature, culture and science are deluding ourselves. The conjectures of the ignorant and the uneducated are closer to reality than ours. Was he really speaking the truth? Are we who are ignorant? Why can't we feel the pulse of the people? Why don't the masses fit in with our concept of them? I insist that things cannot be this way --- people living together for centuries cannot set fire to each other's hovels and homes and standing crops, and then laugh at the sight. They cannot force others to applaud when they smash their own centuries-old traditions.

The fire continues to spread and its getting darker and darker. The raging sanguinary flood of hatred, contempt and destruction has spread in every corner of the two Punjabs, and the two confront each other like Cain and Abel. Don't you want to cry, doesn't your heart want to explode when brother kills brother? Have the pangs of separation turned into stone? How can you tolerate that Muhammad Hasan's laughter should suddenly cease, that Ram Prashad's melodious voice should go silent? Who told you this laughter was not ours, that this melody was that of a stranger?

Standing astride the corpses of this laughter and this melody who are you calling out to? Who are you welcoming? Who are you waiting for with hope in your eyes? Who is this clothed in saffron invoking the name of Shivaji and raising the slogan of Ram Raj; and who is this in green uniform sporting the star and the crescent? What are the two saying to you? Strangle this laughter and asphyxiate this melody? What is this demonic magic that has got hold of you that with blind-folded eyes and sealed lips you are marching like an army of barbarians, a herd of wild animals, and you have shot your Muhammad Hasan, your Ram Prashad, your Ram Singh. You march with spears raised high and guns held aloft in the rat-tat-tat of machine guns, and following you are the armies of *Maharajahs* and *Nawabs* who are supposed to have mutinied to bolster your courage so that your spirit of *jehad* and holy war does not slacken. What a noise! Children scream. Mothers are frantic. Wives have been separated from husbands. Maidens have lost the sense of virginity. Tears dry up before they can flow. Love has lost its mad fervour. Beauty is dead. And you! You!

But what is all this to you. You are paralyzed, blind beggars with some bread of charity in your begging bowls that you are dipping in blood. Tempered by the flames of fire colour is coming into the piece of bread and you are happy, delirious, at piling up dead bodies around you. You have gained victory over the terrorized look of virgins, over the flower-like children impaled on your spears. Making Muhammad Hasan feel like a stranger and pointing a pistol at Ram Prashad you are triumphant that the standard of your beggary is attaining great heights and you are marching towards the highest point of humanity. You have discovered your lost paradise, and we, what have we got?

I asked Arif if he had found his lost cousin. But he too seems to be dreaming, a dream that has broken in mid-air, as if something heavy has fallen on it. Maybe it is Ram Raj. The sequence is snapped, and, like me, he is trying to join the ragged ends. He just shook his head and said, "Then what?" as if trying to recall something. Was it the naval mutiny, or the rebellion of the peasants in Bengal, or the rise of the Free India Army with the slogan "On to Delhi!" reverberating all over the country? Then what?

"Comrade Fikr," he said, "What happened then? There was such a blinding dust storm, I can't even remember its colour --- was it black or blue or yellow? Trees were uprooted. It was a strange dust storm, quite different from the usual kind. It was blowing the wrong way. Strikes and handcuffs were all lost in it and you couldn't hear anything in its shrieking wildness. It was carrying everything with it, and its feel, its touch, left a delicious taste. Some people say it was the taste of freedom. What was it, Comrade Fikr?

I shook Arif by the shoulders and said, "This was the middle link. Don't try to put the dream together. This hymn of happiness has now reached Delhi, and the musician in saffron has commenced playing Holi with innocent blood there too. Buckingham Palace and Shivaji have come to an agreement, Let's go to office."

From today I have started going to office regularly. There are signs of balance returning to life in Lahore, and I am trying to forget a lot under the cloak of this balance, obsessed as I am by the desire to resume my normal life. The arrow has been shot from the bow, and I am trying to get rid of the nightmare that Delhi's grand Jami Mosque may be threatened. I hope the bright school children of Jamia Millia have resumed their lessons, There is a fine air in the shadow of the Qutb Minar, and I am going to office. Escapist! Yes, that is what I am, representative of progressive writers. Escapist! Long live literature!

5 September

Everyone was in a daze, and everyone was quiet. And I was neither puzzled nor silent. I was engrossed in my efforts to bring about normalcy. Nothing surprised me any more, howsoever terrible the news. Today in such-and-such city a thousand Hindus and Sikhs were massacred. Today at X railway station two thousand Muslims were put to the sword. In village Y young women were stripped of their clothes and made to march naked in the streets of India.

Today a train reached here with just two people alive, and left the unnecessary burden of dead bodies on the way. That's all? Come on, tell me some big news. Tell me that that no one is alive in the whole of Punjab today, except the cabinet ministers whom death has left behind to look after the government. Tell me that today bloody hooligans thrashed Jawaharlal Nehru to an inch of his life in Connaught Place, because he had run barefoot out of his bungalow and had ordered the army to shoot the marauders and looters. But in deference to the Prime Minister of India the bullets in the rifles of the army men had gone to sleep. Nehru had defied the ruffians to make a target of his white cap. Tell me, tell me . . . But what us the use? I am now inured to such news.

Today Arif received a severe scolding from Qateel for handing over to the police all the goods in the house of which we had taken possession. He should have followed the example of the police and kept some of the things for himself. A chair, a radio set, a sofa. O foolish man, you lost everything in Amritsar, your house was burned down and here you are displaying your senseless nobility in Lahore! But Arif was silent. There was nothing but darkness before his eyes, and in this darkness mobs passed by him, open-mouthed. They were looting houses and shops, looting entire cities. By the railway line were littered silk veils, ornaments, trunks, bedding and dead bodies, and everyone of the mouth-gaping mobs was trying to assuage his hunger and thirst for worldly goods. Now was the time to become prosperous. The old law was breathing its last, and new laws were being framed. Meantime people looted other people.

On a string bed before me lay a few books, two slates, a couple of copy books, a child's wooden writing board. I had found this loot, this booty, in the house we had occupied, the schoolroom belongings of a fifth class

55

student whose quest for knowledge had been nipped in the bud and who couldn't carry his things with him when he ran away to save his life. Wherever he was he must be saying to his mother, "I want my old slate, my old books on which I had written my name. I don't want these new things. O mother!" But the boy's cries were drowned by the noise in the courtyard on the ground floor of the house. This was the din raised by beggars. The new beggars, the refugees who were shouting for something to eat. The big man of the locality had opened a free kitchen and was doling out *daal* and bread and rice. The crowd was lauding his act and praying for him. May God recompense him for his goodness!

I told Qateel's new wife that God had already rewarded the big man. He has taken possession of four houses. A truly noble person. He was a millionaire even before the riots, says his prayers five times a day and takes hold of empty houses. He distributes food and earns the benediction of the poor refugees.

Today Arif, Qateel and I again had tea in Nizam Hotel and discussed literature and science. The noise in Anarkali was deafening, before which the poetry of Meer and Ghalib could not hold its own. I asked Arif what the noise was all about. He told me how a caravan had arrived that morning from Delhi and had described India's capital as being washed in blood. The instigators in saffron had got there, so had probably the mutinying troops from Patiala with their stolen weapons. They had entered the city like conquerors. The troops of Nadir Shah had commenced the massacre.

Do you know who had cursed Nadir Shah, who had thrown that dirty word at him that set off the massacre? I know, I know. But Nadir Shah was a conqueror. It was different now. The verses of Meer and Ghalib had been enslaved, and slaves had no right to live in a free country. The caravan from Delhi has arrived in Lahore. Jawaharlal is literally begging for peace. His appeal, the appeal of civilization, the appeal of Gandhi, are trembling in that atmosphere. In his loin cloth and his walking staff in hand, Gandhi has run from Calcutta to Delhi. "Listen to me!" he screams, "Listen. Don't kill the Muslims, they are our brothers. If you go on like this then kill me too, kill your Gandhi too!"

"Hn! The fool! What do we lose if we kill you? Go away, don't give us your prayer meetings and hymns and your fasts unto death. Take them and go and sit on a peak in the Himalayas. That is your proper place. What are you doing here anyway? Why do you poke your nose in our affair, an affair between brothers? It's people like you who have destroyed us."

But Gandhi is still enveloped in the senselessness of his simple beliefs and has come over to Delhi. There he stands on the steps of the Jami Mosque resting on his staff. "Come, come," he shouts, "listen to what the Quran says you devotees of the Vedas, you lovers of Krishna and followers of Guru Nanak. Come sing with me in this tune of the Arabs. Sing, you human beings, sing with me!"

But Gandhi sings alone. Arif, Qateel and I go on with our tea. The verses of Meer and Ghalib go on screaming in Anarkali. A caravan is proceeding on foot from Lyallpur towards the Indian border, and is attacked by a blood-thristy horde. There is panic. The screams of the refugees echo in Gandhi's ears and he responds again and again, "Kill me too! Kill your Gandhi too!"

They say there was a king in the old days by the name of Muhammad Tughluq. His hobby was to take his people from city to city and rule over them wherever they halted. My mind goes back to the India of 400 years ago. Muhammad Tughluq is roaming around with his people and every day thousands of them die, sacrificed to his whim. They die of starvation, of trudging with him over hundreds of miles, and there is no water in sight. But Muhammad Tughluq goes on with his work. For he is king, the deputy of God on earth. It seems that even after 400 years the people of today have not been able to rid themselves of that monarchy. They too are dying --- of thirst and fatigue. On both sides the monarchs go about saddled with their people. Nine million of them are to go through an agreed exchange of populations. Nine million have abandoned their houses and fields and their cattle and have come to live in camps. Was it necessary, inevitable? Many wise observers say it was not only necessary, it was naturally called for. Why should a person live in another country as a slave? I am a fool, so is Arif's father who thinks Amritsar is his homeland and refuses to leave it.

What will happen now? Where are we headed for? What kind of monarchs are these, and what kind of people they have. What sort of freedom is this? I am again swamped by questions. Another hurricane of destruction is rising from the border line at Wagah. Hatred has been disguised as truth. People are getting up, being killed, running like mad, having their legs cut off and heads bashed in, losing little children, their virginity ravished, shouting and screaming, but doing all they can to get across this line, either towards this side or that side. On one side of the line floats the Tricolour amid slogans of Hindustan Zindabad! On the other flies the Star & Crescent amid shouts of Pakistan Zindabad! Man has staged a strange drama of life and death for man. The show goes on. On one side of the line is life, on the other death; on one side is death, on the other life. Does this line really symbolize life and death?

Yes, this is that line. The line that is immovable. We have drawn this line, and you can't do anything to us for doing so. We are your monarchs, we are your Muhammad Tughluq. You are just the people and count for nothing. You can go on shouting, but what can we do? We too are helpless. You have made life hell for us. You fight and kill one another and burn each other's houses, for what? We know you are doing this because of us, but we are fully conscious of our duty towards you. We respect your sentiments, that is why we agreed on an exchange of population. If we hadn't done so none of you would have remained alive. It was necessary for peace, for your peace of mind. It is none of our fault. We didn't ask you to loot and kill. We only wanted to rule, and now by the grace of fate we have that opportunity. And if you go on fighting even now, and looking at each other with hatred, then it is better for you to leave your homes, bury the beauty in your lives, strangulate your love for one another and cross that immovable line. You idiots! Barbarians! Brothers! Allow us to govern in peace.

Sahir Ludhianvi is crying out in Delhi and reading out the lament of the Punjab:

"My friends, for you

Over long years I spun dreams of the moon and stars and the spring,

But today my tattered garment holds nothing for you

But the dust of the road we have travelled.

The music in my harp has been strangled

Its tunes are buried under wailing and screaming,

I beg you for peace and civilization as alms, charity,

Return to my lips my songs and their melody."

But who is there to hear Sahir's mournful dirge? How can the tune of the singer regain its melody? We are all beggars today, not singers, and nobody throws a piece of bread at us. Who has the patience to listen to our songs! Nobody wants to be reminded of your pain, your grief and your lament. Go on shouting. Let Gandhi also shout. Let me shout, let Arif shout, let Bari shout. You know that our shouts strike against the wall at Wagah and are reduced to nothing. Sahir, my friend, so what if our Punjab is no more, we have the line at Wagah. The armies of Rajas and Nawabs went on mutiny, but at least the faith of the Hindus and Muslims was saved. Mosques and temples have now been spared by the vandals. And haven't you heard, there is not a single believer in Allah left east of Wagah. People are playing cards in mosques, and copies of the Quran lie in gutters. It is the same west of Wagah. Not a single devotee of Rama and Krishna is left here. Temples and Gurdwaras lie deserted, and idols in shattered pieces decorate the dung heaps. Isn't this enough? And you, the singer of the people, wailing in song for the return of everything you held precious. You are living in a fool's paradise.

Today I came across Maulana Salahuddin Ahmed in Paisa Akhbar. He was simply aghast to see me. "You here?" he exclaimed, "Come into this corner." And then in tones in which surprise was mixed with some sympathy and a little regret, he began to question me. "You here in this horrendous locality? Are you mad? I hope you are all right. Good. But living here is not sane. Come to my place, that is a safer area. But why don't you go away? I'm also thinking of going away to Delhi. How can I live here?"

Obviously Maulana was terribly nervous. I replied as calmly as I could, "Maulana, I don't want to leave Lahore. But why are you going to Delhi? In Delhi it is . ."

"Yes, yes, I know. But how can I live here? One of my houses has been burnt down, the other has been stripped of everything by ruffians. What shall I do? But then, what can I do?"

Poor Maulana, what could he do? If he were a barbarian it would be different. What did he get from being civilized? That his house was looted? And now he was thinking of going across Wagah.

10 September

Arif is given to argumentation. It is not a good habit, but his political awareness and a healthy thoughtfulness has always made me like this habit. Many a time he gets involved in his own arguments in this time of horror, barbarity and terror, and overcome by the prevailing atmosphere he sometimes changes the very tenor of the matter being debated. Then I at once try to correct him. I don't know why but he seems to be influenced by my personality. I sometimes think that this tendency to agree with me may land him in a maze, because nowadays I am again beset by emotionalism. Is it fair that whatever we have been thinking for the last fifteen years, whatever we have written and whatever point of view we subscribed to should become a victim of political anarchy? Is this why we fought British imperialism so that we may have to face the murder of thousands of innocent lives. Should we change our point of view? What is the use? What use is it? It's all nonsense. Friend Arif, I think we should die now so that we should stop losing our way by deceiving ourselves with thoughts of a bright future.

Arif was shaken by my remark. And then his habit of arguing took over and he began to explain things to me in terms of lauding the nation, supporting self-determination and other idealistic complexities. I said to Arif I was a firm believer in ideas based on philosophy, that's why I ask what place has religion in our lives now?

"Religion?" he retorted, "Religion has fought its last battle in this unfortunate land of India and has been decisively beaten." How optimistic of him!

"I feel like writing a poem to show how my laughter and my aspirations and my zest for thought have been strangulated. Then I would join a mosque as a *mullah* or enter a temple to take on the duties of a priest."

"But that is escapism which is poison for our literature and our politics."

"Maybe, but what about the murder of emotions? Don't you remember the constable we met in Nagina Bakery?"

At the mention of the constable tears welled up in Arif's eyes. The man had made love, and his love had blossomed into marriage. Then, before his very eyes, some Sikh hooligans carried off his bride of two months. He was crazy with shock and grief and could do nothing by cry helplessly. Life now meant nothing to him.

"Ah, if I had the power I would decimate these Sikhs. They are responsible for this holocaust, aren't they?"

Arif's eyes lit up. I had seen this shine ten days ago too, but this time there was anger in it. With a tremor in his voice he said, "Fikr my friend, by cursing this community you are behaving like a non-Marxist. This expression of hate for them means you are no longer dispassionate. Are you sure you are not saying this just to please the Muslims?"

Despite the sincerity of my remark I was left astounded by Arif's reaction. He went on, "Just because the leadership is dishonest we cannot hold an entire community guilty. If we do so the real criminals cannot be pinpointed., as is the case with our politics as a whole. In a fit to take sides we are sucking each other's blood, while the real culprits sit in their mansions and estates and in Buckingham Palace. No one Sikh is guilty, neither one Hindu or one Muslim, but this evil spirit, this imperialist selfishness that we can't see."

Oh God, how hard this man is and how cruel is his manner of explaining the truth! But I cannot believe that the mourning constable can emulate his hardness. His destroyer is that Sikh who has ravished his life and vanished. How can I explain to him that the real criminal is sitting in his palace.

It is said that today 1,300 refugees in the Walton Camp died of cholera. Thirteen hundred men and women who had been created to contribute to the beauty of earthly life. But those responsible for the adornment of this world brought them to the camp to die, so that this idiotic work may be better performed. Cholera, to which religion does it belong? "Doctor, give me an injection of religious cholera." And the doctor stared at me with surprise and thought I was a lunatic.

I wanted to visit Walton Camp so that I could watch people die with hands spread out for food. Parched gram was being doled out. An aged man in white got both his hands filled and then flung the grams in the air with a horrible scream of laughter. "Haha! Come on dogs, eat your fill. Rehmat Bibi have ten bags of gram sent to this dog's house!" It was as if he was addressing God.

63

The young man on duty to distribute grams filled the two hands of a girl while she looked at him with thankful eyes. The youth's lips went dry and his eyes acquired a strange yearning. I couldn't stand the sight. My brain will burst. Human beings smell of sex. Oh God, the stench of the camp; the stench of man!

15 September

Today when Qateel and Rahi returned empty-handed from Taunsa, a new hope instead of regret was born in my heart. My in-laws had been amazed. How could they sent Rani and Kailash with two Muslims? Qateel told me that Khwaja Sahib himself was taken aback that I could not distinguish between Hindu and Muslim. What kind of a man must this be who can trust a Muslim in these times and thinks that his Muslim friends will deliver his Hindu wife to him safe and sound!

I was deep in thought. What kind of social contradiction are we living in. Qateel and Rahi undertook a difficult journey of hundreds of miles to Taunsa and had to go back unsuccessful. I could hardly raise my head before them. But Qateel told me that in my home town there was another idiot like me by the name of Khwaja Nizamuddin. He had taken on the responsibility for the safety and protection of all the Hindus in the area and had announced a terrible curse on all Muslims if even one Hindu was killed. Khwaja Sahib is a well-known religious divine of our area. Here is religion shoving the whole of the Punjab into the fire of hell, and the same religion taking on the duty of providing sanctuary to thousands of Hindus in Taunsa. And I am looking into a dictionary to get the real meaning of the word religion.

Qateel tells me there was a terrific rush of passengers on the train on the way back and people were sitting on the roofs of the carriages. There, on the rooftop, a travelling ticket examiner was checking, not the tickets but the "religion" of the male passengers. Anyone found without the sign of his being a Muslim was thrown down from the roof of the carriage. Everyone laughed. I was thinking why Khwaja Nizamuddin did not behave like the TTE. Why is he sitting with heretics in his fold and why is he insulting the *shariat*. Doesn't he know what religion means today? Does he think that after living together for centuries there is no difference left between Hindus and Muslims? And that Hindus don't have to be thrown from a moving train? What a foolish man is this Khwaja. I salute his foolishness.

I also salute the mad Gandhi who, thousands of miles from the foolish Muslim divine, stands on the steps of the Jami Mosque in Delhi and screams, "Don't kill the Muslims, they are our brothers!" But the massacre goes on and Delhi is red with blood. Today Tufail Ahmed arrived from Delhi, in just the clothes he was wearing. His bride is still hiding in a dangerous area of the city. He himself jumped over the back wall of the Anjuman Taraqqi-e-Urdu and kept hiding in a bush the whole day. This expert in politics and economics, slim and slender, a talented artist and writer, was able to save his own life. He told us that only a few days ago Hindu young men had decorated the main gate of the Anjuman with the tricolour, but then later they decided this was not enough so they set fire to it.

How did this mental change come about? They say that the Hindus and Sikhs of Lahore woke up the slumbering people of Delhi when they got there and then everybody got active. Books were burned, priceless manuscripts of art, literature and science were thrown into the fire, because they said Urdu was the language of the

Muslims. Yes. It was part of the Islamic civilization and had walked to India from Iraq and Arabia. Therefore destroying it was a national duty. As a symbol of Islamic culture it had to be reduced to ashes. This symbol, this Urdu, in which Prem Chand wrote his masterpieces (was he a herald of Islam?), in which Krishan Chander wrote his immortal stories (was he a protagonist of the Quran?) the vehicle of literary expression chosen by the great Ratan Nath Sarshar (was he an Arab?). Everything went into the bonfire in the name of safeguarding the Hindu civilization.

Mumtaz has found his Achha and is happy. While returning from Batala he saw countless dead bodies of Muslims on the sixty mile stretch of road. He thinks it is Hindus and Sikhs who killed them. I think the same, and so does Arif. Today Mumtaz has been trying to convince a clerk of our office that Arif and Fikr are wrong, these murders were really committed by Hindus and Sikhs and no one else.

20 September

Today Arif and I went to the railway station. There was a huge crowd of lifeless unfeeling men and women inside and outside the building, lying on their tattered and soiled bedding. They were refugees who had come from India and had been welcomed in Lahore by disease, cholera, hunger and squalor. Their eyes looked like balls of ice, their faces devoid of animation, as if life had left them behind. Their past was lost to them while their present was wrapped in dirt and grief. The future was still uncertain. Where do you want to go travellers? Their dry lifeless lips seemed to say, "We want to die. Have you a bit of poison on you?"

A girl of fifteen or sixteen, her face pale and drawn, arose from a corner of the platform, walked a few steps, and then, in full view of hundreds of shifty eyes, sat down to urinate. Something like a meteor shot in my brain and then lost its light. What was it, Arif, that broke inside me? The concept of virginity? That young pretty girl, what had she been made to give up that she no longer had any idea of shame, right in the midst of a crowd' Come on, Arif, let's get out of here. How rapidly moral values are being transformed. We are crossing a great historic point in the march of civilization, the point where young girls are no longer bothered about virginity, the spiritualism of the East dies a sudden death and the Quran and the Vedas hold their breath with suspense. This point, this stage. Come Arif, let us go back centuries and hide in our caves. Let us bury ourselves in the ground. We don't want to go the way of progress. Let's go back!

27 September

All of us were in a daze. We all felt that something must happen. We were tortured by the thought: where have we reached? Come let us put our heads together and think, let us shed tears on our demise, let us compose elegies on the death of civilization. Abdullah Malik was limp, the usually ebullient Tufail looked like a corpse, Kalimullah was drowned in sorrow, Bari's eyes were heavy with despair; and all of us were thinking, what now?

We gathered at Mumtaz's house. The progressive artists and writers of India and Pakistan were enveloped in a thick cloud of grief. The light of dawn had been overtaken by a frightening darkness at its very birth. In front of their eyes the beautiful garden of the Punjab had been devastated. Nothing was seen on roads and streets

67

except dead bodies. Even the shade of the trees had been shot out of existence by gunfire.

Peace! Peace! This is what these intellectuals craved for. "We despise brutality, we condemn barbarity," they said, though this statement was overwhelmed by their own sense of impotence. But they wanted to overcome this helplessness and do something about it. They were trying to come to a decision in Mumtaz's house. It was decided that a meeting of all the known literary personalities of Lahore be called the day after tomorrow and a programme chalked out. This gave me courage and I felt lights go on in my deep pessimism. I was coming alive again.

Sahir had just returned after spending two blood-soaked weeks in Delhi. What a delightful way he has of describing events, even the gory events of Delhi. He had spent some days in the house of a Sikh comrade, and, in the company of his wife, had made the rounds of All India Radio to see if they could use some of his poems. On freedom day he was in Bombay, and despite a feigned attempt and a put on sense of happiness could not be a part of the celebrations. But Delhi had been terrible. It had awakened the muse in him, and it was there that he wrote that great poem, "O my companions, all these long years, for you . . ." As he read it our, Mumtaz exclaimed, "What a beautiful piece, full of genuine feelings and emotion. Not progressive at all!" We all wondered why he didn't like it.

As the poets and writers emerged from the meeting they were perplexed to see that it was pitch dark outside. I don't know why I thought that the East Punjab government must have switched off the hydroelectric power. The Ravi was in flood and we crossed The Mall in knee-deep water. It was said that the Sikhs had purposely breached the river bank. On top of this someone reported that the Sikhs were going to mount a huge attack on Lahore that night. All this was too much for my nerves. What will happen now? Why are we people bent upon self-destruction? And I couldn't sleep the whole night. Shouts of fear were heard all over Lahore the whole night.

29 September

Actually neither the river bank had been breached nor had power been shut off, nor did the Sikhs turn up with their attack. Fate had taken its revenge on the reactionaries, and the Ravi and the Sutlej were in high seasonal flood bringing devastation to Central Punjab. The deluge was impervious to the game of fire and blood already being played over the area, it was not bothered by the gory acts of the Hindus and the Muslims, it had broken up the refugee camps, trampled over roads and railway lines and, after wreaking havoc in villages and hamlets, it had entered the city streets. The plight of thousands of refugees trudging over miles for shelter was the most pathetic. A 'progressive" fate was trying to teach the murderous people of the Punjab a horrible lesson in equality. In the form of death it had intruded into the homes of everyone --- Hindu, Sikh and Muslim. Habitations were been abandoned, crops had been laid flat, houses were falling. And when the storm subsided the banks of the rivers were littered with thousands of broken down carts and household goods of refugees and non-refugees alike. Hundreds of men, women and children had been washed away.

Today Arif and I went to look at the flood-affected localities of Lahore. It was a terrible sight. These were the areas where refugees had come to take shelter and the flood water had reached the rooftops. There were tragic screams all around. Someone had lost a son, another couldn't find his wife, while someone else was trying to see if his old mother was alive or not. In all this when life was pell-mell and without any sense and order, miscreants had started looting empty houses. I couldn't bear the sight and we came back.

On the way we met Anjum. He looked as if a whole river of tears had dried up within him. One couldn't even say a word of sympathy to him. What was there to say? Two of his young sisters had been abducted in East Punjab while his old father had been shot dead. I knew that if I tried to say anything I would scream, for there was no longer any sincerity to be found in words of condolence. Our emotions had committed suicide, and we had strangulated ourselves.

For the last four or five days I have been faced with a funny reality. It would really be funny if it wasn't so grim. Every day the manager of our office advises me to convert to Islam. He does this in all sincerity, being a practising orthodox Muslim himself. But he lacks political sense and is only moved by religious considerations. I can sympathise with the method he has chosen to help me, but what can move me to take his advice seriously? I laughingly mentioned this to Arif and asked him to recount the social and cultural differences between Punjabi Hindus and Muslims. He counted a large number. But what is the use of dwelling on this pointless idea and worrying myself with it?

4 October

What was to happen tomorrow has taken place today. It seems to me that I am nearing a big accident in my life. Whatever I am doing, this thought does not leave me. History has turned over a new leaf and here I am still craving for the old days. The manager repeated his advice again today, saying in a most confidential manner that it was for my own good. But what is prudent and worldly wise in the eyes of the manager is not acceptable to my mind. I really feel for him as if it is his problem and not mine. I suppose there is no cause for worry on my part.

Even so I couldn't recover the whole day from the mental shock that a dispute with Mumtaz had given me. It was as if a huge electric bulb giving out a bright shining light suddenly had exploded leaving everything in darkness. The bulb did not go off against my expectation, but the manner in which it was smashed was so crude and inartistic that I couldn't speak a word, and I said, "Stop it, Mumtaz, please forgive me, I can't bear to go on."

What had happened was this. Mumtaz had said that if he were the dictator of Pakistan he wouldn't let an Indian Muslim set foot in Pakistan. I concurred with the basic idea and the concept that gave rise to it, but in a disputative mood I asid, "But Pakistan was the result of a combined struggle of all Indian Muslims. Therefore since the struggle has succeeded, every Muslim in the country should be able to benefit from it. The Pakistan movement was a people's movement and not merely a means to form ministries and governments."

Mumtaz boiled up. "I will put up an iron wall at Wagah and prevent them by force from entering Pakistan. This is our country, not theirs." I tried to explain too calmly that the Indian Muslims were hardly at fault. They had done their best for the achievement of Pakistan, and now if Hindu fascists make live hell for them in India and you decide to put up an iron wall at Wagah then where are they to go? After all they are human beings and not animals that they should be deprived of the basic right to live just because they were born in India before Pakistan came into being and because they supported the movement.

"But we cannot allow every Muslim in the world to come and live in Pakistan. If tomorrow the Muslims of Arabia and Iraq and Kabul want to make Pakistan their home, should they be permitted to do so?" His logic was correct, but I felt as if some vital basic consideration was slipping away from the argument. If the fascists and reactionaries had not joined in the slogan for Pakistan the outcome would have been different, and that possible outcome gave every Indian Muslim the right to consider Pakistan as his home. I too feel pleasure in being a citizen of Pakistan but my case is not the same. If anyone else in my place is threatened with being killed then how will loyal citizenship prevail over the desire to save one's life? This was the case with India's Muslims today. The same threat to be killed was there.

Sitting in Lahore Mumtaz could not appreciate the dangers inherent in this threat. He wanted to build another great wall of China. He was ignoring the fact that the homeland of Arab and Iraqi Muslims was not Lahore and then, after Amritsar the terror in this threat was spreading to Delhi and UP and Bombay. Mumtaz looked at me with anger in his eyes. His mental aggression had reached its peak. Controlling himself with some effort he said, "Mr Fikr, don't argue with me on this subject. You talk like a Hindu and I am a Muslim. I may loose my balance, and the result of that might be terrible."

And then another huge electric bulb burst into nothing and its pieces fell on the ground. After this I was silent. What a cheap and inartistic way to explode! The artist had accused me of being a Hindu, and while he also called himself a Muslim, he did not take it as an indictment, while I felt disgusted at the slur thrown in my face. O God! Mumtaz was welcome to call himself a Muslim, but what right had he to call me a Hindu as if it was a smear, a

72

denunciation. He had hurt me terribly, he had challenged my very thinking, my intellectual upbringing.

But I am silent. I was talking frankly with Mumtaz in the confidence that he was an intellectual, an artist, supposedly the mirror of life's realities and truths, whose worship of humanity is a religion in itself and who can probe secrets that are not even visible to others. Can the life of an artist be based on such a frail and changeable foundation as being a Hindu or a Muslim? My mind is in a whirl.

9 October

The attacks on railway trains have started again. It seems that the "rebel deserters" of the armies of the Rajahs and Nawabs have not yet surrendered. Girls and women are still being abducted and paraded in order to be humiliated and shamed. The screams of Gandhi have acquired a kind of balance, and, according to a politician, he is threatening to come to the Punjab to restore peace. In anticipation of this threat the attacks have been intensified., although the frequency and violence of the riots in Delhi has considerably abated.

The Kashmir tangle appears to have reached the final stage. Someone was saying that the Dogra armies of the state are on the rampage. Another comment was that the tribesmen had launched fresh attacks and were engaged in widespread looting, and that is the Maharajah of Kashmir has announced his decision to join the Indian Union. The state is in turmoil. Some people think that the responsibility for the safety of the state's subjects falls in the tribesmen;

others than that only India can save them. The poor Kashmiris are between the two grindstones of the mill. The cancer of native states is a legacy of British imperialism, and both the sides are anxious to adopt this cancer. Arif! Arif! What is this going on?

Arif joins his voice with the cry of my heart and says, "From the geographical angle Kashmir should accede to Pakistan, but is accession the only question? The point is what will become of the people of Kashmir? Why are the people, the chinar trees, the flower-filled valleys, the lakes, being prepared to be thrown into the flames of conflict? Must the juggler play his tricks in this land of beauty and romance? The fact is, my friend, that whether Kashmir becomes part of India or Pakistan, the game of the juggler will go on."

I am again confronted with the mist of vagueness. My mind wants to commit suicide, and in this state comes the voice of Mumtaz: "I am sorry, Brother Fikr that I spoke with you in that manner. Actually I shouldn't have joined that discussion. Actually . . Do forgive me." But I am involved in the juggler's game and my mind has left Mumtaz far behind. In any case I have no longer taking his words to heart.

Mumtaz says to the manager in confidence, "We should all be armed so that we can attack Kashmir from the rear." The manager agrees. "Yes, how can we protect ourselves and what is ours if we are not armed? Haven't you heard what a weapon can do? That poet friend of yours whose collection has been published under the title "Salsabeel," shot so many heretics during the riots with his own gun. He may be a poet but I must say he is a brave man." Arif thinks the manager is not speaking the truth. How can a poet do such a thing?

Last night for the first time in my life I had the opportunity to look closely at the psychological condition of an escapist. Since last evening I am with Sahir, and am cloistered with him. God knows how long this depression is going to last. Arif too was with us the whole night. He was trying to convince me not to take a decision in a hurry and, in any case, not to leave Lahore like this. Sahir was terribly angry, saying he would go away from here, and go to Bombay, while Arif coaxed and cajoled him in his soft philosophic manner to change his mind. As for me, I don't know what I am going to do. I am a prisoner of my psyche. I only know that I feel like a deserter, a coward, and have come to Sahir's house to seek refuge. Maybe I cross the Wagah border tomorrow and then look back with longing at the streets of Lahore. But then there is always the sharp point of the dagger that appears suddenly somewhere into my plans. The sharp point of the dagger!

The manager came and sat with me and said to Mumtaz, "Please advise Fikr Sahib not to be stubborn. A few vagabonds are pursuing him. What is the harm in becoming a Muslim? What difference does it make? After all it's a question of saving one's life." I don't know what Mumtaz said to him, but I began to laugh, and so did Mumtaz. He went out after a while. A minute or two later two roughs walked in and one of them asked me peremptorily to come out with them where two others were waiting, conversing in whispers. His lips trembled as he spoke. This was a truly unique experience for me. I remained calm and asked him what they wanted of me. The man got a little flustered. I extended my hand to take his but he pulled it away. I recited the Muslim *kalima* and he

75

was dumbfounded. He said they knew I was a Hindu, but Qateel and Rahi shook their heads in denial. The young man then asked me to come out so that they could kill me. I asked him what was his religion. When he said, "I am a Muslim," I asked him if he had read the Quran and if he could recite the ritual prayer. He said all this had nothing to do with the matter, and, in any case, he was not a Hindu like me. I told him I was a Muslim, I have read the Quran and I can say my prayers. What else was needed for being a Muslim? This made him really nervous, particularly the assurance by me and Qateel that an affidavit to this effect would be obtained from the *maulvi* of the big mosque and shown to him tomorrow. On this, the rough left the place in a dudgeon, his hand probably fondling the dagger in his pocket.

At closing time the manager again got hold of me and explained that it was necessary to placate "these bastards" repeating his refrain, "After all, what difference does it make." Sahir lost his temper and said, "What the hell do you mean by what difference does it make. You should be handed over to the police along with these men." This threat evoked a return threat and the manager said, "If you will ride the high horse with me you too might get a dagger in your body."

I was thinking. . . . But then, what was the use of thinking? The law had already been beheaded. Jawahar Lal and Jinnah had announced two different versions of democracy --- democracy, that epitome of human progress and development, about which Iqbal's verse said, "The system in which men are not weighed, only counted." Democracy, in which people were being made to emigrate at the point of the dagger. Jawahar Lal was proclaiming the protection of the minorities as the first principle of his democratic state, and Jinnah was announcing that his democratic state could not survive unless it safeguarded the life and property of the minorities. And here was I being given the undemocratic advice of changing my faith to save my life.

Arif talked with me the whole night. I said to him, "Arif, ask me to become a Muslim, and, I swear by all that I hold precious that I will obey your command. But this . . ." Arif's lips were trembling as he cried, "Brother Fikr don't shoot such arrows into my being. Let me think, let me think." And he lay thinking the whole night, without sleeping a wink.

17 October

Lahore is again full of life. It laughs at the corpse of its previous existence and, at the same time, is giving birth to a new self. The gap of history between the exodus of the Hindus and Sikhs and the arrival of Muslim refugees has been closed with great speed. The rule of disorder, fear, arson and stabbing is gradually giving way to peace. But this peace resembles autumn more than anything else, and certainly not spring. The air of regret and nostalgia at the phenomenal change is mixed with the desire to create anew. On the roads, under the trees, whole families in rags, friendless and helpless, stare at the sky. These are the victors. They have come here after winning the battle between faith and heresy and have landed in Lahore to celebrate their victory. They have fled from Ambala and Rohtak, Jullundhur and Kapurthala, Delhi and Saharanpur and come here to participate in the festivities of freedom. They have inflicted a convincing defeat on the joint culture of the Punjab, a defeat that will resound in history.

It is a strange festival, in which moans and groans can also be heard. Ruffians, both local and outsiders, are being applauded for widespread looting. Big people have taken possession of big mansions, so that commoners should not be seen watching the celebrations. As for the middle class, they are content with roaming around. A film director is managing a bicycle stand in a local cinema. A sixty-year old father parades his four unmarried daughters in Anarkali in search of patrons. There is a flood of charity and sympathy and aid for the poor. A painter of world fame who was part of killing and looting during the riots is walking the streets collecting quilts and warm clothing for the refugees. A well-fed poet who set fire to a storehouse of valuable films during the riots has organized a poetic symposium for extending monetary help to the new population. Sahir has given me an invitation to this *mushaira*.

Sahir's mother counsels me not to go out. "These are bad times," she says. The bad times are turning a tramp like me into a recluse. Mother, this is my city, nothing in it can frighten me. I want to see how it has welcomed its new inhabitants. I want to see how they roam in the Lawrence Garden, are they acquainted with the manners of walking on The Mall, are they impressed by the greatness of Anarkali, are they given to discussion of art and literature and philosophy in Cheney's Lunch Home and the Coffee House. I said to Sahir, "I've heard two famous progressive women have come to Lahore. Can I meet them?" "No, my friend," says Sahir, "In Lahore they have started observing *purdah*. You can't even see them." He is busy drafting a proclamation on behalf of the intellectuals of Pakistan.

Today Arif came over thrice to see me. Chaudhry too came. He was sorry I had been subjected to that sorry treatment and hoped I would not go away. The pain in his heart is visible on his face, and sometimes he fails to understand all that is going on around us. Mumtaz too tried

78

to see me but somehow I was never at home. I have finally decided to leave Lahore.

20 October

My dilemma is unresolved. The desire to go away refuses to get out of my mind. What a torture! Is it right for me to go on believing that by living on in Lahore I can falsify the fact of the wholesale exchange of population? This is a personal stubbornness, but behind it a collective feeling also plays its part. If the exodus and influx had not been on this scale, what was the danger to Hinduism in Pakistan, what would Islam have suffered in East Punajb, and, most of all, what loss would it have caused to humanity at large? Am I a foreigner now? Is Sahir a foreigner? All of us have spent the best years of our lives together. How can a magician out of Arabian Nights suddenly wave his hand and brand us as foreigners? It is a strange situation, unprecedented and unthinkable, and the mind refuses to accept the fact that only twenty miles away begins a strange land, an alien culture. Can't some other magician blow that border to pieces?

Yesterday, in the gathering of writers, poets and intellectuals Sahir said in an emotion filled voice, "Come, let us form a new caravan and go to Wagah. From the other side, let another caravan come. Let us then exchange flags and march on, the Indians carrying the Star & Crescent and the Pakistanis holding aloft the tricolour."

It was a romantic proposal and the faces of many writers glowed with pleasure. Those of many more registered incredulity. A veteran poet who had suddenly turned from a loyal servant of the British to a communist, vowed in a resounding voice: "We shall revivify humanity with our pens, our art and our lives. We will warn every citizen that his blood is being drained by the feudals and capitalists and Nawabs and Rajahs and that he should come out of the abattoir."

A veritable hurricane of love and emotion engulfed me. I felt that life was not dead yet, that in this gory cycle of history there were still people around who wanted to kindle the lamp of accommodation and tolerance, and that hatred and degradation had not completely overpowered poetry and music. Who are these people, where have they come from, refusing to be influenced by bloodthirstiness and the flames of communalism? Are you really Indians, you men, asserting yourself in an atmosphere where the concept of politics is based on circumcision? Aren't you bothered by man's hatred for man, the Punjabi's hatred for the Punjabi, the hatred of culture for culture and the hatred of Bhagwan for Allah? What kind of people are you, who insist on singing the melody of love, and how can you see so far and so clearly?

The mist on my brain is evaporating. I can see things somewhat clearly now. Last night I had said to Arif, "Can we, a handful of literary personalities, succeed in making the people forget such a terrible tragedy? Can we really make our broad vision and the echo of our emotions penetrate the bestial and hate-filled hearts of the people?" Arif stopped me. He said I was insulting the revolutionary basis of events by labelling the people as hate-filled beasts. He said, "My friend, it is not the people who are barbaric and animal-minded. It is only that we have crossed a very important stage in history in which imperialism has won the battle. Our work, our duty has reached a very difficult point now and we have to re-educate the people anew."

Arif went on speaking, like an inspired spirit, and I went on listening with an equally inspired spirit. For the moment I completely forgot the killer-ruffian, the dagger,

80

the thoughts of fleeing. Why do I worry so much about these matters? These are only stages in our fresh journey. "Mother, let me go. My companions are waiting for me. Give me your blessing for I am beginning a new journey."

Sahir, who had been going round getting writers to sign the proclamation, came back and said, "Fikr, have you heard? Askari has refused to sign our joint statement. He does not take himself as a writer of Pakistan. Then why did he run away from India and come here? Why?"

24 October

The pressure on Kashmir is increasing day by day. Things are going from bad to worse. A new chapter of hate has been opened. This hate was started before the first round of hate could end so that continuity should not be broken. Thousands of innocent Kashmiris are suffering just because the King Emperor, on departing from the subcontinent, left their destiny in the hands of the Maharajah, and the Maharajah's hands were in the hands of the Indian dominion. Since the foundations of Pakistan and the Indian dominion were laid on hatred what else could be expected? It is as if this had been designed long ago. Waves of emotion are engulfing the streets of Lahore. What will happen now?

From here the threat is, "We shall go to Delhi." From there the threat is, "We shall go to Peshawar." The unrest in minds is never-ending. The mist is overpowering, but within this mist the puppeteer's hands can be discerned. My friends try to recognize these hands. I know you are tortured by memories of Delhi and Peshawar. Do go there, but first of all learn to do things with decency. Do not come down to threats like strangers and aliens

Today Sahir and I had an encounter with a progressive writer and poet in McLeod Road. It is said about him that he has taken possession of some vacant houses so that the valuables in them should not fall in the hands of thieves and vagabonds. He was shouting at the top of his voice, "We must capture Kashmir at all costs, by hook or by crook." Does this progressive poet think that the only solution of the problems of the poor Kashmiris lies in capturing Kashmir? Can't he see the interplay of international politics in this sordid business?

Today the Quaid-e-Azam addressed a crowd of hundreds of thousands in Lahore. The poet who had suddenly turned communist read out a poem to welcome him. Sahir and the other comrades heard it on the radio, and all of us were thunderstruck by the poem of Firdausi of Islam.

27 October

Yesterday Comrade Prasher visited the party office. He had come from Amritsar. He was not too surprised to see me still in Lahore, and I was not too glad to meet him. Why was this? I had not looked at a Hindu face for the last two months and was yearning to do so. But Prasher is hardly a Hindu. In these dangerous times he had come from Amritsar and was frankly discussing politics with the Muslim comrades in the party office. I wanted to look at a Hindu who had run away from Lahore out of fear and did not want to come back. Prasher asked me if I would go with him to Amritsar. I declined. Comrade Rahi said jokingly, "You see, we need minorities in Pakistan, and so far as we friends are concerned Fikr serves the purpose." The jest was actually a grim truth, and everyone in the office became serious. They wanted to light a flame to pierce the fog of darkness and show the faces of the real culprits to the people.

But the real culprits had disappeared with the royal crown on their heads. Others like them were busy taking over big mansions and factories while the real people trod the streets half-naked and hungry, waiting for a magical word to change their fate. These poor refugees did not want religion, either Hindu or Muslim or Sikh; they wanted food and shelter, they needed the will to live which seemed to be absent. Despite all this the situation is not entirely hopeless. What if Sahir has not been able to get his house back even after nearly two months. What if the young girl urinating on the railway platform had lost her sense of shame. What if Maualana Salahuddin's house too had not been spared by vandals. Justice was not yet dead; morality was still alive; happiness could still be found in things. Look at those peasants who, the other day, brought a Hindu family to the party office and wanted its safety to be ensured.

Today Sahir, Rahi and I had tea in a place called Paramount Hotel. The proprietor, a fat, dark man in Peshawari sandals, Punjabi *shalwar* and a red Fez cap sat at the counter like an exhibit. Every minute or so he would get up, walk about the restaurant, even go out for a moment, and then come back to his appointed place. To me it looked as if he was making his presence felt by this exercise. I continued to look at him with curiosity till Rahi told me that a month ago he had been a Hindu and was a new convert. I enjoyed this revelation and wanted to say to him, "Friend don't wave the tassel of your Fez cap so much, otherwise you will be exposing your Hindu past. This tassel does not prove that you are a Muslim now, nor do your features and demeanour show that you were once a Hindu. I know the likes of you. You cannot be a Hindu or a Muslim. I salute you!

I have never taken kindly to political parties, feeling greater kinship for things spiritual. But I now see that politics has invaded my being and its mad dance and lunatic music have affected my peace of mind. I can feel the fight going one between spiritualism and politics inside me. For instance, for two days I have been thinking about the Communist Party. Nowadays I am living in the party office, as are a few others. I don't know what kind of magic moves them but they give the impression that these few men are holding up the globe. Outside there is a terrible conflict and millions are suffering from an upheaval, but they are at peace with themselves, as if this unprecedented disaster had left them unaffected because, all-knowing as they are, they are aware what it is due to. I too know something about the origin of this holocaust, but there is a difference between my knowledge and theirs, for I lack their certainty, their self-confidence. I was thinking whether I could acquire this self-confidence if I became a party member, but then, I am not a believer in miracles and instant changes. It is better to be stunned than being subjected to a miracle.

These friends of mine are true representatives of the modern machine age. Everyone of them is a robot. Mansoor is talking to someone on the telephone, "Hello, hello! Two of our comrades are working as doctors in the Wagah camp, they look after refugees coming from East Punjab. Hello, what did you say? There are no more injections? All right, I'll do something about it."

The telephone rings again. "Yes, you are speaking from the DAV College camp. I heard you. There are five of us working in that camp. What is your problem? Your wife

84

and children are marooned in a house inside Shah 'Almi? I'll send a comrade there at once."

A half a dozen Muslim Jats have entered the party office with a Sikh family. Comrade Aslam is talking to them. The Jats say they have saved this family by putting their own lives in danger, and they want them to be conveyed to the camp in safety. Two fair-complexioned good-looking young men from Kashmir are sitting talking about the Kashmir issue. Everyone is attentive to what they say. They are a little nervous for they are trying to justify the tribal violence in the state. Comrades Shaukat, Aslam, Mansoor and Mirza exhort them not to become tools in the hands of international imperialists. The two look at these Muslim comrades with suspicion as if they were agents of the Indian government.

This goes on every day. There is the same activity, the same sincerity. I look on with gaping eyes at these comrades of stone working in this stone building without becoming emotional. Can I ever acquire their spirit? Should I become a party member and see? But the glances that Comrade Mansoor throws at me seem to be saying to me, "Nothing will avail by being a poet or a party member. You should become a member of the struggle for life. We don't join the party for fun or romance or as a fashion. Once you enter the struggle for life you too will acquire this spirit that you admire in us. Get up and join this storm that will give you meaningful happiness and love --- lasting and everlasting."

3 November

My desire to leave Lahore is intensifying. But now there is no stubbornness behind this desire, no aorry and no escapism. In fact a new shining line has overlain itself on these considerations. Every day I see on The Mall truckloads of Hindu and Sikh refugees, and they give me the feeling thast they are all being pulled by the graveyard.. None of the occupants of the trucks betrays any feeling of life from their faces. God knows what picture these long drawn faces have in mind about the future. Sometimes I feel like stopping one of the trucks and saying to the inmates, "Take me with you so that I may see you in your new homeland begging for food and solace, so that I may witness your little children and your women giving up the ghost at the threshold of the goddess of freedom. I wish you knew what you are going to get in that homeland where your own faith flourishes. It will be nothing less than the fires of hell."

The trucks speed on without waiting for my words. Along with them my wish to get out of Lahore also gathers speed. I wish I could go to India and see the fate of these long, drawn faces. I would collect a group of writers and poets and artists and take them to every city, every village, every refugee camp and say to them. "Look, these are the characters of your masterpieces. Can you see their fate? Look at them and write for them. Tell them that you want well-filled, contented characters for your writings, not these withered, lifeless and failed faces."

This evening the Quiad-e-Azam was in Lahore. It is now four months since we got freedom and since Lahore has been wallowing in blood. Maybe he has heard about it recently. It seemed as if the whole miserable and unfortunate city was going to hear him speak. Everybody was curious to see what he would say. My companions and I decided to liston to the broadcast over radio. The Firdausi of Islam read out his introductory poem, The master-of-ceremonies was speaking in his usual flattering manner as if an emperor was being made welcome. I asked a comrade why this was so in a democracy. He said, "We have become free after 300 years, therefore we must show proof positive of our having remained slaves for so long." The Quaid, in his speech called on the nation to be ready for further sacrifices. The crowd was altered by this; will this cycle of sacrifices never cease? We were ready to lay down our lives for freedom, why are we being asked to make more sacrifices? Now we want happiness and contentment. Everyone in the crowd thought so, but no one voiced this thought.

Then the Quaid said, "Now I will speak in English because the foreign correspondents who are present here do not understand our language." All our comrades were thinking if the occasion was specially for foreign correspondents or to impart courage and solace to the devastated masses who were listening to the speech like deaf-mutes. The speech went on and the crowd was attentive because the words were being spoken by its beloved leader and must mean something good for the nation.

6 November

Last night I stayed with Rahi in a grand building. This was not his, but only in his keeping temporarily, for Rahi and Hameed hold its charge. Hameed is very musical and has a very fine voice. The whole night, between puffs of *beedis*, he regaled us with the melodious songs of Sehgal and Shamshad. We were carried away by the music for we too were in search of escape. Then Hameed sang a Punjabi piece, "My veil is in tatters," and I said to Rahi, "Yaar, tell me, which culture are these words from? Is it Muslim? Is it Hindu? After all why does it pull at our heart-strings and why does it go deep inside us and strike an emotional

87

chord? Why doesn't the Quran affect me similarly, why do the Vedas and the Granth leave me cold that way? Does West Punjab have a vested right to it, or does it also represent the culture of East Punjab? Can we divide these few words too like the two Punjabs?"

Rahi was close to tears as he responded, "Comrade Fikr, the Punjab too is in tatters like this veil. It was once beautiful when it was in one piece. Now it is in shreds. Can we join the shreds to make it whole again? Can this veil wave in the air of the Punjab again, the land of five rivers? Hameed, for God's sake sing something else. Anything but this veil in tatters."

But Hameed was silent, for he had finished his bidis, and had no money to replenish his stock and keep the music flowing. This rising young writer, the pride of new literature, didn't even have a few paisas to buy more beedis. Yesterday he was saying to his younger brother, the artist, who had saved himself from the killings in Amritsar, and had been looking for a job in Lahore ever since, "Ask that blasted publisher of yours to make you some payment, or stop working for him."

After this Rahi talked about his life in Amritsar with his eyes wet with tears. He knew every inch of the city, for it was his birthplace, and its very air had given him breath. Whatever had happened to him, romantic or unpleasant, was associated with Amritsar. He couldn't even sum up courage to ask if it was possible for him to be in Amritsar again, for his eyes betrayed the improbability.

I wanted to say to him, "Rahi, yes, you'll go there. Its streets await your return for they carry your imprint. It was there that you sang the songs of liberty for the starving and the wretched of the earth.. You will go. You have been served with a terrible deception in the guise of freedom. Comrade Rahi, they wait for you in Amritsar in the factories and mills." But Rahi continues to stare at the ceiling, as if thinking how he can plunge through it to attain his heart's desire.

7 November

A short Gurkha soldier stopped me, "Hey, where are you going? Who are you?" Chaudhry, Arif, Sahir and Rahi looked at me with smiles and something sang within me, "Life has come to the crossroads." The Gurkha protector of Hindu faith and the Hindu way of life at the DAV College camp wanted an answer. Why have you come to this camp? And if you are a Hindu then what are you doing in Lahore? You should have come to this camp on 15 August." I showed my forearm to the Gurkha with the childhood tattoo of Om on it. He allowed me to go into the camp, leaving my friends on the other side of the Hindu line. They were not allowed to cross it. For the first time in my life I despised my faith. Before this I had never considered religion worthy of my hatred. I was startled. I was truly at the crossroads. On a sudden impulse I threw my things aside and went back into the arms of Sahir who was saying, "Comrade Fikr, I apologise to you on behalf of the whole world of Islam that you couldn't live here."

My friends didn't know how to react. Chaudhry wanted to smile his usual twisted smile but couldn't. Arif didn't know whether to laugh or cry. The others were in a gloom of stunned silence. We sat together for more than an hour. The inmates of the camp stared at us in wonder. They must be thinking: what kind of a Hindu is this who can have faith in these Muslims, for Muslims are snakes in the grass. This Hindu must be a fifth columnist. Then the Gurkha felt we had had enough of each other's company and ordered me in. We embraced, one by one, and, with bent head, I ambled slowly towards the Hindu sheep fold.

What happened after that? Amid that scene of hellish horrors I sat silent for about half an hour. Huge trucks came in, maddened Hindus and Sikhs ran hither and thither. There was an impatient crowd in front of the camp commandant's office. Some wanted food, others fuel to cook something for themselves. Still others were crying for their lost daughters. I got up and went around the place. It was a terrible sight. Everyone had his or here tale of personal torture to tell. An old woman was wailing, "I don't want to go to India. My son has been killed her. Bring me my son, somebody. What will I do with freedom?"

Four soldiers brought in two dead bodies on stretchers. A village woman was dragging herself behind a lady doctor entreating her to do something for the child she carried in her arms. The doctor looked around helplessly. "What can I do? The child died last night, but this woman will not let this bundle go."

There was dirt and squalor beyond description in the camp. Thousands of refugees were living in this stench, encouraged by the thought of going away to a free India, maybe tomorrow, maybe the day after. Trucks were not easy to obtain, for they cost money, and most of them had no money. A well-built young man from the Frontier was quarreling with a barber who refused to trim his moustache the way he wanted it because that was the Muslim way. The young man insisted and said he didn't care whether it was the Muslim way or the Hindu way, he must have his own way. He must be wondering what was wrong with these people in Lahore. In Peshawar it had never been like this.

The scene made me smile. Here was a joint culture dying at the hands of its votariesh. The flaming eyes of the custodians of faith were bent upon smouldering everything beautiful to ashes. A culture born of centuries of living together was being destroyed. Is this why we had fought the conquering British for three hundred years? Only to go back a thousand years on winning our freedom?

Fatigued by the flood of emotions I went and sat with the Gurkha soldier. In his broken Urdu he sympathised with my lot and then asked me what I did. I told him I was a poet. He was excited at talking to a real poet and wanted to know for whom I wrote my poetry. I said nowadays it was only for the refugees. "Then give them your poetry," he said, "They are very sad. They are killed by the Muslims who loot them and burn their homes. Console them."

I touched his rifle and asked the Gurkha, "Do you know who gets these refugees killed and their houses looted and burnt?" "I know, I know, but what can I say? I am a servant of the government. If I say anything I'll lose my job." It was as if he was voicing the belief of the people. "We know, but what can we do?"

Chaudhry was standing at the main gate, calling me. He carried a basket of fruit and Mumtaz stood by his side. Mumtaz was overcome with emotion and wouldn't let me out of his embrace. Chaudhry laughed. He had brought Mufti to meet me. Mufti had brought a tin of cigarettes for me. We sat eating the fruit and smoking the cigarettes. The Gurkha went on looking at us with a meaningful expression, as if saying. "I know everything. But what can I do? I am a servant of the government. I know what you are doing."

As they took their leave, Chaudhry took out a pen from Mufti's pocket and put it in mine. "Just a souvenir," he said and laughed again.

Today I am sitting as a refugee in the Khalsa College camp in Amritsar. For almost two miles around me there is a concourse of men, women and children and trucks and household goods. Amritsar is not new for me, but for these people it is a new place, a new country where they can breathe in peace. They are celebrating *Diwalin* in the camp. There are lights everywhere and sermons on love and peace. But the crowd is in no mood to listen to sermons. There is no peace of mind for them. Their homes stand destroyed, their beloved neighbours have been converted into enemies and snatched from them, their children have rolled in dust and blood, their elders killed before their eyes and there is no knowing where their young daughters are. The lights of *Diwali* cannot illuminate their hearts which are engulfed in darkness. What do the organizers think? They are welcoming Rama the conquering hero back to Ayodhya? A leader-type nationalist was declaiming, "We have defeated the British today. This is the first *Diwali* of freedom. Let us celebrate." The crowd responds with shouts of "Shut up! Give us rations! Give us something to eat and wear. We are starving. We shall not celebrate *Diwali*."

It set me thinking. Yesterday, in the DAV College Camp in Lahore, these very people were yearning to get to a free India. With what excitement they were loading their things on the trucks and suffering the taunts and chides of the soldiers who were pushing them into the trucks mercilessly. But in the strength of their faith they bore everything with patience. The trucks were accompanied by Muslim armymen, so the throats of all the sheep were dry with fear. Who knows, the Pakistan army may turn on them and slaughter them! On the way the trucks had to stop at many places for routine checking. Every time the sheep thought their last moment had come. After a three-hour journey to cover the thirteen miles to the Wagah border, their hearts leapt with excitement on seeing the Indian tricolour and they shouted in unison. "Hindustan zindabad!" "Pandit Nehru zindabad!"

They were hollow slogans. There was no real joy behind them. I couldn't join in them, so everyone in my truck looked at me with suspicion. I looked the other way where the Star & Crescent was waving in the air. Just below it were the words "Government of Pakistan." Just then, from the Indian side, a truckload of Muslim refugees reached the border and new slogans rent the air, "Pakistan zindabad!" "Quaid-e-Azam zindabad!"

Soldiers brought down the corpse of a withered old man from this truck. He couldn't bear the strain of holding on to the bars for two days and died. Death found many bizarre ways to show its presence. No weapons were needed to kill. You could die of stiffness on a truck, you could die of stench in the refugee camps, you could die of hunger and thirst, you could die of watching your young daughter being raped or at the sight of your child skewered on a bayonet. But before dying you had to join in the slogans: "Hindustan zindabad!" "Pakistan zindabad!" "Jawaharlal Nehru zindabad!" "Quaid-e-Azam zindabad!"

This went on from Wagah to Amritsar, the air resounding with slogans raised by the refugees in the trucks. Till they ended in the chaos and confusion of the Khalsa College camp. There may be darkness in the hearts but the camp was ablaze with the lights of clay oil lamps. The bitterness showed that the sweet concept of freedom had been smashed to bits, while the future was drowned in the dimness of uncertainty. Where shall we go from here? What shall we do? Who will give us bread and who will cover our nakedness? Who was it who had promised us the moon and the stars that lay hidden behind freedom and independence? That beautiful vision of life as free men and women! Where is it?

Where is that future? Where is that dawn? Where is that freedom?

Come, my friends, we are victims of a cruel hoax, a dangerous conspiracy, that has led us astray from the true path and frozen our ambitions and our search. Come, this is not the dawn for which we have journeyed this far. Let us march on, forward. Ever new mists, ever new walls, new oppressions are being erected before us. Let us tear them apart and ram through them and find that dawn that has tantalized the innermost recesses of our hearts for 300 years. But nobody heard these words and the crowd went on shouting

Give us bread!

Give us clothes!

Give us a place of our own!

We will not celebrate *Diwali*!

(Translated from Urdu)

3

PAKISTAN IS BORN

ALYS FAIZ

We had half a house on Racecourse Road, Lahore, in the early summer days of 1947 when our parents came to India.

It was an old house and we met up with scorpions and a host of other crawlies. Parents had to be warned about bathroom walls and crevices, walking barefoot. But we forgot things like snakes and falling fans. I suppose we almost lost a younger daughter when the fan fell. Grandpa was playing with her - he would call her 'my little gel'. On that almost fateful day she rolled over towards him, suddenly, with a laugh, and then with a terrible thud the fan fell from the ceiling onto the bed, in the exact spot where 'little gel' had been Iying and gurgling. We were all so shaken, so overcome with the thought of what might have been, that we decided there and then that our parents should leave for Kashmir, where they were later going anyway. So a car was booked, from Lahore to Srinagar, father loved his little luxuries. We reserved their rooms at Nedou's Hotel in Srinagar by the side of the Dal Lake. Our last luxury together were plates of strawberries and clotted cream - the strawberries came from Ludhiana. Father's 'little gel' was soon smothered in red juice!

Their letters from the side of the Dal Lake were ecstatic, and as the days passed we, too, planned to leave -

Faiz's fate was to stay in Lahore running the 'Pakistan Times'.

But the rumblings of Partition were on and as Rajgarh burned, and as train after train pulled into Lahore Station loaded with its dead and injured, the girls and myself were packed off by train to Rawalpindi, from thence on to Srinagar. By this time tales of horror had reached us, and as Faiz loaded us onto the bus for Srinagar, our hearts were heavy.

Our parents had hired a large airy house for us all, the Taseers and ourselves, and the family was united, as the country moved towards its destiny of Partition.

The house had a large garden full of fruit trees and to keep mother busy she was put in charge of the unloading of the laden trees, organising the packing of the fruit into boxes for the market. Her helpers were many, but still piles of fruit lay rotting in the grass, and we filled our larders and ate to our hearts' content. Cherries came and went, all kinds of currents, raspberries, more strawberries, plums, apricots and peaches. We were amazed at the abundance.

It was a very hot summer and even Srinagar was sweltering. But misfortune seemed to dog us. Mother suffered a very severe attack of blood pressure followed by a haemorrhage, the girls were shockingly ill with whooping cough, our younger one being hospitalised and the bloodbaths went on in the Punjab and elsewhere. News was appalling. Faiz came and decided to move us nearer to Lahore in case Kashmir was cut off, one could hardly guess at what might happen. We left for Murree while the rest of the family remained in Srinagar. Their tale of hiring the last truck down to the plains and their evacuation is a harrowing one

Murree was still full of Sikh refugees awaiting transport and a way out. Friends were all anxious to try to arrange for a safe exit for the Sikh families, so we banded together, and somehow buses were arranged to take them all the way to Amritsar. There was a large convoy with as much luggage as could be accommodated. It was a sad and devastating sight for us all as they boarded the buses in the centre of the town, and bade us farewell. We had done for them what was humanly possible. We gathered on that fateful morning in good spirits, our hopes were high for them all. They all smiled bravely, we touched hands, said all would be well, it was but a short journey to Rawalpindi and there army personnel would join the convoy. We stood watching the last bus trundling down the hill on its way to safety. We went home, not yet at ease.

Before night the news had spread throughout the city. Who does not know the small village of Tret on the way along the Murree-Rawalpindi road? A stream runs the length of the main street, and that day it ran with blood, for tribesmen raced down from the surrounding hills upon the convoy, and all was lost.

One tells the story as the part of history now, one's own recollections, one's piecing together of a fabric, a little torn here and there, patched in places, but still whole, with a beauty which has not been lost through the years.

So we, too, later made our way along the same route to a new Lahore, now in a country named Pakistan, to look for a home, where we would spread out our humble belongings, heal wounds, begin a new life, with our children named 'Pakistanis'.

We found this home opposite the Lahore Radio Station, with the Governor as a neighbour at the end of a short road, with Masud Khaddarposh as a another neighbour and the stars and stripes of the U.S. Consulate waving next door.

Strange days came to pass. We lived in a home once occupied by a wellknown Lahore doctor, and below us, we looked down from our front balcony into what was his garden, strewn with the clinic's iron beds, bottles, chairs, syringes, in fact all the contents of what had been one of Lahore's finest private clinics.

Our accommodation was still full of the late occupant's possessions, fleeing in a great hurry. We stacked them away and then spread our belongings. Our parents arrived and the room to the right of the long, wide verandah earned the permanent name of Grandma's room! So our two dear parents stayed until it was time to start on the last lap of their long journey to Africa to meet a son, a daughter-in-law and grandchildren.

No. 41 Empress Road was ours until 1962, when the first long self-exile took us away. The fabric was again torn a little, no patch this time. It was farewell to a much-loved home and to Grandma's room.

(Excerpt from her autobiography *Over My Shoulder*)

4

ANOTHER DOLLAR CITY

IBRAHIM JALEES

Lahore. Another dollar city!

A man from a hotel came up to me. "Will you be staying in a hotel, sahib? Come with me. Brand new hotel, real Pakistani hotel. Best rooms, fine furniture, shower, flush, everything. Excellent arrangement. (This in English). The building was looted from Hindus."

The last detail was probably recounted in order to wake up in me the dormant spark of religious hatred and exploit it for his benefit. I followed him.

I deposited my luggage in the hotel and went over to Radio Pakistan in search of my friend Ibn-e-Insha. There I learned that he was on leave. Already in fever, this news raised my temperature by another degree. On the strange roads of Lahore I now began to hunt for a dispensary instead of Ibn-e-Insha. After roaming about quite a bit I saw a signboard *Daily Inqilab*. I thought I might find out the whereabouts of Ahmed Nadeem Qasmi from here. But not only was the office closed, but the paper itself had been shut down for many days. That drained the last bit of energy out of me and I could hardly walk. Feeling helpless I sat down on the platform of a closed shop in front of the office. Who would know me here that I was Ibrahim Jalees? A Pathan, who stood outside the gate of *Inqilab,* and had been staring at me for some time, came up to me and asked in his typical accent, "Who did you come to meet here?"

I told him I was looking for Ahmed Nadeem Qasmi. The Pathan, obviously educated and respectable, was stoutly built and was dressed in a baggy cotton *shalwar* and a dark striped tweed coat. On his head was a starched turban with a rising *turrah.* He said, "Ahmed Nadeem Qasmi is a famous man. It shouldn't be difficult to find him. I came here to meet Ghulam Rasul Mehr. Come with me, I'll help you to locate Qasmi."

I couldn't even stand up and narrated my unfortunate story. He was duly surprised and said, "Oh, you belong to Hyderabad Deccan? I have lived there in 1944. The people of Hyderabad are good and noble. Don't worry, as long as you don't meet Ahmed Nadeem Qasmi you'll be my guest. Just now I'll take you to a *hakeem* friend of mine. He'll rid you of your fever in a minute."

On this my new benefactor hailed a *tonga* and took me to his house. There an aged *hakeem* felt my pulse and tapped on my chest, and after making me drink a potion in an earthenware cup, made me lie down on a string bed. In about an hour I felt as if I was completely well. My benefactor, whose name was Mubarak Shah, then made me get up for breakfast.

After this refreshment this free citizen of the freedom-loving Frontier, whose heart seemed as big as the peaks of the Himalayas, took me in a *tonga* to a bungalow in Muslim Town. In the verandah sat an old scholarly-looking man smoking a *hookah*, with piles of books on a table beside him. Maulana Ghulam Rasul Mehr did not know Ahmed Nadeem Qasmi's address, but he didn't disappoint me. He called out to someone in the adjoining bungalow from which emerged Maulana Abdul Majid Salik who told us, "Qasmi lives on Nisbet Road behind the clinic of Dr Qavi Luqman and it is there that he spins his short stories."

We went back. At about four o'clock I was standing outside the house of the story-spinner, but the man himself was absent. But his sister Hajira Masroor was there and was happy to see that I had reached Lahore safe and sound. In the meantime the spinner also turned up. Looking at my haggard appearance he exclaimed, "What! Ibrahim Jalees?" As if he could not believe that a man with such emaciated features could be Ibrahim Jalees. Of course Ahmed Nadeem Qasmi is as handsome looking as his heart is beautiful which keeps its doors open even for the commonest stranger. My case is different. I may look like a scarecrow but I am still Ibrahim Jalees.

Hajira and Qasmi Sahib both asked why I was putting up at a hotel. "You should have come here straightaway," they said. "This is embarrassing for us."

I replied, "You two are lesser artists than I am. I want to be the guest of someone of my own status. Give me the address of the bungalows of Hameed Akhtar or Ibn-e-Insha." Qasmi Sahib's face lighted up with his typical smile as he answered, "I am sorry I don't know the addresses of these two great writers, but they can be found out. Come with me."

Our *tonga* trotted for some time over unknown ways, and at last stopped. We were in front of the Paradise Cold Drink Restaurant. On the upper storey hung the signboard of *Savera*, the famous, exquisite and progressive magazine of Chaudhry Nazir Ahmed. Leaving me and Mubarak Shah to eat bread and butter in the Paradise

101

Restaurant, Qasmi Sahib went upstairs to the journal's office and came back after a while. "Found it," he said.

Soon we were standing outside a Chinese pagoda opposite the Odeon Cinema. Qasmi Sahib knocked on the door and a slim, be-spectacled Confucius-looking man came out. That was not Confucius, that was Ibn-e-Insha, and the place was not a pagoda but his house. Qasmi Sahib used to say it was portable and could easily be stolen, or transported anywhere else.

It was a very small house, but for me it was as big as Lahore, for I could live there and find shelter in it. I brought over my things from the hotel. After that my other benefactor, Mubarak Shah, took leave of me at the shop of Sindbad the Tailor at the crossing of Beadon Rod and McLeod Road. I am not likely to come across Mubarak Shah again, but I shall never be able to forget him.

I shall be grateful to you for ever, Mubarak Shah!

Good bye, Mubarak Shah!

After that we went out in search of Hameed Akhtar. In the whole of Lahore Hameed Akhtar is one man who can never be traced. That is, every progressive writer in Lahore complains that it is very easy to know of Hameed Akhtar's address but not so easy to find him. After failing to meet Hameed Akhtar till six o'clock, we returned home after meeting his address, because Qasmi Sahib and Hameed Akhtar had to attend the weekly meeting of the Progressive Writers' Association. How fine! The very day I get to Lahore there is the Association's get-together the same day. I didn't want to inflict my non-progressive presence on the meeting, but Qasmi Sahib promised not to introduce me to anyone there.

As we stepped into the YMCA Hall, I stood rooted to the spot, for there was Muhammad Safdar, my friend of

Bombay, playing the chairman. In order to escape his notice I sat crouched behind Qasmi Sahib. Zuhair Siddiqui had just finished reading out his piece on the reactionary aspects of Iqbal's poetry and Agha Shorish Kashmiri was indignantly replying to his accusations, while I was trying to keep out of sight of Safdar's terrifyingly big eyes. But there was no escape.

After the meeting all the progressive cronies gathered in the tiny sitting room of Ibn-e-Insha to have a look at this reactionary communalist who had fled from the Islamic state of Hyderabad in order to draw breath in the Islamic Republic of Pakistan. Muhammad Safdar shouted, "O you fascist, you have come here too?" Then the other progressive writers were introduced to me.

This is Ahmed Rahi.

Here is Nazir Chaudhry.

And this is Arif Abdul Mateen.

I was feeling quite non-plussed on making their acquaintance, but I managed to say that it was a great pleasure to meet them. At the same time I was thankful to God that Abdullah Malik was not one of them. The Almighty was probably still considering my expression of thanks when a handsome young man of 25 or 26, in a chocolate-coloured suit, entered the room, and, advancing towards me with his hand held out, and without an introduction, said, "Jalees Sahib, I am Abdullah Malik."

All that I could mutter was "Oh . . . you mean . . .you!"

He added at once, "Yes, I mean Abdullah Malik."

That left me even more nervous, and everybody laughed. My good fortune that soon all the Punjabis began to converse in dialect and I tried to bring my nerves under control by lighting a cigarette.

103

When everybody had left, and I lay down in my bed after dinner, I asked myself, "Why am I afraid of Abdullah Mailk? What is it about him that makes me nervous? I am better known as a writer. In the whole of India and Pakistan people respect me more than Abdullah Malik. He's not a patch on me. It's like from the sublime to the ridiculous."

But, at the same time, somebody was saying to me in my heart of hearts, "Abdullah Malik is not the name of an individual. He's a movement. He possesses a balanced and highly developed sense, and all that you have is a sorry pen. He knows mankind. He stands before man, looks deep into his eyes, while you only gaze at his reflection in a hall of mirrors. He is not just Abdullah Malik. He is progressivism itself. And you are not Ibrahim Jalees. You are reaction, regression. He is Jules Fucek, Louis Aragon, Ilya Ehrenburg and Howard Fast, while from inside you are just Baudelaire and Andre Gide. When the chips are down, and the ground is pulled from under the feet, Jules Fucek keeps standing and Andre Gide falls to the ground."

But my ego, my vanity goads me. "Even when you fall you are taller than Abdullah Malik. Never bow your head. It'll be your defeat. Abdullah Malik's steadfastness is not art. Your faltering footstep is art. Literature with an aim is sheer nonsense. Its only art for art's sake that matters. Be careful, never bow your head." And, as usual, I went to sleep in the dark.

Next morning I was still in bed when Ahmed Rahi and Nazir Chaudhry came to see me. The circle of my acquaintance began to widen.

This is the office of the daily *Imroze*. Ayub Ahmed Kirmani is writing the editorial. "Hello Jalees. Thank God you've got here alive. Have a cigarette." I am looking at him with amazement, and I say to him, "Kirmani Sahib, you are the same Ayub Ahmed Kirmani who was captain of the Hockey Eleven in the Osmania University?" He laughed and said, "Come, have some tea. Are Jigar and the rest of them OK? I say, tell me about Hyderabad. I am missing it badly. Ausaf, Ashfaq, Aaqil, Yusuf, Nazim, Raza, Baqir and the rest of them. Are they all alive or have they been killed?"

It is getting on to evening. I am standing before Paradise Hotel. Ahmed Rahi says, "Meet Qateel Shifai." We fell into each other's arms. My presence has lighted up Qateel's healthy, florid face with the lightning of a smile. With him are Jamil Malik and Hasan Tahir. "Come on. Let's have tea and talk."

India Coffee House is ablaze with noise. The intellectuals of Pakistan are engaged in heated discussions. On one table are Maulana Chiragh Hasan Hasrat, Bari Sahib, Maulana Salahuddin Ahmed, and Shorish Kashmiri. Around another Sher Muhammad Akhtar, Salahuddin Akbar and Ahmed Bashir are having cold coffee. On a corner table Qayyum Nazar, Yusuf Zafar, Riaz Qadir, Mukhtar Siddiqui and Zia Jullundhri are trying to interpret the latest poem of Meeraji. Someone, possibly from the CID, is saying, "We can't have India Coffee House in Pakistan. It'll have to be Pakistan Coffee House." Maybe that is why the well-known short story writer Muhammad Hasan Askari is going out of India Coffee House with Chaudhry Rashid Ahmed of Maktaba-e-Jadeed Publishing House.

There is a man standing in front of Bristol Hotel. I ask Ibn-e-Insha, "Is Jan Nisar Akhtar in Lahore?" "No, no," he replies, "This is our own Abid Hashri." We are introduced. Abid Hashri is a great friend of Shaukat Siddiqui, the short story writer from Lucknow. Because of Shaukat Siddiqui the chance encounter is transformed into friendship.

This is the office of *Adakar*. Ahmed Rahi says, "Let's go and see Qamar. He and I are writing the songs of a new film." "Which Qamar?" I ask. "You don't know Qamar? Qamar Ajnalvi." "Oh yes, I know him. He also knows me well."

Enter Tanveer Naqvi. Qamar introduces us. Tanveer Naqvi, the famous revolutionary poet of the Indian film industry. He invites us to dinner that evening. I demur. I don't drink. But what's the harm? I am impressed by Tanveer Naqvi and he is impressed by me. Its not only pleasure that one looks for in drink.

Tired after roaming about the whole day, we are poring over old and new journals at Chaudhry Sultan's "Kitabi Duniya." Inside the shop a short and stout young man, something like a British Tommy, is either sitting or lying down. This is Riaz Javed. An unforgiving critic. He has been a side-kick ofkick of Maulana Salahuddin Ahmed, and is now wallowing in Marxist criticism. Even famous critics quail before him. Let's go for a moment to the office of *Imroze*.

This is the only newspaper populated by youthful, intelligent, progressive writers. Meet Hasan Aarafi. He is as yet unknown, but, mark my words, soon he will be a poet of the people and become the idol of thousands. And meet this young man, He's Hameed Hashmi. You know Anees Hashmi? He's his younger brother. Very useful if you are interested in foreign progressive literature, or if you want anything translated.

The night is half over. I am alone, passing before the girls' hostel of the medical college. There's a cigarette between my fingers but no matches. All the shops are closed. A well-dressed young man is nearing me. He is smoking. I stop him under a lamp-post. "May I light my cigarette with yours?" I say, that's Zaheer Babar. "Hello, chain-smoking critic, where are you coming from at this time of night? And why are you loitering near the girls' hostel?" A smile hovers on the handsome face of Zaheer Babar, "You are mistaken," he says, "I live in the boys' hostel nearby."

Zaheer Babar threw away a half-smoked cigarette and lighted another.

Imroze has published an article of mine. Five columns. Oh, good! Seven rupees per column. Thirty-five rupees! Come on, let's go to the office of *The Pakistan Times* and get the money. We'll meet Faiz Sahib there. Faiz Ahmed Faiz. He's the editor of *The Pakistan Times*. What an attractive personality. An ever-smiling face. Humming thoughts. And yet every feature of the face is articulate. I was so over-awed by Faiz Sahib that I came away promising to meet him again.

I continued to roam the streets of Lahore. Lahore became bigger and bigger. It was no longer a strange city. As it expanded, I saw in one of the faraway streets Hameed Akhtar standing by a fruit-seller's barrow eating a banana. Ahmed Rahi, who is the loudspeaker of the Progressive Writers' Association, shouted," I say, Ibrahim Jalees, there stands Hameed Akhtar."

I enveloped Hameed Akhtar in my arms. We had lived together in Bombay for a whole year, and then separated as if never to meet again. There was no hope of another encounter, for Punjab had been divided and Hyderabad had been devastated. But we did meet again.

Hameed Akhtar arranged for me to stay with one Abdur Rahim, an aristocratic friend of his. Ibn-e-Insha resented this and asked, "Jalees, are you uncomfortable here?"

"No, my dear Ibn-e-Insha, nothing of the sort. The fact is that I am a scholar gipsy, I don't remain rooted to one spot. What possible discomfort can there be in your house. There are your loving parents who treat me with tender affection as if I am Ibn-e-Insha. Your younger brother, Riaz Ahmed Khan, who insists on talking to me in Punjabi knowing full well that I can't speak your language, and every day brings new kinds of cigarettes for me. Sometimes "Gold Flake", sometimes "Scissors", sometimes "Passing Show" and sometimes "Red Lamp", and on the excuse of buying a packet for me keeps me informed of the entire range of cigarette brands. But seriously Ibn-e-Insha, what a large family you have. About a dozen people, and you the sole bread-earner. I don't want to add to your burden. However, if Pakistan had been a land of Ibn-e-Inshas instead of feudals and capitalists, and your father had got the lands here that he lost in East Punjab, or if your department was paying you adequately for your literary efforts, I would have lived with you for ever."

"There is another thing too," I added. "Your house reminds me too much of home. When the world comes to life in the morning, the waking-up noises made by your little brothers and sisters, Riaz, Sheedu, Meedu, and Bibo, take my mind back to the noises of Shehryar, Zoya, Lily, Iftikhar and Zubaida and I am smitten with nostalgia. It is as if I wake up in Hyderabad and spend the day in Lahore. The way you, your parents and your brothers and sisters have looked after me, is going to remain unforgettable. How can I ever thank you!"

I shifted to Abdur Rahim's house. What a place, a veritable refugee camp! There's Hameed Akhtar who has come from East Punjab, Rashid Hasan has migrated from Lucknow, and I have fled from Hyderabad Deccan. Even our servant Sher Ali is a remnant of the destruction in Kashmir.

There is only one thing common among the four of us. The pain of living. We brought nothing with us from East Punjab, UP, Hyderabad and Kashmir, except for a frightening past which makes us frustrated with living and the future of the world. Only Hameed Akhtar stands in our midst like a rock. Despite wading through many streams of human blood from Ludhiana to Lahore, he has not lost his mental equilibrium. Unlike us three, he never looks back at the past. His eyes only gaze at the future. He is looking for the coming world and the new man who is to arrive. He says, "The bourgeois system is just the frost, the mist, that is keeping the new world away from our sight. We shall melt this frost, this mist, with the warmth of our eyes, and then we'll be able to see the roofs and cupolas and walls of Moscow. Moscow is not just the capital of the USSR. It is the name of a colony of human beings. It is a symbol."

Sometimes when I am very sad, Nazir Chaudhry pats me on the shoulder and says, "What is this gloom? If you really want to pass your days pleasantly then do it the way Ahmed Rahi does. The fellow is simply living it up."

Then I begin to think seriously about what Nazir has said. Ahmed Rahi is a poet. The whole day long he indulges in hollow laughter on the roads of Lahore, in restaurants and the meetings of progressive writers, as if that is all that writers, poets and artists of the Repulic of Pakistan are expected to do; and that they have no other occupation, no other hobby. Or as if Pakistan was created for feudals and capitalists and its doors are closed for artists and workers and ordinary human beings.

Ahmed Nadeem Qasmi has given up his job with Radio Pakistan. Hajira Masroor and Khadija Mastoor have stopped writing radio features. Qateel Shifai has given up his radio contract. The reason is that Radio Pakistan was devoting itself to propaganda for the Nawabs and landlords of Pakistan. Abdullah Malik has relinquished his job in *Akhbar-e-Muhajireen* and Tufail Ahmed Khan has disassociated himself from weekly *Istiqlal* and daily *Nawa-e-Waqt*, because the two of them felt that feudals and capitalists were hiding behind the pages of these two newspapers.

Then what are progressive writers going to do? How are they to solve the economic problems of their families and their dependents? What are they to live on?

It is said that the government made many lucrative offers to Zaheer Kashmiri, but it could not divert his gaze from the fields and factories. The government run by the feudals and capitalists was not able to buy his gaze and his conscience. It failed to buy his brain, his pen.

Ahmed Rahi is asking Nazir Chaudhry to give him a key to his office so that he can sleep there, for Ahmed Rahi's father has said to him, "If you can't bring any money home, why come home at all?"

Hameed Akhtar's trousers are almost in tatters, and he has no other pair. No money too. He just had two cups of tea in the morning. His lips are parched, but he has kept his embrace around the progressive ideology of life. He is dressed in rags. He hasn't eaten. But his footsteps are steady. There is no shaking him out of his determination.

Ahmed Nadeem Qasmi, known for his good clothes, is in a shirt with a frayed collar and has been yearning for a cigarette from somewhere.

Muhammad Safdar has been smoking *beedis* made by Kale Khan-M.Hanif and singing in his deep voice the Punjabi verse, "The rocks of the mountains are weeping on hearing our laments."

Ahmed Rahi is ever ready to share the tribulations of his friends. Ahmed Rahi, who turned his body into steel by doing 400 push-ups at a time in Delhi's Qarol Bagh and Amritsar's Katra Sant Singh, is a very soft man at heart. He seems to have been born for his friends and lives for his friends, and maybe he'll die for his friends. His own grief doesn't matter where the problems of others are concerned. Thus when he saw the South Indian Ibrahim Jalees shivering in the winter of the Punjab, he took off his pullover and gave it to me. "My friend, put this on," he said.

I demurred, but he said, "Don't feel shy. We are the artists of Pakistan, writers of a bourgeois country. Our time too will come and we'll take revenge from these mighty landlords and capitalists. Today we are shivering in this cold. Tomorrow capitalism and feudalism and imperialism will die of the same cold."

I put on the pullover. Hameed Akhtar said, "There is no need to feel embarrassed. I'll ask Tufail Ahmed Khan today to write an article on the economic condition of progressive writers in a bourgeois democracy."

Everybody laughed. Meantime Riaz Javed came in and shouted, "Good news! Good news!" We all turned to him. He said, "Congratulations gentlemen. This is to announce that Russian wheat, Russian cloth, Russian soap, Russian oil and Russian cigarettes have arrived in Lahore." This was greeted with exclamations of "Good! Very good news!"

Arif Abdul Mateen interposed, "But do you know that all the big traders of Pakistan have protested strongly against this, because they say that Russian wheat and Russian cloth will promote the spread of communism in Pakistan."

111

We all burst into laughter, but the news was true and had also appeared in the newspapers. Ahmed Rahi was very happy and said, "Well. Now I shall have a suit of Russian cloth stitched, and after washing my face with Russian soap and eating bread made out of Russian wheat, I'll walk into Volga Restaurant and in future sit there, smoking a Russian cigarette. Good bye to Paradise Restaurant!"

Safdar retorted, "You cannot leave Paradise Restaurant, for where else can you go? All your private letters come to that address."

A broad smile breaks on the rugged features of Ahmed Rahi as if a canal had sprouted from rocky land. But Nazir Chaudhry has started a quarrel with Safdar. There is every possibility of it becoming acrimonious, but suddenly Zaheer Kashmiri walks in and everybody is quiet. The progressive poet oozes from his golden locks and ruddy face, his hooked nose and Shakespeare-like beard and his dark blue suit with white stripes, and he declaims in a thundering voice:

"Communes are coming up today in every corner of Telangana land,

"The breeze of life is flowing today in its dust-laden existence,

"Today the Telangana man is waving the colours of love's victory,

"Today the Telangana man is announcing the revival of the East,

"Today the Telangana man is connecting Bidar with Greece and Java."

Tea arrives. A proposal is presented that a group photograph of progressive writers be arranged which should not only show their faces but also depict their economic plight. This group photo should be inserted into Pakistan's political history. But Ahmed Rahi suggests that Zaheer Kashmiri's picture should be separate from the group, in an inset.

Ibn-e-Insha makes an amendment. "It should be like this. The pictures of Zaheer Kashmiri and William Shakespeare should be printed on the same page, with the caption: 'Let us see towards which flame the moth goes'"

But Ahmed Rahi continues, "No camera can portray Zaheer Kashmiri properly, because I know for a fact that Pakistan does not have cameras that can make technicolour portraits."

In a rage Zaheer Kashmiri pounces on Rahi in his best rhetoric. "In this mortal world it is long since beauteous good sense took leave of Ahmed Rahi in the dark of night. That is why, obsessed with his limited sight, and waiting futilely for the inspiring light of the morning, he confuses the negative with the positive and, in interminable accents, goes on spouting sheer nonsense every moment of the day." And, in order to change the mood of the gathering, he begins to recite his latest poem.

As the poem ends, the daily informal gathering of the Progressive writers also concludes. Coming out, I light a cigarette and begin to think. Where am I to go? Did Zaheer Kashmirir speak the truth, that there is no other lunatic asylum but this life?

I stand alone. No, I'm not alone. There is my beloved with me --- hunger. Hunger which is the lifeblood of Pakistan. Nowadays I am entrapped in her love. I have just six annas in my pocket. When everybody is gone I proceed stealthily to a man selling *kababs* on the *pavement* of the McLeod Road crossing and buy two *kababs* and two *naans* from him. Rolling these up in an old newspaper I go to the house of a friend and there I quietly eat my meal and thank God that no one has seen me. Then I go public and stroll on The Mall smoking a cigarette as if I have just had dinner in Stiffles or Metro. Whereas the fact is that Falettis and Lorangs and Stiffles and Metro are located far away from Pakistan. The common man of this country can't reach them. How many rupees separate the people's Pakistan from Metro's Pakistan? I don't know.

But in the first days of the month when Ayub Ahmed Kirmani gets his five hundred rupees we do spend some evening in Metro Pakistan too. Metro Pakistan is completely different from Hira Mandi Pakistan and Shah 'Almi Pakistan. Everything in Metro Pakistan is different -- - the population, the culture, the politics and even the climate. When I step into Metro Pakistan I feel an inferiority complex overcoming me because my only coat is frayed at the elbows and the crease of my trousers disappeared long ago. Otherwise too I look more like a coolie of the Nizam State Railway or a snake-charmer from the Vindhyachal mountains, or an Indian secret agent.

Metro Pakistan is a very romantic place. When you come out of Shah 'Almi Gate or from the narrow, twisting and stinking alleys of Abdullah Malik's Koocha Chabuk Sawaran and suddenly enter Metro Pakistan you feel as if you have emerged from the war-battered ruins of China's Nanking city that you see in news-reels and have reached Rainbow Island in the company of Dorothy Lamour.

In Metro Pakistan you see the women of Islam in colourful dresses dancing with their boy friends, breast to breast, and even lips to lips, while in Shah 'Almi Pakistan a frenzied Muslim may be out with a pair of scissors ready to snip off the plaits of young girls not in purdah. That is why you don't see any women in Shah 'Almi nowadays, only *burqas*. And yet, in crowded Anarkali Bazaar when sometimes a fairy face lifts the veil of her *burqa* to look at

114

something, it is as if the Kaaba has been illumined by celestial light.

The dance of wealth goes on. Wine-glasses are tinkling, and, on the floor of Metro Pakistan, feudalism and capitalism, drunk in each other's arms, are pirouetting like in a cabaret. It looks as if they will stumble, fall . . .

Ha ha ha!

Beer and gin!

Gin and whisky!

Whisky!

Ha ha ha! Come on Kirmani, let's get out. This Metro Pakistan is not for us. Everything here is a fraud. Look! The blood of seventy million humans is being poured into wine-glasses. The wide expanse of life has been contracted in this narrow place for a few persons, while outside, darkness and death have been made the fate of thousands upon thousands. Hold me tight. My head is whirling. I can hardly breathe. The glare of lights from London and New York is blinding my eyes. My sight is dying, my heart is dying. I am falling. I am about to die. Take me out of here. And tell how far I am from the people's Pakistan. How far?

(Excerpts translated from *Doa Mulk Ek Kahani*)

REFERENCES & NOTES

1. *Two countries, one story*, a long forgotten, and perhaps out-of-print, book by Ibrahim Jalees, is the story of the subcontinent's partition, revolving around Hyderabad Deccan, his home in India, and Lahore which he visited, and Karachi, the city where he finally settled.

When the British rule ended, and India and Pakistan became free and sovereign, Mir Osman Ali Khan, the Nizam of Hyderabad, then reputedly the richest man in the world, decided that he would accede to neither of the two dominions. Accordingly he declared his independence, although the landlocked state of Hyderabad was populated overwhelmingly by Hindus who wanted to be part of the new India. Legally he was entitled to do so, but in the modern world you cannot ignore the wishes of 15 million of your Hindu subjects just because you are a Muslim yourself.

On the other hand, his Muslim subjects were jubilant and bent upon protecting and preserving the Osmania state which they characterised as "Southern Pakistan." However, this was not to be, and India over-ran Hyderabad after a few months. In this crisis, Ibrahim Jalees, a staunch supporter of the state's Muslim culture, had to flee, and was assisted by his communist friends in somehow getting to Bombay. After staying there in hiding for some time, he purchased a "permit" for Pakistan and flew by air to Karachi. After being homeless and aimless in Karachi, Jalees caught a train to Lahore to be among his friends in the Progressive Writers' Association. This is a sentimental account of his encounter with them and with the city of Lahore, and graphically captures the atmosphere of 1947-48.

5

THE WAGAH CANAL

FIKR TAUNSVI

Wagah.... It is neither located on a plateau nor on a river bank. Neither does it produce cotton to be sent to Vassawar. Nor is it a port for which the British and the French fought for years. Wagah is a plain and simple canal--silent, gentle and calm. It watered the fields before the formation of India and Pakistan and breathed life into swaying fields of corn. But the moment the bugles were blown to herald Independence, it seemed as if the Wagah canal had turned into an arid wasteland. Instead of milky-white cascading waters, the troops were stationed there. Guns, cannons and armoured cars brought news of freedom to Wagah and relieved the canal of the burden of cultivating the fields. Henceforth, the fields around Wagah canal were not to wait for the streamlets carrying life-giving nectar. Instead, they were to get used to the weight of cannons and armoured cars. The fields, in any case, were not servile to either the canal or its glistening sweet water. Nor were they bonded to the farmer who ploughed them or to the ears of corn that swayed over them. They were, in reality, only a few pieces of dry land. And land either belongs to God or the King. No one else has any claim over it. And the King, the deputy of God on this earth, can dispose it of any time and anyway he likes. If he so wills, he can destroy the ears of corn and replace them with guns and bullets. He can change the face of the earth. He can turn a jungle into a flourishing country and then divide it into two and call one Mangal (Mars) and the other Sanichar (Saturn). Having done that he can proclaim before the whole world to the beat of drums that Mangal is Mangal and Sanichar is Sanichar. That is why the twain will not be allowed to meet....

And then to emphasize the divide between the two, huge signboards were installed. Colorful flags were hoisted, a green one on this side and a red on the other. Now they had separate names.

Separate flags, separate uniforms and separate cannons. That is how the world came to know that the canal which watered the fields, both on the east and west, would now be used to divide east from west, and henceforth historians would call it Wagah.

I could have easily called Wagah, the border between India and Pakistan, but I feared--and I had solid and valid reasons for my apprehensions--that all the leading historians and geographers would have immediately censured me for doing that because, for them the old concept, according to which there used to be only one border between the two countries, had now become redundant. Moreover, a few astrologers in 1947 made the heavenly bodies revolve in such a scientific manner that instead of having one border between them, India and Pakistan had two. Actually the word 'two' had befuddled their minds in such a way that now neither the stars moved in an orderly manner nor did their predictions come true. Exasperated by this very 'two' and swayed by their animosity to 'one' they became oblivious of the fact that the new unit they were trying to create was by itself a derivative of 'one'.

Consequently you may be exasperated or annoyed, but I can't deny the two borders between India and Pakistan. One is Wagah and the other.... But what have I to do with the other one? I only want to convey a few things about Wagah crossed by over ninety lakh people during the last few days in the name of safeguarding their religions. I chanced to cross the border three times during the last few days.

The first time my status was of a regular citizen, i.e., I entered the territory of India as a regular refugee, riding a regular army truck, and with proper pomp and show. I say 'pomp and show' because our grand caravan, consisting of trucks, was given a grand reception of a fluttering red and yellow flag, an extensive army camp approbation and applause, and slogans shouted by the refugees themselves. The first thing I did was to try and search for that dividing line. To define it, the pages of the Quran, the Vedas and the Granth Sahib had to be reinterpreted so as to bring out altogether different meanings from what they actually stood for. On this the Prime Minister of Great Britain said: 'It is not merely a line. On the contrary, it is a sacred link which will strengthen the bond of friendship between India and Pakistan.' Consequently I was disappointed when I looked for that strong bond. There was no formidable mountain, sea, river or jungle on the border. But almost immediately I repented having thought so foolishly, because having a river, a sea or a mountain for a border was a concept associated with the Stone Age. Man was afraid of man then, one state was against the other, and the borders existed as defence barriers against the enemy. Wars were fought to vanquish adversaries and gain dignity and honour. As far as I could understand, there was no earthly reason for India and Pakistan to be enemies. Whenever the elites of the two countries met, they embraced one another like brothers. That the commoners of the two countries always pounced on one another like hungry wolves was an altogether different matter. The downtrodden people are by nature wolves, eternally hungry and bloodthirsty. Why should anyone raise walls for the sake of people like that? Actually the real cause of a war was the clash of interests between the elites. Otherwise, how else can one explain that when the commoners are virtually tearing each other apart like wolves, the elites, overflowing with love and affection for each other, sit together in cozy comfort over tea, rub their snouts with each other like goats, and work out how to bear the crushing burden of the extra millions raked in as profit under the new industrial policy.

I was shocked to see the border guards of both countries indulging in idle gossip-mongering outside their camps. I felt like shouting at them and telling them: 'Aye soldiers! What's the use of posting you here? Don't you know you are there to strike terror in the heart of the enemy? And here you indulge in meaningless chatter, as if you have been trained since childhood just to do that! How comfortable you look playing cards, as if you were born masters. '

But before I could learn more about the Wagah border, our caravan set out on the road to India, the land of paradise. My desires remain unfulfilled.

The next time I went to Wagah on a lorry from Amritsar. This one too, like other lorries, collected a fixed fare from the passengers and took them to the border. The passengers were either Hindus or Sikhs. Almost all were traders. All of them cursed Pakistan during the journey. I got angry several times. One person deliberately picked a quarrel with me when he heard me say that I was going to Wagah to meet Ahmad Nadim Qasmi, a Muslim friend of mine. When I asked him: 'Are you going to Wagah to sell the bundles of Kashmiri cloth to your Muslim friends?' he told me truthfully that the merchant in question was no friend of his. He was just a merchant. And as far as he was concerned there was not even remote connection between trade and friendship.

This time, I was shocked to see the way the two governments functioned. There was no sign of the Wagah Canal on the border. Nor did I see the flags or the soldiers. There was just a three-mile long sea of people who had swallowed up the marks which demarcated one country from the other. This sea was pulsating with the same people, who until only a year ago were enemies. Now, they could be seen sitting together under the shade of the trees having a friendly chat, sharing a sliced melon, enjoying a joke, guffawing and hugging one another. A man donning a Turkish cap was slicing a mango and offered pieces of it to a Sikh. A Muslim woman had brought homemade *keemaparathas* and was laughing and affectionately feeding a *dhoti*-clad gentleman. Thousands were crossing the border at will without fear of being stopped. I really felt sorry for the way the two governments functioned. What could be more absurd than this: that these thousands of people seemed to have absolutely no feeling and regard for the dignity and honour of their respective governments! They hardly remembered that only a few months ago they did not carry melons, mangoes and *keemaparathas* for one another. Instead, they had daggers, swords and bombs to destroy one another. I wondered how the intensely violent religious hatred in their hearts had subsided. I wished to God they had the sense to keep their religious feelings alive for a few more days so that their respective governments could prove to the world that they were two different people prepared to destroy each other! But that had not happened. Yesterday's enemies were sitting together recounting their tales of woe. The tales of ransacked homes. Tales of how their women were dishonoured, how their flourishing businesses collapsed, how their homes were set on fire, how their children got separated from their mothers and the wives from their husbands. All these tales were shocking and full of anguish. They brought tears of sympathy to every listener and carried with them a faint glimmer of hope that one day they might go back to their homes and live together once more. Now, those tales had no meaning. At the most they could provide raw material to the future historians. And there was also the possibility that future historians might refuse to include them in histories because they had more melons, mangoes and *keema-parathas* in them than daggers and swords. Such non-political aspects had no place in history books.

The history of Wagah of those days is absurd because it was against the basic ideology of a government, and encouraged disloyalty towards the government. And the truth was that the down-trodden people have always rebelled against the ruling classes and betrayed their trust in them. That was why I felt like descending on their camps and giving them a piece of my mind: 'Gentlemen! Stop this cursed friendly intercourse between these people. Otherwise, if people keep on meeting one another like this, they might begin to understand the reality and all that has been achieved so far would go down the drain.'

The most interesting feature of the Wagah border were the shops set up for the organized sale of religion. A bearded *Maulvi* sat there with a huge pile of books, including the Vedas, Shastras, Granths, Geetas and Upanishads and many more works in Hindi and Sanskrit. Sitting next to him was a Sardarji who sold copies of the Quran Majeed, Fiqh, Hadith and dozens of other writings in Arabic. All those books were a part of the loot which the two gentlemen had brought to sell. Otherwise, they would have been at each other's throats by now. But at Wagah they were selling their books peacefully, the *Maulvi* selling the Hindu scriptures and the Sikh works on Muslim theology. In their heart of hearts they were thinking that

122

once the books were sold, they would sit back and live comfortably for at least a few months. If by selling religion one could have two square meals everyday, what could be better.

Next, I met the writers. They were Muslims. They had come to Wagah from Pakistan. Their group consisted of Sahir Ludhianvi, Ahmad Nadim Qasmi, Ahmed Rahi, Abdul Matin Arif, Ibne Insha, Barkat Ali Chowdhury and Salahuddin Akbar. We just rushed and hugged one another. The earth under our feet did not shake with this. Nor did it protest that the earth which the Hindu and Muslim writers trod was either a part of India or Pakistan. As such it should have cried out in protest against the aliens treading on its bosom. But it remained quiet. How dumb this earth was! Actually, we were totally oblivious of the religion of the soil, stones, straw and grass underneath our feet, though we ought to have been more aware. In fact, if we had made these mute elements conscious of the greatness of their religion and their regional cultures, there was every chance of their revolting against us!

Anyway, we writers were not bothered about the protest or lack of it. Ours was a meeting of writers. So we poked fun at one another's writing and enjoyed *kababs*, *korma*, rice and tea at an exclusively Muslim hotel. We almost forgot that we were sitting at a place called Wagah which divides Pakistan from India. We laughed at the folly of those thousands who wanted to forge an intimate relationship between the two dominions. Then, we informed one another about the major achievements of our respective governments so that we could convey the information to them and thus perform the literary duties of fifth columnists. All sorts of suggestions were mooted to strengthen each other's governments, so that they could join hands to wage war against the half-naked and the semi-starving masses and suppress them. A couple of writers suggested they should raise a wall of tigers on one bank, and a wall of elephants on the other bank of the Wagah border so that people who regularly sat on either side and devoured melons and mangoes should learn to stay put in their own homes.

Anyway, we noted these absurd and impracticable suggestions and dispersed. The evening was drawing near and the military post on the border had sounded their bugles, warning people to return home. Gradually, the dividing line at Wagah emerged more clearly. We suddenly realized it was time to part, and walked to the border together Neem trees were lined on one side of the Grand Trunk Road. One stood bang on the border, almost as if it were a communist, otherwise it might have easily grown a little away, on either side. How boldly it stood there, as if no one could touch it! Had this been reported to the authorities of either country, the tree would have been surely felled. But why do that? Why not divide the leaves and branches equally between India and Pakistan? Why not tell the tree which of its branches and its leaves are Hindu or Muslim?

Sahir said to me: 'Why bother about this tree? Come let us go to Lahore.' And then all the Hindu writers went over to the other side of Wagah to the enemy country.

No one knows which politician forwarded the suggestions we had aired at Wagah just to have some fun at the expense of the lawmakers in both countries. When I went to Wagah for the third time, I was glad to see that the hall-marks, signs and symbols that distinguish one country from the other were in place. There was no trace of melons, mangoes and *keema-parathas*. Silence and desolation prevailed. All those guffaws, echoes of laughter, those tears and tales of woe had retreated to where they belonged. Their place was taken by tigers and elephants. Realizing the special importance of Wagah canal and fearing that this 'beauty' would become world famous and start attracting hordes of lovers from all over, it was hidden from their prying and unwelcome eyes. About half a mile away on this side of the border a lion spotted me and gave me a look which seemed to say: 'Sir, your daily incursions have made the border an object of ridicule. Don't you know, the border came into existence after long and serious deliberations. You should know the difference between taking this fact seriously and mocking at it?'

Following this, I and many other fun-loving people like me raised their heads and fluttering their eyelids attempted to catch a glimpse of the Wagah canal. But we could see nothing except army camps and the outlines of some familiar sights. One of the tigers told me that half a mile away, to the west of Wagah canal, an elephant was an expert in constitutional and international law. He prevented people from crossing over and informed them that the outmoded and uncivilized way of friendly social intercourse among people belonging to different countries was prohibited. Now, only regular passportholders could touch the 'Wagah beauty'. The government had to be convinced that the person claiming to be a lover was 'genuine' and that he was not a threat to the security of the 'beauty'.

I quietly took the army sentinel aside and asked: 'Well sir, a tree stood on the bank of Wagah canal. Can you tell me whether it has been felled and thrown away or. . . ?'

The sentry pointed his bayonet at me and staring at me said: 'Who are you to interfere in this business which concern the two governments? '

And in the core of my heart I said: 'Listen good man, after all I am a branch of the same tree.'

(Translated from Urdu by A.S. Judge and Mushirul Hasan.)

6

"The Infidel Comes. Where's My Dagger!"

BY GOPAL MITTAL

The civil disobedience movement launched by the Punjab Muslim League against the Khizr ministry remained peaceful on the whole. This was mainly due to the organisational ability of the province's League leaders. But there was also another reason. The movement never met with serious confrontation, either from the government or from any other direction.

If a campaign had been launched by the supporters of the ministry it was quite possible that the government could have strengthened itself by taking strict action against both the parties, but Sir Khizr Hayat did not have the guts to proceed only against the Muslims. Moreover there was some kind of talk at the highest level which was not exactly in favour of his ministry. The establishment of Pakistan looked like a certainty. In the event it was neither profitable for Khizr Hayat to remain in power nor did it meet with the changed perceptions of the Government of India. Thus he tendered his resignation. It's a different matter that even this did not result in the formation of the new ministry by the Muslim League, and Governor's rule had to be imposed.

Then all of a sudden Master Tara Singh got it into his head that he must make a show of aggression. Before a large crowd of Hindus and Sikhs he unsheathed his *kirpan*, his symbolic sword, and warned them that the time had come to do or die. After his harangue, when the procession was passing through Anarkali, night had fallen and I was on my way back from office. The processionists were really incensed, and wherever they saw a Muslim League flag they tore it down. If a flag was beyond reach a man would stand on another's shoulders and bring it down. If it was even higher than that the *kirpan* was used. It was more than evident that the peace and calm of Lahore were no more.

Like many other things, our *qalandars* of Lahore (as we called our group of intellectuals who were more spiritual than worldly-wise) did not realise the grimness of the riots. As I would step into the bakery, Bari Aleeg would shout, "The infidel comes. Where's my dagger!"

Even when the disturbances took a turn for the worse the area of Anarkali remained safe, and so the gatherings in Nagina Bakery went on as usual. Why was Anarkali safe? Because the Hindu and Muslim shopkeepers had made a pact that they would not allow the bazaar to be destroyed. Thus even when the city was burning, nothing untoward happened in Anarkali, although even here business remained suspended. Except for eating places no other shop was open.

One afternoon as I was playing cards at home, someone came and gave the news that arson and looting had started in Anarkali too. Some miscreants were breaking open the establishment of Raja Brothers and were also trying to set it on fire. In those days it was not easy to secure assistance from the police and the fire brigade, and it was apparent that, built as it was, the whole of Anarkali would be enveloped by the fire. But the presence of mind of the proprietors of Bija Mall & Sons, the famous crockery

127

mart, enabled them to contact the British Superintendent of Police on telephone. He reached the spot at once along with some constables, and with his own gun, shot down three rioters. The rest ran away. The fire had started, but it was prevented from spreading. Incidentally the only shop that was destroyed by it was that of a Muslim.

The dead bodies of the three arsonists were allowed to lie in the bazaar even the next day, perhaps to create a lesson. From their clothes and looks all the three appeared to be from the lowest class of Muslims, and were apparently hired hooligans.

While it was the intrepidity of a single Englishman which saved Anarkali, it was persistently being rumoured that the British were themselves responsible for the disturbances.

The compact among the traders of Anarkali remained intact, and, except for stray cases of stabbing, there was no unlawful incident in the bazaar. In any case, the Hindus were apprehensive, and somehow knew that this relative calm was only the harbinger of the coming storm. Reports about secret preparations for bloody riots placed suspicion on the sons of a Muslim landlord who owned extensive property in Anarkali. One of them was in the habit of paying an occasional visit to Nagina Bakery. A few days after the above incident, he accosted me on the way and said, "Mittal Sahib, why not have tea with us today?" His home was a large mansion, and his own room on the top floor was reached by going up a number of staircases.

As we reached the room, he asked me, "Do you know why I have brought you here?" I said, "To kill me?" He burst into laughter which sounded like an echo of genuine happiness, and said, "I am happy that at least one Hindu does not take me for a murderer. I have brought you here to rid myself of an emotional burden, and to tell you that the accusation that I am secretly preparing for killing and looting is false."

Admitted that Anarkali was undisturbed, but in the walled city hell had been let loose and the bazaars of the Hindus were being put to the torch turn by turn. As long as the Hindus had the assurance that Lahore would be part of India they stuck to their positions, but as soon as it became known that the city would form part of Pakistan, they lost their nerve. And when, somewhere at the very top, though not openly, it was decided that there would be an exchange of populations, and official trucks began to be provided for the movement, there was no question of Hindus remaining in Lahore.

My daily life was spent among Muslims, so most Muslims who were not personal friends, took me for one of them. Once a bizarre situation was created. It was the 15th of August and I was having breakfast in Nagina Bakery where the usual jolly crowd was gathered, when three rough-looking Muslims entered the place and sat down at the next table. Gradually they joined us in our conversation and then regaled us with stories of their loot and murder in a triumphant manner.

One of them was addressing me all the time and narrating the tale of their attack on a *Gurudwara*. He said the inmates of the *Gurudwara* had sufficient ammunition and they continued to defend themselves by firing at the attackers all the time. But then their ammunition was exhausted and these young fellows jumped over the wall into the *Gurudwara* and killed the Sikhs one by one.

I don't know whether it was complete trust in my Muslim friends or a streak of the devil in me that I told him that he was narrating all this to a Hindu. His tone changed at once, and he said, "If I had met you two days ago I would have certainly killed you, but yesterday Pakistan came into being and now you are my guest. Come with me to my house and I shall treat you like one, and if anyone so much as raises a finger at you I'll cut off his head." Then, taking out a few bullets from his pocket, he added, "Look, these are some of the bullets that your brothers have been firing at us."

The impact of the bloody riots on the *qalandars*, the intellectual denizens of Nagina Bakery, was only to the extent that Bari Aleeg stopped raising the slogan, "The infidel comes. Where's my dagger!" and would simply threaten to treat me as a *zimmi*. On this I would say, "Go on, you are just a running dog of some Nawab Mamdot." We were still optimistic about the state of affairs and believed that the Hindus who had run away would come back and Lahore would be its old self again.

But this optimism did not last many days. It was not only that the Hindus were fleeing from Lahore, new Muslims were being added to its population. The image of Lahore was being totally transformed. Now, instead of threatening to make me a *zimmi*, Bari began to express the fear, "I say, friend Mittal, I hope we don't have to grow beards."

Whether the riots were pre-planned or spontaneous, there were various conjectures. Some people averred that the killings began when the hooligans of Amritsar sent women's bangles to the hooligans of Lahore to indicate their contempt for the latter's inactivity. Another version was that the Muslim League leaders had themselves provoked them. But then there was also the story that Nawab Mamdot and some other Muslim Leaguers were going from mosque to mosque begging their brothers-in-faith to abstain from violence.

Possibly there was some truth in the various versions. Possibly the leaders had instigated rough elements among the Muslims, but when the intensity of the riots reached unmanageable proportions they tried to call them off. However, one thing was beyond comprehension. If the riots were according to a plan, why were the hundreds of shops and houses put to fire when they were an asset of Pakistan?

When the rioters attacked the locality in which Professor Brij Narain lived, he had tried to restrain their urge for arson and loot and murder by presenting this very argument before them. It was stated that the attackers were convinced of the professor's logic and had gone away. But then another group arrived to commit mayhem he failed to convince them and was the first to get killed.

Professor Brij Narain was an eminent economist. But where most economic experts claimed that Pakistan could never become consolidated as an independent economic entity, and that it was being built on sand, his was the lone voice that had faith in its economic integrity. He had written many articles in support of his thesis that Pakistan would be sustainable on economic grounds. He had decided to live on in Pakistan, and even the most rabid Muslim Leaguers believed in his dispassionate attitude. Maybe if he had lived he would have been invited to contribute to the economic strength of the new country, but fate willed otherwise.

The professor's death was a terrible shock for me. He had been my teacher and was responsible for moulding my personality. My family was already set against living on in Lahore, and now I too became unsteady and unresolved. Thus as the last caravan of trucks left Lahore I was one of its passengers. Some Muslim friends turned up to see me off, and many an eye was moist with tears. One passenger whispered in my ear, "The bastards! first they kill and turn us out of our homes and then they weep." I was incensed by his remark and told him to shut up. I have not been able to decide till today whether I was snubbing him or blaming myself. For the truth is that inside my heart I was feeling somehow that I was leaving my *qalandars* in a lurch.

As we reached Amritsar we again saw burnt houses. Though I had managed not to play the role of a martyr in Lahore, here, in Amritsar, I could not refrain from feeling ashamed.

I found that Raj Baldev Raj was also in this caravan. Where it halted the place had become a regular bazaar. We washed the dust of the journey from our faces and sat down to have tea. Those who had travelled with us had been deprived of whatever valuables they carried, but it transpired that there were looters among the refugees too. Some poor chap couldn't find his trunk, another complained that his bedding was missing. We were caustically commenting on this state of affairs when we heard a voice say from nearby, "Now we'll go and attack Lahore." I asked Raj when we were going to do that. His reply was, "Some day, but it will probably be to participate in a *mushaira*."

(Excerpts translated from his autobiography *Lahore Ka Jo Zikr Kiya*)

2

Lahore Goes Up In Flames

7

LAHORE 1947

B.C.SANYAL

Pre-Partition Agonies

The World War came to an end and the war at home began. We began to hear slogans about the rights of the linguistic and religious minorities. The dreadful consequences of the partition of the country could not even be dreamed but the air was rife with conjectures about the great divide. From my studio window agitated processions were seen one after another. A temper of violence was generating like a subterranean rumbling. The shape of things to come was yet diffused, but the fate of this city was the focus of discussion. The city of Lahore, enriched by the wealth and cultural heritage of the Hindus, Sikhs, and Muslims, the destiny of this city of stout heart became the burning question on every mind. Census and assessment of population and property had begun. Hindus had made large investments in educational, medical, industrial and religious institutions. Sikhs and Muslims had deep ties of history and indelible sentiments wrapped in the din and dust of the city. What would be the fate of the different communities in the hands of the arbiters ? It was no longer an imaginary fear but conceivable possibilities of a reality.

There was a perceptible increase in the number of sword-carrying Akalis in the town. The landlord of the

Regal Cinema building being a Hindu, had employed a couple of hefty *sardars* with naked swords in their hands to keep watch over his property. We made good use of them as models in my studio.

In the midst of this agitational atmosphere, the public of Jat dominated Rohtak, then a district headquarter of Punjab, decided to erect a statue of Sir Chhotu Ram. Chhotu Ram certainly deserved the honour and I needed the commission to execute the bronze statue. The memorial committee invited me to come to Rohtak and sign the agreement. The seretary of the committee, Chaudhry Kedar Singh, was a tough and shrewd negotiator, and he sensed my desperation in getting some work in hand and I gave in to his terms.

Lahore was hot in every respect. The summer in June with its dust storms and the dust raised by the political contest was hardly agreeable for concentration on serious work. So, my good and friendly pupils decided for me that I proceed to Kashmir. Chaudhry and Sir Chhotu Ram could wait till I returned refreshed. I, with my family of two and Hamida Begum, boarded a bus to Srinagar. Finally, we pitched our tents on the Pahalgam plateaux, at my favorite site. It was here, with the joyous assistance of Hamida we celebrated the first birthday of our daughter in August 1946.

But our joy was short-lived as Hamida brought ominous news from the Kashmiri hotels in the bazaar that Hindu-Muslim riots were imminent. We read about the dreadful communal killings in Calcutta. Hamida's anxiety infected us as it infected the rest of the holiday crowd on the plateaux, irrespective of caste and community. We organised a meeting of the tent-dwellers in the manner of a social get-together to relieve tension. Kashmir, a Hindu state with majority of Muslim subjects, could easily become a danger spot in the current atmosphere. In fact, the cordiality enjoyed between us, Hindus, Muslims, Sikhs, and Christians, was beginning to show the strain of the ugly riot news. At the meeting, controversial statements were made and questions raised. An air of gloom descended upon us. At the time in a holiday mood I had stopped shaving and sported a nur on my chin. To make light of the developing heavy air at the meeting I suggested that one way of lowering communal tension could be by sporting beards like mine by the Hindus and cultivating *beedis*--the tuft of hair--by our Muslim friends as a gesture of communal good-will.

My proposal was greeted with laughter and applause, and people relaxed. But an act of indiscretion on the part of the *tehsildar*--a Kashmiri Pandit--whom we had invited to tea at the meeting, vitiated the atmosphere. Normally, the Kashmiri Pandits are above the narrowness of social or caste behaviour, but our *tehsildar* guest rather ostentatiously chose to sit apart from our Muslim friends to sip his cup of tea. This was taken as an affront and tempers began to run high.

We returned to Lahore. The press was full of exaggerated news and views, truths and half-truths about the Calcutta riots. One could read between the lines about the shape of things to come. Our *ayah* Hamida Begum left us. I shaved off my beard.

In this disturbed state of mind I kept on postponing my work on the Chhotu Ram statue. Endless processions and shouting of slogans became the routine of life. We heard that India's independence was at the threshold, but at the cost of political amputation of the country. We also heard about the appointment of the Radcliff Commission and that the Punjab was to be partitioned into the East and West. No one knew yet which side would win the trophy. Justice Bakshi Tekchand, Sri Gokul Chand Narang and other prominent Hindus issued statements justifying the inclusion of Lahore in the East. Well-to-do people and men of means had already begun negotiations for transfer of property, exchange of assets and withdrawal of bank accounts.

All my assets were what I had in my studio and other household effects.

The Crack of Dooms

Stabbing, killing and burning had begun in restricted areas in Lahore. One evening, some friends had gathered at Khushwant Singh's house. Khushwant was then practising law, and his wife and he were good hosts. I and my wife also happened to call on them. G. D. Khosla and Azim Husain, both in the Indian Civil Service, and Manzoor Qader, a barrister-at-law, were present. The conversation inevitably turned to what individual decision was contemplated in the event of the declaration of Pakistan and India as two different entities. Those who were in government service had to opt for one or the other, and naturally, religious sentiment was to be the rationale of the choice, since the idea of Pakistan had been mooted on the basis of religion. Azim Husain said he would throw in his lot on the side of secular India. For me, it was not the question of secularism or theocracy, but the place I had learnt to love in two decades--through work, play and friendship. It was Lahore that mattered.

I sought counsel with P. N. Thapar who was then the commissioner of the division. He was interested in the arts, and I was pleased to make his aquaintance. Thapar's friendly advice to me was that during the disturbed period it would be better for me to be away. Since, however, I had a wide circle of friends among Muslims--officials and intellectuals--there should not be any need to uproot myself from here. Reasonable advice, I thought. Simultaneously,

Jawaharlal Nehru and other leaders proclaimed that it would not do to be panicky, that no harm would come to anyone. Stay where you are and carry on with your normal life. But in the face of the administration breaking down, arson and loot occurring unabated, the populace turned cynical and could not rely on the sermons delivered by the leaders.

As days went by, I saw from my residence on McLeod Road, streams of people heading towards the railway station, situated at the far end of the road. Occurrences of stabbing and attacks by mobs on *mohallas* inhabitated by one community or the other were reported. I was living in the midst of a mixed residential area, *Qila'* Gujar Singh of the Sikhs on one side, Hindu *havelis* in the middle, and at the back predominantly Muslim locality. At midnight we would wake up, aroused by the terrifying shout of 'Hara Hara Mahadeo', 'Sat Shri Akal' and 'Allah ho Akbar', emanating from different directions.

It would appear as if my area of residence was the target of attack and meeting ground for the three communal brigades of miscreants.

The rulers had taken resort to curfew and shooting, being unable to control the mobs, or were not just concerned about the carnage that was unleashed. The Dogra Regiment was withdrawn and replaced by the Baluch.

We saw flames coming up from the Shah 'Alim section of the walled city inhabited largely by Hindus. The inmates of the burning houses ran out to face the bullets of the Baluch Regiment for infringement of curfew regulations!

Night after night we kept awake, anticipating trouble, till it was rumoured that our turn would be the next. My next-door neighbour were Dr. S. N. Kaul, the well

138

known eye-surgeon, and his barrister brother. The barrister took the initiative to organise the neighbours to keep watch by turn. My house being adjacent to the entrance gate of the Khanna Haveli, it was decided that the terrace of the house would be the most strategic place to mount watch from. When my turn came, barrister Kaul handed over his gun to me. Long past midnight, the familiar cry by now was heard, but I could not help feeling amused as it suddenly dawned upon me that I never learnt how to pull the trigger. The mob was sporting enough not to attack that night.

Stories of unprecedented violence spread like wildfire. Two of my oldest Bengali acquaintances in Lahore were murdered. One was Sarkar of the police service and the other was the priest of the Kali Bari, a giant of a man. Rumour was at its height that Lahore was given to West Pakistan by the Radcliffe Award. At this, the Hindu and Sikh population was obsessed with the fear that in Islamic Pakistan there would be no place for them. The baser element of the other community became quite active in grabbing what they could and looted the properties of non-Muslims.

In the meantime, reaction had stimulated ghastly reprisals in Amritsar, Patiala and other places of the East Punjab, with the result that large number of Muslims began escaping to Lahore. At such a time of anxiety and indecision, one day at the dead of night a friend of ours, Mrs. Sarin, knocked at our door and held out two air tickets to Delhi. She said, "Shah 'Alim is burning to ashes, we cannot leave till we have some news of our relatives living there. I have the car and the driver and curfew passes with me. Go to the Walton airfield immediately. There is no time to lose".

In a few minutes, we left for Walton. It was decided that I would put Snehalata and the child in the plane and return. At the airport, Snehalata argued that since we had

139

two tickets, we should both leave for the time being. So, I also boarded the plane as I was. Snehalata's parents were in Delhi and were happy to see us, but I returned to Lahore the day after.

The situation was worsening day by day. There were more passengers than the railways could cope with the two-way traffic of uprooted people. It was difficult now to meet friends. No one to talk to, seek counsel or sympathise with. I managed to reach my studio and stay there for a while. During these disturbed times I painted a canvas depicting the horrors of communal riots, of man killing man. The painting was exhibited at Calcutta at the Academy of Fine Arts' annual exhibition, but it was removed, I was told, at the behest of Suhrawardy who was then the Chief Minister of undivided Bengal.

Words went round soon that the railway traffic between Lahore and Delhi might be discontinued as passengers of both communities were butchered on the way.

Delhi's Bloodbath

Snehalata arrived before the week was over. The child was safely left in the care of her parents in Delhi. For us the moment had come for the momentous decision. Either we both stayed on, come what may, or we both quit. Even Muslim comrades thought it would be wise to stay away till the dust settled, and we should leave by train which might be the last train from Lahore for Delhi. We left. Before leaving, hastily packed two trunks with silk *saris* and warm clothes and left them with Dr. Charles Fabri at the Museum. He was then the curator. There was no time to make any other arrangement; besides, the idea of returning was very much there at the back of our minds. I had locked the studio earlier with years of my work in it, and now locked the doors of my home which we so lovingly had set up, and handed over the keys to comrade Karimullah at the commune.

It was a repetition of what we thought we had left behind, beyond the Wagah border, when we arrived in Delhi. I was staying at Havelock Square, where each Punjabi home was overflowing with uprooted relatives from the West Punjab. There was gloom, sadness and bitter complaints everywhere. I felt I had come from one cursed city to another. The same atrocities, killing, looting and burning were going on, only the venue and the perpetrators were different. From Havelock Square the Birla Mandir, a distance of few furlongs, I saw dead and half-dead bodies lying on the roadside. Some sadists had built up a fire around a body yet breathing. Primitive desire for revenge was writ large on the faces of some young Sikh boys I saw, who must have lost all, including their dear and near ones and arrived as destitutes. Hindu chauvinists were freely proclaiming "Hindustan for Hindus."

The Muslim population concentrated in certain areas were also well organised and equipped with guns and other weapons. The destination for them was either Pakistan, or kill a *Kafir* and go to *Behissht*. Dr Joshi fell a victim in their hands at Pahargunj.

Small police forces could be seen looking on helplessly. Gandhiji was grief-stricken, Maulana Azad sad and remorseful, Jawaharlal upset and angry. Eventually, riot-control was handed over to the army. Most of the soldiers were from down South. The authorities decided that Muslim population desirous of crossing over to Pakistan should be escorted and given protection. Transit camps were set up at Idgah, Purana Qila' and at Humayun's Tomb. It was a heart-wrenching sight at Daryagunj to watch the long procession of men, women and children with bundles on their heads and under their arms, dragging feet under military protection, towards the transit camps.

They were mostly from the poorer section of the Muslim populace, leaving their hearths and homes. Even so, they were pounced upon, unnoticed by the military guards and dragged in the side lanes by refugee youngsters who then robbed them.

I saw the nauseating sight of truckloads of rotting dead bodies taken away for mass burial.

Is this the civilisation humanity is proud of ? And where are the culture and progress we are never tired of talking about ?

Even before the deadline of the declaration of independent sovereign Pakistan, momentum had gathered in the voluntary exchange of population. Now it was undertaken under the aegis of the government. The basic cruelty of mankind was manifested in the butchering of train-loads of Hindus, Sikhs and Muslims while in transit from one side lo the other. The only silver lining to the clouds was the knowledge from my personal experience and from what I heard, that there were a few people among Hindus, Sikhs and Muslims who were not blinded by communal hatred and risked everything to save some fellow human beings.

The stage came when the movements of trains were not disclosed and the public was forbidden entry to stations. Soon after, railway communication was totally disrupted .

Who was responsible for this man-made catastrophe and what forces had brought about the colossal disaster and suffering ? The question still remains unanswered.

Bewildered and dazed, I remained in a kind of animated suspension. Had I really arrived at the point of no return to my home and studio ?

At Kingsway in Old Delhi, a large camp was established to receive refugees from the Sind, N.W.F.P. and the West Punjab, with a view to helping them in their rehabilitation. Snehalata volunteered her services to work for the camp. But what about our own rehabilitation ? We had not yet registered ourselves as refugees. The idea of becoming a refugee in your own motherland was repugnant yet.

Not far from Havelock Square, Gandhiji was camping in the Harijan Colony. With him was Abdul Ghaffar Khan, also camping there. I began attending Gandhiji's evening prayer meetings. Day after day, I heard him appeal to Indians irrespective of caste and creed to shed their communal outlook and become human and compassionate. It sounded more like the wailing of an agonised soul than someone delivering sermons.

I began sketching at the prayer meetings and asked his secretary for permission to sketch Gandhiji from life, outside the meeting hours. He told me a day later that I could do so when Gandhiji would be resting. I went prepared with my sketchbook and saw him seated with writing material in hand. Hardly had I begun when he looked at me and like a naughty boy he stretched himself and turned his face away.

The 15th of August

News reached us that Amritsar and beyond had been devasted by rainstorm and flood, and all communications had been practically cut off.

Then came the 15th of August. In the afternoon I witnessed the unimaginable sight of Lord Mountbatten in the horse-drawn carriage, proceeding towards the Parliament House in a procession of glitter and gold of liveries. Unlike any representative of the British Empire of yesterday, he was bending down with stretched arms to shake the extended hands of Indians, most of them, I was sure, were the uprooted natives of India that was; now called refugees of nameless, faceless anonymity.

At midnight, I heard the famous speech of Nehru about his tryst with destiny.

I acknowledged the reality of the accomplished fact that Hindustan and Pakistan were two different countries, but did not find anything in it to revive my spirit.

It was now impossible, however, to leave everything to fate and remain inactive. The stark realities of life were staring in the face. Accommodation, employment, earning and the rest of it, all were of the same priority. It is true we found immediate shelter at Havelock Square, but it could never be the final solution. To start life all over again from the scratch, with a brush in hand, seemed a tremendously uphill task. At the approach of winter, I desperately thought of means to recover at least our warm clothes left behind in Lahore.

This is Lahore Calling

As if my silent thought was transmitted across the border, I heard from Fabri that things were now normal in Lahore. He further added, "Come back, your friends are waiting with open arms to receive you".

Comrade Karimullah also wrote to say that we were very lucky that though many houses of the evacuees were looted and emptied, no one had touched the lock of our home.

He added, however, that he had allowed a Muslim refugee family from U. P. to occupy the upper storey of the house, which consisted of the terrace-kitchen and the store room.

I was impatient to reach at Lahore, but how? I took the plane from Safdarjung airport to Amritsar. Luckily met the sister of one my pupils who invited me to her home and began exploring ways and means to reach my Eldorado. The very next day was lucky. I was watching the exodus of the displaced on the Grand Trunk Road when an army van stopped, and a young officer in khaki stepped down, saluted and asked, "What can I do for you, Sir? I am Captain Luthra". Looking at his face I remembered he was one of my students at the Mayo School of Arts evening class. I explained to him my mission. He simply said, "Jump in, Sir". I jumped in. Luckily I was carrying my stop-over bag, but felt a little uneasy not having informed my hostess.

Luthra said he was on evacuation duty. A brigade of Indian army was stationed at the Lahore cantonment under the command of Brigadier Mohite, for whom I was carrying a letter from my friend Bhardwaj who was the Director of Press Information in New Delhi. The Indian army contingent was engaged in the task of escorting evacuees from the deep interior of Pakistan in convoys to Amritsar. I noticed evidences of decay, devastation and destruction by human hands, flood and elements of nature. Carcasses of animals, dead human bodies and stink kept me stunned throughout the way. At dusk, Captain Luthra opened the door of the van in front of Falletti's Hotel, saluted and said, "God look after you".

Now, Falletti's Hotel was hardly the place for a beggar that I was, but Luthra had told me that that would be the safest place for me then. I walked in, and again luck seemed to favour me. Two young gentlemen exclaimed how I happened to be there. I vaguely remembered having met them. Some of the Hindu employees of British firms were lodged at the hotel till they could be replaced by Pakistanis. There was not the ghost of a chance to find accommodation at the Falletti's since the rich Muslim refugees from India had occupied all normal places available, and all improvised accommodation possible.

Both the gentlemen suggested that they would ask the management to put an extra bed in one of their rooms. The management agreed to do so.

October can be chilly in Lahore. I felt cold in my cottons and longed to open my trunks lying with Fabri. I began telephoning to friends. Gradually, one after the other came. Iftikhar-ud-din, popularly known as Mian Baghbanpura, was the first to call. Iftikhar was a devoted Congressman with leftist leanings, who had joined the Muslim League little before the Partition and was now a minister in the Punjab government. He very kindly offered me hospitality at his home and any help I needed, but I decided to stay put at the hotel in view of other conveniences. Friend Niyazi, a professor at the Government College came and warned me not to move out alone unless he or someone else accompanied me.

Then came Fabri and proposed his plan of action. He said it would be necessary to obtain permission of the Deputy Commissioner to remove my household effects and objects of art from the studio. He promised to take an appointment with the D.C. I met Prof. Bukhari, Principal of the Government College and Faiz Ahmad Faiz, now editor of The Pakistan Times, the next evening at the hotel lawn, where they were hosting a dinner to the Governor, an Englishman. Bukhari offered to store all my paintings and studio equipment at the college premises for safe custody. What I gathered from friends I met that the welcome with open arms was true, they all hugged me warmly, but advised that time was not ripe yet to return. Throwing cautions away I ventured out alone in the streets of Lahore to have a look at my studio even from outside and call on Manzoor Qader and Asghari, his wife. I had been only three months away and I felt like a stranger in this city where I had lived for eighteen years. Faces and persons then gave me a feel of familiarity. I saw now people crowding the streets who did not seem to belong. Every one was looking suspiciously at the other and at me. Manzoor was away but Asghari was happy to see me. She said she herself felt as I did and dared not go out alone as mischief was around the corner everywhere. She asked me to be with her out shopping and we had a *tonga*-ride. Fabri came the next day and took me to Mr. Ehsam, the D.C. Mr. Ehsam gave me the permit to remove anything I wanted and advised me to seek the assistance of police while doing so. While parting, he said, "Mr Sanyal, I hope you are not leaving Lahore for good. Do come back".

Lahore, My Lahore !

My friends, however, instructed me particularly to avoid the police as they thought the police were in league with the looters. While they came to protect, they actually had you robbed. Fabri brought his car and Dr. Gorie, the Chief Conservator of Forest, who was friendly towards me, sent his station wagon to collect my things. Thus equipped, I collected my door-key from comrade Karimullah, but found my doors open to receive me. An old Muslim, the present occupant of my house, very graciously told me to take away what was mine, but there was nothing left to take away except the heavy furniture I had made with exquisite workmanship from the Mayo School of Arts. I pulled the chest of drawers, each one of them was empty. Between two drawers I found stuck the bronze plate with Mohen-jo-daro Bull I was awarded at the Simla Fine Arts Exhibition. One gold and two silver medals were not there. In fact, the entire household stuff, crockery and cutlery, provisions of food and clothes were removed. Surprisingly, not a single book was touched. I remembered my wife had asked me to

147

bring all her books. At that moment Fabri rushed in and said excitedly, "Sanyal, come away at once. The goondas are coming". Bewildered, I snatched two books from the shelf and jumped into the waiting car and was whisked out.

The two books I held in my hands were *The Story of Philosophy* and the *Lust for Life*.

I met Rashid Ahmad, the Deputy Director-General of Radio Pakistan, an old friend. He told me he had left behind in Delhi his set of household furniture with a friend. Would I mind exchanging mine with his? I happily agreed to part with mine. The next take-over remained to be done at the studio. Mr. Bashir Qureshi, the young I.C.S. officer then in charge of the Industries Department, was the controller of evacuee industrial properties, including cinema houses. Qureshi was an enlightened person and appreciator of the arts. Without a moment's hesitation he instructed Ghulam Nabi who had the key of my studio in his custody to open it for me.

In the meantime, I had met Brigadier Mohite at the cantonment and requested him if he could arrange to transport my paintings across the border. Very bluntly he told me that they were occupied with evacuating human beings and could hardly be bothered with articles of art. He softened a little and said he could perhaps consider carrying small packets if they were delivered at the cantonment daily. I thanked him and parted.

Now, this Ghulam Nabi was certainly not the Ghulam of Nabi of old, the little that I had known of him. He was the headmaster of a carpentry school and had taken over the charge of the Mayo School of Arts on the retirement of my friend Mohammad Hussain. He proved to be troublesome. For the successive few days he would ask me to come and wait at the doors of my studio at an appointed hour, but would never turn up. The doors were sealed and he alone was authorised to break the seal. It was risky yet for me to loiter around.

Frustrated, I went to see Faiz at the old premises of the *Civil and Military Gazette*. He sympathised with me and wrote a stiff note to Ghulam Nabi. I discovered a student of mine working there as a cartoonist for *The Pakistan Times*. He volunteered to meet Nabi and brought me a letter from him to suggest that I should hand over the studio to his son in writing. That way the studio and its contents would be in safe hands. I knew by now there was remote chance of my returning to Lahore, so I sent him a message to say that as long as I was away his son could use the place.

A date and time was fixed. I informed Fabri. He and Gorie arrived with their vehicles and also the student. This boy was displaced from Ludhiana. It was not possible to remove everything, so I picked up a few paintings that I liked more than the others and also of such dimensions that could be handled with ease. We left out the sculpture pieces and heavy plaster casts, fixtures, equipment and books and proceeded to the Museum. Fabri made out an inventory, signed and gave it to me in case I wished to claim them in future. I made a gift of a Tirupati wood carving and a painting to his Museum. Nothing more was left for me to do in Lahore except wait for an opportunity to exit. The Art School was an extension of the Museum building, so I walked in. Some of the teachers were surprised to see me and most of them showed concern about my safety. Latif and Ata Mohammed told me, "Sahib, things are not as they were, do go away from here for your own sake".

In times of distress you learn the value of friendship. On the other hand, there are villains ready to exploit your adversity. I met a briefless barrister, a Hindu, who lived not far away from my studio. He said he had a truck and an armed Gurkha at his disposal. If I gave him five hundred, he would see me across with my movables. The barrister found it more paying than practising law. Usually, he charged a thousand, but I was a neighbour !

I called on Fabri once a day to explore any possibility of crossing the border. Fabri was full of praises of the new administration in Pakistan, but I found him a little preoccupied one day. I thought probably his unconventional manners might have upset the officialdom, for I had found him once half-naked in his office chair during the summer months of Lahore. There were no air-conditioners those days. However, he told me that over the weekend he was going to Amritsar to fetch Ratna who was waiting for him at the convent. I knew he had been courting Ratna in my studio whenever he visited and began to paint there. Charles said they were going to be man and wife at Lahore. He further said that Ratna's parents were also at Amritsar, but were not aware of Ratna's presence there. He further asked me to meet the parents and tell them that he would do everything to make Ratna happy and they did not have to worry.

So, I prepared to leave with him. The evening before the departure, at the backyard of the Museum, unnoticed by any, we loaded the two trunks. Fabri said that we might also find room for a couple of paintings. So in the afternoon he picked me up from the hotel and proceeded to Wagah border. The sentry at the border with his bayonet-mounted gun cried, "Halt". He said that the border was closed indefinitely. No one could cross. Even Fabri seemed to be at his wit's end. I told him he was a government servant and white-skinned at that, and had better walk up to the commandant's camp yonder and get clearance. He left the steering wheel and walked up to the tent. While I was waiting for him to return, the Baluch soldier was fuming with foul remarks about the Hindus across the border, not knowing that one was sitting right under his nose. Fabri came back flurried and said it was true that the border was closed. I told him to tell the sentry, "Hukam mil gaya" and press the accelerator. He did so. We were not shot form behind. He dropped me near the railway station at Amritsar and parted company. I did not know where to stay.

(Excerpts from his autobiography *The Vertical Women* Vol. I)

8

Lahore Goes Up In Flames

SATISH GUJRAL

Returning from Bombay in 1946, I set up a graphic art studio at Lahore. Instead of reducing my father's financial burden, I squandered whatever remained of his savings. This was very foolish of me as life in northern India was fast deteriorating into chaos. No one could be certain of what might happen the following day.

I wondered why my father had not stopped me from this misadventure that wiped out all his savings. When I had suggested it to him, he had simply nodded and let me go ahead. Instead of receiving customers, I would sit in **my** studio and watch never-ending lines of *tongas* loaded with Hindu and Sikh families going towards the railway station with their trunks and bedding-rolls. They were in a hurry to transfer whatever they could of their possessions to the side of the border they felt would fall to India, and thus be safer for them.

At about this time my father was elected to the newly-formed Constituent Assembly representing Rawalpindi division, of which Jhelum was a part. His membership was transferred to Karachi as soon as the country was divided into India and Pakistan. He was in Karachi awaiting his turn to take the oath of loyalty to Pakistan when both sides of the Punjab erupted in civil war on an unprecedented scale, leaving no doubt in anyone's mind that Hindus and Sikhs were not wanted in Pakistan.

I stayed on in Lahore watching different parts of the city go up in flames. The fires and rioting came nearer and nearer towards my home, which was close to the Nishat Cinema. I had just enough time to escape before hooligans came to loot whatever little I had. The only safe haven I could think of was Lajpat Rai Bhavan where my father's friend Lala Achint Ram and others associated with the Servants of the People Society were staying. I covered the distance of five kilometers at a run. There were many others also fleeing Muslim mobs who were venting their fury on Hindu and Sikh life and property.

After I was safely inside the Bhavan, I realized the magnitude of the calamity that had overtaken the city. The Bhavan and the adjoining DAV College hostel were overflowing with distraught families; more were pouring in every minute. The buildings were converted into the Central Refugee Camp and a contingent of the Dogra regiment was provided to stand guard. We were still more than a fortnight away from the fateful day of 14 August when Pakistan was to become a sovereign independent Islamic state. But we still did not know the fate of Lahore. Would it come to India or go to Pakistan? We tensely awaited the Radcliffe Award which was to decide the issue. The air was thick with rumours. Most newspapers had ceased publication. This further added to the confusion. Those who stayed on in their homes came to the camp to get authentic news. But none was available.

Finally, on 13 August 1947, the Radcliffe Award was announced. It ceded Lahore to Pakistan. The next day the country of Pakistan officially came into being as an independent entity.

For my father, the culmination of what had been his life's mission was, to say the least, ironic. He had worked and suffered for the freedom of his country. Now freedom had come, but instead of one country there were two. Where did he belong? Like many others, he was confident that once the anarchic tide of violence subsided, the warring religious communities would return to living in peace on both sides of the newly-drawn frontiers.

He had friends among the leaders of the new dominion, and was close to its founder, Mohammed Ali Jinnah. He had been given to understand that Jinnah intended to invite him to join his cabinet of ministers. He arrived in Karachi expecting to take the oath of allegiance to Pakistan, and perhaps be the first and only non-Muslim to be included in the governing council. But by the time he took the oath as a member of the Pakistani parliament, the two nations were on the brink of war. Communal riots had spread all over the two Punjabs, Pakistani and Indian.

My father was flown to Lahore in a military plane in the hope of salvaging a murderous situation aggravated by ruthless arson and plunder. In the evening when he met the Indian Prime Minister Pandit Nehru and Lady Mountbatten who had flown in from New Delhi, he was a very shaken man. So was Nehru. Neither of them had any illusions about the two countries being able to live as friendly neighbours. Nevertheless, to my father's surprise, Nehru asked him if he thought there was any chance of stopping the communal carnage and preventing forced migration and the exchange of populations. There were many at the table when Nehru put this question to my father. Why he singled him out when he had only a nodding acquaintance with him remains a mystery. Or perhaps, as my father tried to explain to us later, Panditji only happened to turn towards him but was putting the question to himself. This was the state of bewilderment of all who

154

sat round the table, including Raja Ghazanfer Ali, a newly appointed minister of Jinnah's cabinet. Ghazanfer Ali belonged to Jhelum. He had accompanied my father from Karachi to demonstrate his friendliness. The meeting ended on a note of frustration and despair.

The next day Raja Ghazanfer Ali drove with us to Jhelum, a hundred miles away from Lahore. Political differences had not affected the friendship between the two men. This was odd, as they were of completely different temperaments. My father was a recluse and somewhat puritanical; the Raja was a jovial extrovert, and an unabashed womanizer. He had been a member of Sir Sikander Hayat's Unionist Party. When Sir Sikander died, Ghazanfer Ali joined Mohammed Ali Jinnah's Muslim League and became its only representative in the Punjab Assembly. After he had been inducted into the new cabinet, he suggested my father's name to Mr. Jinnah for a ministerial post.

The drive to Jhelum was a nightmarish reminder of what had happened. At every milestone the faces of the two men became even more grim and anguished. Before we came to the bridge on the Jhelum river, Ghazanfer Ali asked my father if he was still against non-Muslims leaving the district. Without waiting for my father's response, he leaned on his shoulder and said, 'Well, Lalaji, let us do our best to keep them here.' Though my father did not react, the Raja concluded that his silence meant approval.

Both seemed to have overestimated their hold over their followers. The joint statement they issued on reaching Jhelum received wide publicity in the national media of both countries. Gandhiji and Jinnah approved of it. However, the actual situation made mockery of their efforts to restore normalcy. Everywhere they spoke they got a hostile reception. Hindus and Sikhs were incensed by my father's appeal to not leave their homes and accused him of making them *qurbani ke bakrey* (sacrificial goats). Although relations between local Hindus and Muslims had never been very close or relaxed, their differences rarely resulted in violent confrontation. Nevertheless, in small towns and villages, the divide was real and persistent. Hindu-Muslim estrangement was both cultural and social. Except for the Civil Lines which existed only in district headquarters, the two communities lived in clearly demarcated localities; their occupations were also different. Muslims lived off the land; Hindus and Sikhs in the towns of western Punjab were largely professionals, shopkeepers, moneylenders and traders. Even in the Mayo School hostel which never had more than a score of residents, Hindu and Muslim sections were clearly demarcated. Though a facade of bonhomie was kept up, there was no conscious effort to bridge the ethnic and religious gulf that divided the students. Though we met on the playing fields, sat side by side in the classrooms and occasionally went to each other's rooms, we were housed in different wings of the hostel building and had separate kitchens and dining rooms.

Jhelum was no different from other towns in the region. Its population of about fifteen thousand was half Hindu and half Muslim. The Sikhs were considered a part of the Hindu community. Despite the segregation there was a lot of friendly give and take in everyday life, because the communities depended on each other for their survival. But this was rarely, if ever, extended to visiting each other's homes to share meals. Hindu taboos against eating with Muslims were the biggest stumbling block to social mixing. To the orthodox Hindu, some Muslim dietary habits rendered that community as unacceptable as Hindus of the lowest caste.

My father did his best to get the towns, people to overcome their prejudices, but he gathered very few followers. He established a branch of the Indian National

Congress in Jhelum; it received no active support from the Muslims.

The fact that Hindus had responded with enthusiasm was all the more reason for Muslims to keep aloof. More galling to my father was the discovery that Hindus who had joined the Congress were very enthused by its call for national independence, but were unwilling to befriend Muslims or change their attitude towards untouchables .

My father accepted Raja Ghazanfar Ali's suggestion to appeal to the Hindus and Sikhs of Jhelum to stay on. But as the violence escalated, he came to the conclusion that there was no option for non-Muslims except to leave for India.

We were in Jhelum when suddenly hoards of *kabailis* (Afghan tribesmen) descended on the town. They were on their way to Kashmir to drive Dogras, Brahmins and Sikhs out of the state and annex it to Pakistan. Since Jhelum was the closest station from Mirpur, the border town of the state, it had been chosen by the Pakistani army commanders as one of the staging points for the invasion of Kashmir. The Pakistani leaders were wary of taking personal risks and hoped that the frontier tribesmen, ever eager to plunder and to abduct non-Muslim women, would do the job for them.

The tribes who lived in the no man's land between Afghanistan and Pakistan recognized neither law nor government. Their very presence struck terror into the hearts of the Hindus and Sikhs of north-western Punjab. For many centuries the main occupation of the tribal hordes was looting and kidnapping for ransom. Their chief targets were Hindus and Sikhs because in the tribal consciousness killing and robbing infidels elevated marauders to the status of *mujahideen*, warriors of Islam. Even the British with all

157

their military resources had been unable to subdue these unruly tribesmen, and had left them to be controlled by their *jirgahs* (tribal councils).

The day the first band of tribals descended on Jhelum was unforgettable. They eyed our refugee camp as predators assess their quarry. They began with their traditional *khattak* dance, going round and round our terrified camp to the beat of drums, firing rifles in the air while they danced to warn us of our impending fate. Had it not been for the pleading and cajoling by local officials led by Raja Ghazanfar Ali, neither I nor anyone else would have lived to tell the tale. The experience finally convinced Ghazanfar Ali that it was time for non-Muslims to depart from the 'Land of the Pure '--Pakistan .

As the conflagration spread, Hindus and Sikhs in their thousands sought refuge in our *mohallah*, which soon became a refugee camp. Every newcomer had his tragic tale to tell each bloodier and more spine-chilling than the last. I lost all sense of time. Death became a gruesome reality in our daily lives.

My introvert father rarely allowed anyone to witness his emotions, but there were moments when he seemed to sweat tension from each pore. At such moments he would sit huddled with his eyes shut. He was a God-fearing man, but seeing what God's creatures could do to one another shook his faith. Here were human beings behaving worse than wild animals. I wondered to whom my father now addressed his prayers.

With the ferocious *kabailis* having effectively increased the resolve of local Hindus and Sikhs to migrate to India, we began the evacuation, which turned out to be as bloody as the carnage that followed. Almost twice a week I would accompany a convoy consisting of dozens of trucks packed with several hundred people on the journey that for many would turn out to be their last. In spite of the armed Dogra contingent we were provided during each trip, the Muslim ambushes were difficult to withstand because the attackers outnumbered our guards.

The assaults varied in their character and intensity. If we were lucky, we were just ordered at gunpoint to surrender all our belongings. Those who resisted or showed any signs of reluctance, especially women who did not want to give up their jewellery, were seized and forcibly deprived of their valuables with horrifying brutality that left them badly injured and terrorized beyond belief.

Still, this was nothing compared to the escalating incidents of planned genocide. These not only resulted in the almost total annihilation of men, women and children, but were carried out in such a ruthless and bloody manner that they numbed the senses of those who were helpless witnesses and survivors.

Once at Lala Musa, a small town roughly fifteen miles from Jhelum on the way to Amritsar, the ambush ended in the general slaughter of all the men, the rape of women on the spot and the abduction of a few before the rest were butchered. The murderers celebrated the carnage by impaling infants on spikes and going into a frenzied *bhangra* dance, accompanied by wild drumming.

The fact that this gory event took place in a location that happened to be part of Pakistan did not mean that such atrocities were restricted to that part of the divide alone, or that Hindus and Sikhs were the only ones who were subjected to such demonic treatment. I witnessed no less inhuman scenarios enacted in areas that had become part of free India, the only difference being that the victims were those who happened to belong to the Islamic faith.

The trips I made with refugee convoys often did not terminate at Wagah, a hamlet that had become the border post between India and Pakistan, nor at Amritsar which had become the terminal for depositing refugees. I had to make sorties to Jalandhar, sometimes to drop off the stray girls and children we rescued from the kidnappers, and at other times to seek sorely needed assistance from the newly established East Punjab government which was camping at Jalandhar. Since my father was a government official, he gave me a letter of authority that enabled me to cross the border easily. We took an armed contingent with us to rescue women, but I escorted them directly from the recovery sites to camps on the Indian side on my own. This way my father ensured that in case there was any retaliation, at least my life would be saved, if not his. This made me an unwilling witness to the slaughter on the Indian side. The worst among these was the attack on a Muslim girls' hostel in Amritsar. The inmates were stripped and forced to march in a procession through the Hall Bazar, the town's main market. There these girls were gangraped and subjected to the most perverse treatment that any sadistic imagination could devise, before being murdered .

Our car was forced to a halt as the thoroughfare was packed with crowds who wished to watch this gruesome *tamasha*. Sitting in the car, I searched for signs of horror or compassion on the faces in the crowd. I could trace none.

The agonies of Partition left their impact on all those who were witnesses. Over time, the horrific scenes I saw no longer created in me the same intensity of revulsion I used to feel in the beginning. My senses succumbed to a gradual hardening. No calamity seemed to affect my numbed perceptions, which had frozen into a block.

One redeeming phenomenon of the sordid Partition epic was the way the unfortunates who formed refugee convoys would treat each other in an encounter. Though the instances of such encounters turning into massacres were not uncommon, these were outnumbered by instances when both sides sympathized with their common fate. They supplied each other with drinking water and other crucial necessities, but more significantly with profound emotional understanding.

One such encounter ended in the so-called 'Beas catastrophe'--a calamity enacted not by humans but by nature, which that year seemed to be as hellbent on destroying mankind as mankind seemed on destroying itself. There had been torrential rains and floods. An incessant spell of rain flooded all the five rivers of Punjab in the month of September 1947, when the evacuation and migration of refugees was at its chaotic height.

Displaced and exiled people did not escape only in trucks or trains; a much greater number was struggling on foot and by bullock cart towards the borders that had just been carved into the subcontinent. These convoys were dozens of miles long, stretching so far that the vanguard would have crossed the border while the rear would still be several days from safety. More often than not the convoy disintegrated under ambush; rarely would an entire convoy successfully reach the other side in tact.

The 'Beas catastrophe' affected not one but two convoys coming from opposite directions. They camped on the stretch of road that lay between the Beas river and one of its seasonal tributaries, about five miles away.

Pounded by torrential rain, and without any shelter, these afflicted souls were soon relieved of their suffering. Both the Beas and its tributary rose in spate and sucked thousands of humans and animals into a foaming, thundering, watery grave.

Even weeks after the catastrophe one could not pass this stretch of road without burying one's nose in layers of towels, so overpowering was the stench of rotting corpses.

No burial or cremation was ever performed. And like most people, each time I passed the area I was more anxious about not catching some disease by inhaling the foul air than about the fact that so much life had been tragically destroyed here.

Fifty years after that fateful day, as I sit down to write these lines, I wonder which was the greater casualty: the loss of millions of lives and the uprooting of still many more from their homes, or the loss of compassion in myself and in other people. Compassion is the trait that distinguishes humans from animals. How many survivors of Partition, from all faiths, could have retained this, after experiencing so much terror and anguish?

By March 1948, we had managed to send to India most of the families who had been brought into the camp from the area entrusted to my father. The task seemed endless, as there still remained young women who had been abducted, children who had gone missing and others mercifully given shelter by their Muslim friends. The exercise of rescuing Hindus and Sikhs was made perilous by the fact that our region had large numbers of retired soldiers who had been allowed to keep weapons and ammunition with them. The local administration was not equipped to deal with this kind of armed and dangerous populace. Despite the intense danger that the rescue missions involved, my father refused to abandon victims to their fate and escape to India. Most families of these missing people, who were in our care, also refused to leave till their relatives were found.

To add to our difficulties, the army personnel allotted to us for security were replaced by lightly-armed Pakistani policemen. The war in Kashmir had hardened the attitude of the Pakistan government towards us. Because of Jhelum's strategic importance in the Kashmir operations, the government wanted us out of the way as soon as possible. We refused to budge and continued our efforts to rescue the lost and the abducted for another three months. We were able to save nearly three hundred people and despatch them to India. How we did it is a long story. Each case was a tragic drama in itself.

I have never been able to erase the episode of Jaswant Kaur from my memory. She was recovered from Khewra, a place known for its salt mines. The village lay about fifty miles deep in the ravines. Jaswant Kaur, a Sikh girl of fifteen, was saved by her neighbour Ghulam Ishaq when her home was attacked one night by mobs from the neighbouring villages. In the mele her father and two brothers were killed. Her two sisters were abducted but her mother and a teenage brother managed to slip out to safety and joined a party of Hindus heading for the refugee camp. Presuming that all her family had been massacred, Jaswant Kaur had hidden herself in a shed at the back of her house. Ghulam Ishaq found her two days later when he took over the abandoned house for himself.

Ghulam Ishaq was a friend of the girl's father. He also presumed that Jaswant Kaur was the lone survivor of her family. Having daughters who were Jaswant's age, Ghulam Ishaq looked upon the young girl with paternal affection. This alone could not have saved Jaswant Kaur's life in the atmosphere of frenzy and phobia that prevailed in the region. So he announced his intention of marrying her. A *nikah* ceremony was performed but the marriage was not consummated. This was only known to his immediate family.

Kartari, Jaswant Kaur's mother, was brought to the camp in Jhelum with her son. Both were in a dazed state. Kartari was inconsolable and refused to leave the camp till her daughters were found. She had seen her husband and two sons murdered before her eyes, but she was convinced that her daughters were still alive.

We had no soldiers or policemen to help us recover abducted women. My father tried persuasion. He had been legal adviser to the salt mines administration and had sorted out some family disputes in Khewra, so he decided to approach the villagers personally. One of his clients was Ghulam Ishaq. When my father called on him he did not know that Jaswant Kaur was in Ishaq's custody. He asked Ishaq to help in the recovery of three Hindu girls known to be missing from Khewra. Ghulam Ishaq pleaded ignorance of their whereabouts. To reassure my father of his sincerity, he came to Jhelum.

Jaswant Kaur's mother fell at his feet and broke down. Ghulam Ishaq commiserated with her without divulging anything. Much as he was moved by Kartari's grief, he was not willing to part with her daughter because he had fallen in love with her. He returned to Khewra promising to do his best to find the missing girls.

It did not take long for my father to discover that Jaswant Kaur was in Ghulam Ishaq's house. His faith in Ishaq's sincerity was rudely shaken. He also came to know that Ishaq had married the girl and was powerful enough locally to resist any pressure from the administration. The only way out was to somehow inform Jaswant Kaur that her mother and brother were alive and staying in the Jhelum camp, and then plot her escape .

Anwar Khan, a police constable in the small contingent provided to us by local authorities, had been with us from the beginning and had become quite involved in our mission. He was the one who had told my father of Jaswant Kaur's whereabouts. He now managed to inform the girl that her mother and brother were alive and expected her to join them in the camp at Jhelum.

He told no one how he managed to reach her. By then Jaswant Kaur had gained Ghulam Ishaq's confidence

164

and persuaded him to let her see her mother and brother, promising she would return to him. The night before they left for Jhelum they consummated their marriage.

Once re-united with her mother, Jaswant Kaur went through another trauma. She found it hard to part from her. She confessed to feeling torn between her love for her widowed mother and her loyalty to Ishaq, who had been so protective and trusting. Ishaq had moved to Jhelum and visited her every day. The situation was fraught with danger. Ultimately Jaswant Kaur accepted my father's suggestion. One afternoon, she left with her mother and brother and a few others for Amritsar.

My father sent me with the group because he feared Ghulam Ishaq's wrath would fall on us. He then broke the news to the jilted husband. Much to my father's surprise, instead of exploding with rage, Ghulam Ishaq broke down and wept unrestrainedly. He was a giant with a glowing pink complexion which betrayed his Afghan ancestry. To see such a strong man so reduced by grief was a spectacle my father found hard to bear. It took a while for Ghulam Ishaq to compose himself. Then he told my father what he had gone through. He thanked my father for sparing him further embarrassment.

The story of Jaswant Kaur did not end there. Like several other women and children we 'rescued', she was left with my mother who had taken charge of a temporary refugee camp she had set up for rescued women awaiting others of their families to join them. As days went by their chances of leaving Pakistan became bleaker and bleaker. Many of them were pregnant, and their families refused to take them back. The stigma of having unmarried girls bearing illegitimate children was not acceptable to their kith and kin.

This was what happened to Jaswant Kaur. The results of her cohabitation with Ghulam Ishaq began to show. At first her mother Kartari accepted the inevitable. But her teenaged brother Bhagwan Singh was adamant. The family *izzat* (honour) had been sullied. They would have to suffer the taunts of others for the rest of their lives. Kartari came round to her son's views and the two decided to abandon Jaswant Kaur to her fate. My mother's threats to expel them from the camp had no effect. They slipped out of the camp, leaving Jaswant Kaur to survive as best as she could.

It was the fate of women like Jaswant Kaur that determined the future course of my parents' life.

****

By this time my father's membership in Pakistan's parliament had been transferred to the Indian parliament. My mother was unwilling to abandon the women under her care and let them go to government-run refugee camps which had rapidly become like brothels. My father had very little choice in the matter. He could not think of being separated from his wife and spending part of his life away from her in Delhi. He decided to make his home in Jalandhar.

He resigned from the Indian parliament and started the Nari Niketan (women's home) at Jalandhar. It was gradually opened to women other than victims of the Partition. My parents jointly ran this institution for destitute women till my father's death in 1979. Then my mother took over and ran it single-handedly till she died in 1988. The Niketan did not pull down its shutters. My father left his savings to the Niketan Trust. It carries on its good work

166

under the supervision of my brother Inder. Apart from providing food and lodging, it also runs a high school for the children of its inmates, and for orphans.

The citizens of Jalandhar expressed their gratitude by naming the road that runs in front of Nari Niketan after my father. My mother, who survived my father by eight years, refused to accept any honours from the citizens or the government. She was happy that her husband had been honoured and was content to bask in his posthumous glory.

(Excerpts from his autobiography *A Brush With Life*)

3

Through Smoking Towns

9

LAHORE, PARTITION, AND INDEPENDENCE

KHUSHWANT SINGH

Having spent two carefree years in Government College, I was no stranger to Lahore. But coming there to earn my living was a different matter. I had everything laid on for me--a well-furnished flat and office, membership of the two leading clubs, the Cosmopolitan, meant for the Indian elite, and the more exclusive Gymkhana, which was largely an English preserve with no more than a dozen Oxbridge educated 'natives'. My father's and father-in-law's status opened the doors of judges and ministers to me. With my young and attractive wife, we soon became the most sought after and photographed couple in Lahore.

The only thing missing was the clientele. I spent a couple of hours in the morning in my office pouring over law books, then went to the Bar Room for gossip. I went to the Courtrooms to hear important cases being argued, spent an hour or so in the Coffee House for more gossip, and returned for lunch. For the first few months not a single litigant crossed my threshold. For a while I worked as a junior to Kirpa Narain, who had moved from Delhi to Lahore. One day he collapsed and died while arguing a case. I shifted over as junior to Jai Gopal Sethi, who had the largest criminal practice in the Punjab. He occasionally got his clients to throw a few crumbs as junior's fees at me. I was told that I should acquire a good *munshi*, or clerk.

They are quite an institution in the Indian legal profession. Where there are no solicitors, as in the Punjab, they do the soliciting--talking to clients, sorting out their papers, fixing the fee to be extracted, extracting it along with their *munshiana* of ten per cent. Many did much more. They went to the railway stations and bus stands as hotel agents do, spotted litigants and persuaded them to take on their employer as their advocate. All manner of persuasion was practised: their master's wife was the judge's mistress, or vice versa, or he was the ablest 'England-returned Barrister', who played tennis and bridge with the Sahibs, drank and danced with their mems.

The first clerk I hired was a sharp little fellow from Himachal. He persuaded me to let him go on tour in Punjab's districts to do propaganda for me. He was away for a month, presented me his travel bills, and assured me that many leading lawyers of the district courts had promised to send their appellate work to me. None came.

The second one was a Shia Muslim. He got me a brief as a junior to a leading lawyer from Lucknow in a case involving two branches of rich Shia zamindars of Bahraich over their property in Lahore. I got a small fee but lost the friendship of the Lahore head of the family. We also lost the case. Thereafter having nothing to do, I let my *munshi* hire a *maulvi* who taught me the Koran for an hour every morning. Some time later the *munshi* left me on the pretext that taking a salary from a non-believer who was not only not a Muslim but who did not believe in God was *haraam*, unlawful.

In sheer desperation 1 hired the most expensive *munshi* in Lahore. He was a strapping, six-foot Sikh Jat who was a renowned tout. I paid him Rs 10,000 as advance--a sum unheard of to secure his services.

He was familiar with Sikh villages in Lahore district. Whenever there was a murder in any village--and there were at least three or four every month--he went to condole with the bereaved family as well as call on the family whose members had been named as accused. He managed to get a brief from one side or the other. Instead of the tenth due to him as *munshiana*, he took a third of my fee.

However, criminal cases started coming my way. I won some, lost others. I also discovered that hiring renowned lawyers at high fees did not really make much difference in a criminal case. If a magistrate or judge was friendly towards me, I got bail for my clients. And often a lighter sentence. There was an Anglo-Indian lawyer who knew hardly any law but managed to get cases through his touts because he was a sahib. Also a Parsee who wore a monocle, hummed and hawed his way through his briefs in a fake upper-class English accent, and managed to make a reasonable living. There was a Muslim lawyer who gained notoriety for never preparing his briefs and throwing his clients on the mercy of the court. 'Who knows the law better than Your Honour? Who am I to tell you the real facts of the case? Your Honour will no doubt grasp them better than I and do justice to my client!' Believe it or not, he did better than most lawyers who burned the midnight oil pouring over their briefs and wrangled with judges.

It was a hard, back-breaking, soulless profession I took on undefended cases in Sessions Courts for a fee of Rs 16 per day; I appeared free of charge in cases against communists; I took on part-time teaching at the Law College; I was put on the panel of defence lawyers at the High Court and then on the panel of the Advocate General. I hardly ever made more than a thousand rupees a month. My father continued to subsidize me. He bought me a larger apartment with property which brought me some rent; then a large house on Lawrence Road facing Lahore's biggest park, Lawrence Gardens, (later renamed Bagh-e-Jinnah). None of this made me change my opinion of the legal profession.

Perhaps it was my failure to make it in a big way that soured me. I kept asking myself, 'Is there anything creative in practicing law? Don't I owe more to the one life I have than making money out of other peoples' quarrels? A common prostitute renders more service to society than a lawyer. If anything the comparison with the whore is unfair to her. She at least serves a social need, and gives her clients pleasure for their money; a lawyer doesn't even do that.' I have little doubt that if I had stuck to the law a little longer, I would have made it to the Bench and perhaps even to the Supreme Court. Jokers with less practice than me and lesser legal acumen were elevated to the Bench; a couple ended up as Judges of the Supreme Court. Never did I regret chucking up the law; my only regret was that I wasted five years studying it and another seven trying to make a living out of it.

****

Having not much to keep me in the law courts, I began to read books which I should have read in my years in college: anthologies of English poetry, Shakespeare's plays and sonnets, Tolstoy, Oscar Wilde, Aldous Huxley, Hindu philosophy by Radhakrishnan. I also began to review books for *The Tribune* and wrote a short eulogistic booklet on Stalin for the Friends of the Soviet Union, of which I was a founder member. When on vacation in Mashobra I did little besides reading in the mornings and taking long walks in the afternoons. Every afternoon I strode alongside my wife, who was on a bicycle, six miles down to Simla. We had tea at Wenger's or Davico's, watched the pageant of English officials, Indian Ministers, and their over-dressed wives strolling along the Mall. And then six miles back to Mashobra. Once Sir Charles Carson, Finance Minister of the Maharaja of Gwalior, spent a couple of days with us. He told me that he had walked to Tatapani hot springs, on the banks of the Sutlej 5000 feet below Simla, and back, in a day. The following weekend I did the same. I bathed in the sulphur spring, drank a bottle of beer cooled in the icy, fast-running Sutlej, and was back home in time for dinner. Once l took a bet with my sister's husband, Jaspal Singh, who was as tough a Sikh Jat as I had met, that I could outwalk him. We set out on a full-moon-lit night on the Hindustan-Tibet road. He had two of his nephews with him, both in their early twenties, and two Kashmiri porters to carry our provisions. After fifteen miles, the two boys and the porters refused to go any further. We left them at a dak bungalow and proceeded towards our destination, Narkanda. Later that night we stopped at another dak bungalow in the midst of a fir forest to refresh ourselves. Jaspal drank milk by the gallon; I took hot tea laced with brandy. It was eerie in the moonlit stillness. We were talking very loudly when out of the seemingly untenanted bungalow came a loud yell, 'b...off!' We did. We arrived at Narkanda early in the morning. We took whatever the *chowkidar* could give us: *ghee parathas* and over-sweetened tea. We started our journey back home. We kept pace all day and late into the evening. My feet began to bleed. At a dak bungalow about ten miles from Mashobra I stopped to tie them with rags provided by the *chowkidar*. Jaspal decided to go ahead to claim victory. I followed a hundred yards behind him. He got to Mashobra at about midnight, told the family that I had given up on the way, and went triumphantly to bed. I went straight to my bedroom. He was boasting about his feat at the breakfast table when I joined him. Technically he had won. We had done seventy two miles more or less non-stop. Both of us spent the next few days nursing our sore feet. 'If you had worked for seventy-two hours instead of walking seventy-two miles, you would have been a wiser man,' was the only comment my father made. I was not allowed to undertake any more long walks. But a fortnight later, when my father was away in Delhi, I had to return to Lahore on some business. I decided to walk down to Kalka, which was sixty-five miles away, downhill most of the way. I left Mashobra while it was still dark. I got to Dharampur (fifty miles) by the afternoon and was having tea at the rest house when suddenly my father turned up and joined me for tea. It occurred to him that I did not have a taxi waiting for me. 'Where is your taxi?' he asked me. I had to admit I had walked down all the way. He lost his temper and ordered his chauffeur to get a taxi to Kalka and saw me ride away in it. A great pity! The one thing I looked forward to after the marathon walk to Kalka was a shower at the railway station followed by a bottle of chilled beer and a sumptuous meal.

****

I have the happiest of memories of the summer months I spent in my parents' beautiful house in Mashobra. It occupied an entire hill, giving a spectacular view of snowclad mountains to the north and deep valleys on the other side. My mother had a large cement platform raised which overlooked the road running from Simla to Mashobra bazaar, Gables Hotel, past the estate of the Raja of Faridkot, to a nine-hole golf course at Naldera. We spent most of our mornings and afternoons on this platform, sunning ourselves, or in the shade of a holly-oak which stood alongside it. The bird-life was fantastic. Barbets cried all day long. Flocks of scarlet minivets flew among the cherry trees. Sibias nested in a creeper-covered elm. Flycatchers, including the spectacular silver-white paradise flycatcher with his two ribbons of tail trailing behind him, were not an uncommon sight. Lammergeiers and Himalayan eagles floated in the air. Early mornings and late evenings blackbirds perched on our roof and broke into song. All through moonlit nights, nightjars called to each other. A family of flying squirrels had their nest in our eaves; we often saw them float down from tree to tree and hop about on the tennis court.

Sundays were special. We woke to the peal of bells from St Swithin's Church at the entrance to Mashobra Bazaar. It had been built by Allen, a leather-merchant of Kanpur, and was named after the patron saint of cobblers. It was exactly like a village chapel in England, with a lych-gate, stained glass windows, and High Altar. English folk staying at Gables Wild Flower Hall on the crest of the hill trooped in their Sunday best for the morning service. Thereafter they strolled about the bazaar exuding the fragrance of lavender and French perfumes.

My father was an Anglophile and loved entertaining. Once he sent invitations to all the European residents of Wild Flower Hall and Gables. They came in their dozens because it was wartime and nothing very exciting happened in Simla. We hung Chinese lanterns all the way from the entrance gate up to our house. We had a Goan band to play dance music. The *Sahibs* introduced themselves and their mems, drank our Scotch and wines, ate our curried meal, danced, and departed. The next morning I asked my father if it had been worthwhile blowing up thousands of rupees entertaining total strangers. 'English people never forget anyone who is hospitable to them,' he replied. He was right. A few days later, when he was going down to Delhi, an English officer came to him in the rail-car and introduced himself as one who had been at his party. They got talking. My father landed a very lucrative contract to supply provisions to the army.

The Raja of Faridkot was also very fond of entertaining white people. Every autumn he would arrange bull-fights in an open arena. Villagers came in their thousands bringing their champion bulls. Foreign and important Indian guests sat on sofas watching the bulls tangle with each other. After the show, the Raja entertained his guests at a banquet with his private band playing. Since we often had English friends staying with us, we were often invited. The Raja could be as generous as he could be mean. He served champagne to everyone, but when it came to whisky, his bearers served Indian whisky to Indians, Scotch only to the whites. I discovered this one evening when we took Evan Charlton, editor of *The Statesman*, and his wife Joy with us to one of his parties. When I complained to Evan about the quality of the whisky he snorted, 'You are a suspicious so-and-so! My whisky is okay.' We exchanged glasses. He wrinkled his nose when he tasted mine. The Raja could also be very uncouth. Whenever my father invited him, he would drink himself silly and stay on after all the other guests had left. He made passes at my nieces, then only in their teens, and at other young women around. My poor parents, who usually retired at 9 p.m., were kept up till midnight.

More than anything else I loved my long evening walks. When not bound for Simla, I explored other mountain roads. There was a solitary, shaded path which ran through a pine and fir forest to an Italian monastery called San Demiano. Another went steeply uphill from Mashobra to a small orchard called Danes Folly towards Wild Flower Hotel. From the top of the hill you could see the mountain range with Shali peak rising to above 10,000 feet and a broad stream dividing the two ranges. During the rainy season, the Valley was often covered over by mists. Mysteriously the mists would lift and the sun break through, lighting the rain-washed, emerald green hillsides and setting the stream that ran between them sparkling in the sunlight.

Once a year in the autumn there was a fair in village Sipi, a mile or so below Mashobra bazaar. Villagers brought their nubile daughters and young sons to arrange marriages for them. It was rumoured that pretty girls-- Himachal girls can be fair, petite, almond-eyed and wanton--were put up for sale to the highest bidder. I saw many pretty village lasses but never saw one being taken away by any outsider.

*****

Not having much to do in Lahore and yet possessing a nice home and a lovely-looking (though by now somewhat over-assertive) wife, I had no dearth of visitors. Foremost among these was my friend Mangat Rai, who was posted there. Being in the ICS he was much sought after by Christian fathers with marriageable daughters. He also wrote pieces which he read out to an ever-admiring circle of friends. One which received encores was about a hen which laid eggs in a drain. It was always heard with open-mouthed admiration. He became a daily visitor to my apartment. Every evening after his office he hauled his bicycle up the stairs and often stayed on for drinks and dinner. Whatever reservations he had about my wife vanished; it was evident that he was getting quite enamoured of her. To leave me in no doubt he wrote me a letter confessing that he was in love with her and seeking my permission to continue visiting us. I passed this letter on to my wife. I could see that she was highly flattered. I treated it as a joke and wrote back assuring him that he would be as welcome as before. I had reason to regret my magnanimity. Mangat Rai had enormously persuasive powers to bring people round to his point of view. Most of it was destructive and designed to reduce others to plasticine that he could mould in whatever shape he wanted. My wife at the time spent some hours every morning at a painting studio run by Bhubesh Sanyal. He began dropping in at the studio and persuaded her that painting was a futile pastime. She gave up painting. She was a very keen tennis player and always spent the evenings playing with me at the club. He persuaded her that cycling was more fun, so she abandoned tennis and went cycling with him. She was very punctilious about religious ritual: opening the Granth Sahib every morning, reading a hymn or two, and wrapping it up in the evening. He convinced her of the futility of ritual. She began to miss out on her daily routine of prayers and ritual. He had become a hard drinker. My wife took to drinking hard. He was very open about everything he did. He told my wife that one evening, when seeing off his sister at the railway station, he had run into a young Christian girl known to us. She had no transportation. He offered to ride her back on his cycle. She sat on the front bar. He invited her to his apartment without any conditions attached. She accepted. They spent the night in the same bed. He admitted he felt a little guilty because he loved her and not the girl he had bedded. Instead of feeling let down, my wife admired his candour and was more drawn to him. Inevitably their association came to be much talked about.

Amongst others who became regular visitors to my home were Justice Gopal Das Khosla, also of the ICS, and his wife Shakuntala. He was taken with my wife; I with his. So we were on the level. Then there was the Canadian couple, Wilfred Cantwell Smith, Scholar of Islamics working on Indian Islam, and his wife Muriel, working for

178

a doctor's degree at the Medical College. There was P.N. Kirpal, then lecturer of history at Dayal Singh College. He was destined to stay in our lives for the rest of our days. There were others like Nawabzada Mahmood Ali Khan and his Sikh wife Satnam; Wilburn and Usha Lal who were distantly related to Mangat Rai; Professor Inder Mohan Varma, lecturer in English at the Government College; Bishen Narain and his wife Shanti, both friends of the Khoslas. Others came and went. Occasionally, when he was in Lahore, there was Arthur's younger brother John Lall, also in the ICS. John was a bit of a playboy with an incredibly British accent. He was given to making wisecracks at my expense. 'Kaval,' he said to my wife one day, 'if you have a sister let her marry your bearded husband and you marry me.' I was the target of witticisms from both the Lall brothers. With John I settled scores when he brought his fiancee Hope, a dark, pudgy girl, to introduce to us. The next day he dropped in he asked me what I thought of her. 'She will be a perpetual exercise in faith and charity,' I told him. He made no wisecracks thereafter. My day of reckoning with Arthur had to wait some years.

Two people who I met in my early years in Lahore deserve mention. One was the painter, Amrita Sher Gill. Her fame had preceded her before she took up residence in a block of flats across the road from ours. She had recently married her Hungarian cousin, Victor Egan, a doctor of medicine who wanted to set up practice in Lahore. Amrita was said to be very beautiful and very promiscuous. Pandit Nehru was known to have succumbed to her charms; stories of her sexual appetite were narrated with a lot of slavering.

I didn't know how much truth there was to gossip of her being a nymphomaniac, but I was eager to get to know her. I did not have to wait for very long. It was

179

summertime. My wife and six-month-old son had gone up to Kasauli to stay with her parents. One afternoon when I came home for lunch I found a tankard of beer and a lady's handbag on a table in my sitting room and a heavy aroma of French perfume. I tiptoed to the kitchen to ask my cook who it was. 'I don't know,' he replied, 'a *memsahib* in a sari. She asked for you. I told her you would soon be back for lunch. She looked round the flat and helped herself to the beer from the fridge. She is in the bathroom.' I knew it could only be Amrita Sher Gill. And so it was. She came into the sitting room and introduced herself. She told me of the flat she had related across the road and wanted advice about carpenters, plumbers, tailors, and the like. I told her whatever I knew about such people. I tried to size her up. I couldn't look her in the face because she had that bold, brazen kind of look which made a timid man like me turn his gaze downwards. She was short in stature and sallow complexioned (being half Sikh, half Hungarian). Her hair was parted in the middle and severely bound at the back. She had a bulbous nose with blackheads showing. She was full-lipped with faint traces of a moustache on her upper lip. I told her I had heard a lot about her paintings and pointed to some water colours on the wall which my wife had done. 'She is just learning to paint,' I said by way of explanation. 'That's obvious,' she snorted. Politeness was not one of her virtues; she believed in speaking her mind however rude or unkind it might be.

A few weeks later I had another sample of her rudeness. I had picked up my wife and son from Kasauli and taken them up to Mashobra. Amrita was staying with her friends the Chaman Lals, who had rented a house a little above my father's. I invited them for lunch. We were having beer and gin slings on the open platform under the shade of the holly-oak. My son was in a playpen learning to stand on his own feet. Everyone was paying him compliments: he was indeed a very pretty little child with curly hair, large eyes, and dimpled cheeks. 'What an ugly little boy!' remarked Amrita. Others protested their embarrassment. My wife froze. Amrita continued to drink her beer without concern. Later, when she heard what my wife had to say about her manners, and that she had described her as a bloody bitch, Amrita told her informant, 'I'll teach that woman a lesson. I'll seduce her husband.'

I waited eagerly for the day of seduction. It never came. When we returned to Lahore, my wife declared our home out of bounds for Amrita. Some common friends told us that Amrita was not keeping well. One night a cousin of hers came over to spend the night with us because Amrita was too ill to have guests. He told us that she was in a delirium and kept murnbling calls at bridge--she was an avid bridge player. Next morning we heard she was dead. She was only thirty-one.

I went over to her apartment. Her old, bearded father Umrao Singh was in a daze, her mother in a state of hysterics. They had just arrived from Summer Hill (Simla) and could not believe that their young, talented daughter was gone for ever.

That afternoon a dozen of us followed her cortege to the cremation ground where her husband set alight her funeral pyre. When we returned to the Egans' apartment, the police were waiting for him. England had declared war on Hungary as an ally of Nazi Germany. Egan was an enemy national. He was lucky to have been taken into police custody.

It took some time for Amrita's mother to get the details of her daughter's illness and death. She held her nephew and son-in-law responsible for it. She bombarded ministers, officials, friends (including myself) with letters accusing him of murder. Murder. I am certain it was not.

181

Carelessness, I am equally certain, it was. My version of her death came from Dr. Raghubir Singh, then a leading physician of Lahore. He was summoned to her bedside at midnight when she was beyond hope of recovery. He believed that she had become pregnant and had been aborted by her husband. The operation had gone wrong. She had bled profusely and developed peritonitis. Her husband wanted Dr. Raghubir Singh to give her a blood transfusion and offered his own blood for it. Dr. Raghubir Singh refused to do so without finding out their blood grouping. While the two doctors were arguing with each other, Amrita slipped out of life.

Many people, such as the art critic Karl Khandalawala, Iqbal Singh, and her nephew, the painter Vivan Sundaram, have written about Amrita. Badruddin Tyabji has given a vivid account of how he was seduced by her. Vivan admits she had many lovers. Her real passion in life was another woman--she was also lesbian. And she was a superb painter.

*****

Among the guests who stayed in my apartment while my wife and son were away for the summrner was the Communist Danial Latifi. He had been in and out of jail and the food they gave him at the Party headquarters did not agree with him. Being at the time close to the Party, I invited him to spend some weeks with me to recoup his health. Danial was then, as he is today, a compulsive talker. His flat, monotone voice retains the same soporific quality. One evening two of my friends dropped in. Both were very drunk. Danial converted their polite queries into a long monologue on dialectical materialism and the class struggle. I went out to take some fresh air. When I returned

182

half an hour later, Danial was still holding forth. Both my friends were fast asleep. Through Danial I received two other visitors in turn. The first was Sripad Dange, then on the run from the police. He had to pretend to be my servant. He spent most of his time reading my books. When anyone came to see me he would disappear into the kitchen. Another was Ajoy Ghosh, also then underground. He was a dour, uncommunicative man. His mistress and later wife, Litto, dropped in every day and spent many hours with him when I was at the High Court. Many years later, in England, I asked my friend Everette of the CID if he had known of these men having stayed with me. He said he had, but it had been decided not to arrest them, only to keep a watch on my apartment and note down the names of people who came to visit them.

****

A person who dominated my life in my Lahore years was Manzur Qadir. He was a couple of years older than me, had done his Bar in England, and had practised in the district courts at Lyallpur. He had picked up a considerable practice and a reputation as an upright man of uncommon ability. His father, Sir Abdul Qadir, had been a judge of the Lahore High Court and a litterateur: as editor of *Makhzan* he was the first to publish poems of Allama Iqbal. Manzur had married Asghari, the daughter of Mian Sir Fazal Hussain. She had been married earlier to the profligate Nawab of Hoti Mardan and had a daughter by him. The daughter had died and she had divorced her husband. She was a great beauty--the Russian artist Svetoslav Roerich had used her as a model for his paintings of the Madonna. At the time Asghari considered Manzur below her 'imperial' status and felt she had done him a great favour. He was a short, balding, beady-eyed man wearing thick glasses. He was evidently very much in love with his wife and patiently suffered her tantrums. They moved to Lahore with their daughter Shireen, who was the same age as my son Rahul. In Lahore they had a son, Basharat, who was two years younger than Shireen. It did not take long for Manzur and I to get acquainted and become friends. Fortunately our respective wives, both equally prickly characters, also hit it off well. We began to eat in each other's homes every day. My wife shared Manzur's enthusiasm for the cinema: they saw at least one picture together every week; also his passion for mangoes. Between them they would demolish a dozen at one sitting with great gusto.

Manzur was by any standards a most unusual character. He was without doubt the ablest up-and-coming lawyer in the Punjab. He and his uncle, Mohammad Saleem, the famous tennis player who represented India in the Davis Cup for fifteen years, spent hours arguing points of law after they had done a day's work in the High Court. Both men observed the highest standards of rectitude. They took their fees by cheque, or, when paid in cash, gave receipts for the full amount to their clients. They often paid more income tax than was due from them and had some of it refunded. Manzur was the only person I met in my life who never told a lie and took great pains to avoid hurting people's feelings. In due course, he became a kind of litmus paper by which his friends tested their own integrity. When in doubt over a course of action, we could ask ourselves, 'Will Manzur approve of this?' Like me he was an agnostic.

What Manzur and I also shared in common was a love for literature. In his case it was entirely Urdu poetry, to which he re-opened my eyes. He knew the works of many poets and could recite by the hour. He also tried his hand at writing, but without much success. He was best at composing bawdy verse which he recited with great verve to his circle of male friends, although he was extremely proper when women were around.

We spent many vacations together, sometimes at Patiala, where my father-in-law Sir Teja Singh Malik was a minister; other times in Delhi or Mashobra with my parents. Our friendship became the talk of the town as instances of such close friendships between Sikhs and Muslims or between Hindus and Muslims were very rare.

What proved to be a turning point in my career was Mangat Rai's desire to score over others of our circle as a man of letters. He suggested that, instead of him alone reading his pieces to an admiring audience, everyone should read something he or she had written. Our first meeting was in his home, a portion he had rented on Warris Road. The theme suggested by him was 'I believe'. We were to write down our beliefs on the values of life. About ten short papers were read out. I put down my reasons for disbelief in God and religion, and talked about friendship, love, marriage, death, and theories of life thereafter. There was nothing very original in what I wrote but just as it came to me. My main achievement was that I emerged as a rival to the hitherto unrivalled Mangat Rai. To be fair to him, he was generous in his praise. The next day I received a note of appreciation from Wilfred and Muriel Smith. It was my first fan mail and did a lot to boost my morale. Perhaps there was a little more to me than I thought.

The literary circle became a weekly feature. We met in different homes by rotation. A lot of liquor (mostly Indian brew) was consumed as poems, short stories, and essays were read and faithfully applauded by everyone. The two who contributed most were Justice G. D. Khosla and myself. Khosla was more anxious to establish himself as a writer than as a jurist. I had much less to do than any of the others. I used my visits to Sikh villages, from where my clients came, as background for my earlier stories. Mangat Rai's contributions as well as his attendance at our meetings began to dwindle. There were other reasons besides work for his absence.

Having come to the conclusion that he had little chance of wrecking my marriage as long as my wife's parents were alive, he began to cast around for a wife. The first to attract him was a very pretty girl, Lajwanti Rallia Ram, who belonged to a Nationalist Christian family. She was as fair Kashmiri Brahmin, large-eyed, tall, and slender. She got the top position in her MA English exam (her father happened to be Registrar of the University). I don't recall how they met, but since Mangat Rai was the most sought after bachelor in the Christian community, the Rallia Rams could not have had much trouble discovering him and getting their daughter to meet him. The two often met in my apartment when we were away at the club. They announced their engagement and the wedding day was fixed. Wedding cards were printed and sent out. Lajwanti had her household linen embossed with the initials LMR. A few days before the marriage was to take place in a local church, Mangat Rai called it off. Lajwanti was heartbroken. Almost on the rebound she married Mohammed Yunus, a handsome Pathan who was active in the freedom movement. The marriage proved to be disastrous for both.

I could not make out why Mangat Rai had behaved the way he did towards Lajwanti. He had earlier got engaged to Indira Sarkar, younger sister of Professor K. M. Sarkar, and ditched her just as peremptorily when he got into the ICS. As soon as he was free of the second entanglement he resumed paying court to my wife and coming over to see us almost every day. I did not resent his visits as my wife had become extremely possessive, jealous, and demanding of attention. Her pre-occupation with Mangat Rai gave me relief.

A year or so later, Mangat Rai met another young Christian girl, Champa. She had also topped in the MA English exam when her father S. P. Singha was Registrar of the University. He was then in politics and had been elected to the Punjab Assembly from a Christian constituency. Champa was a very different kind of girl from Lajwanti. She was dusky, animated, and unihibited. She was known to have had quite a few affairs. Mangat Rai was drawn to her because of her vivacity. Champa and her parents knew that our opinion mattered a great deal to Mangat Rai and paid us a courtesy call. I did not tell them that I did not think their daughter and Mangat Rai would make a good marriage; she was too hot-blooded for him. However, they got engaged. Champa took no chances with a prolonged engagement and the two were married in church. Though invited, we did not attend the wedding. Champa made a few half-hearted attempts to befriend us. We did not respond. She decided to drop us.

As I had foreseen, the marriage proved to be a mesalliance. Mangat Rai resumed calling on us, and when we were away, writing to my wife regularly. However, his marriage went on the rocks in a more bizarre way than I had expected. One summer we were all together in Simla. The Mangat Rais were staying with his sister Sheila and her husband Arthur Lall in a house near the Lakkar Bazaar. We were, as usual, in my father's house in Mashobra. We cycled down to Simla every afternoon and spent the evenings strolling up and down The Mall with them. It was evident that Champa and Arthur were hitting it off very well. Arthur was not getting much out of his rather frigid wife and Mangat Rai was proving somewhat inadequate for Champa. Plans were made for a week's trekking into the interior. A party was formed and porters hired. On the last day Mangat Rai backed out. So did his sister Sheila. Arthur and Champa had a week together in the Himalayan fastness, spending their nights in deserted dak bungalows.

They made up for what they had missed in their marriages. They returned from the trek convinced that they were made for each other. Mangat Rai readily agreed to divorce his wife; Sheila, a little reluctantly, conceded Arthur's wish to be free of her. It did not quite turn out that way. When the Singhas heard of it, they came down with a heavy hand on their daughter. Champa asked her husband to forgive her. He did so as readily as he had agreed to divorce her. But for all practical purposes the marriage was over. So was the Lalls'. After having bullied his wife into helping Champa get her passport (he had been given a posting in London) Arthur begged Sheila to return to him; he threatened to commit suicide if she did not forgive and forget. The high drama was to continue in the lives of all four of them. I was at times a spectator, at others a part of the cast.

****

My Lahore days were coming to an end. Almost from the day I had come to live there, war had been raging in Europe and the Far East. I had strong anti-fascist views and was convinced that Hitler, Mussolini, their European allies, and the Japanese had to be defeated before India could become free. Most Indians exulted in the victories of the Axis powers more out of spite for their English rulers than love for Nazis and Fascists. I wasn't quite sure of Japanese intentions after Subhas Chandra Bose took over command of the Indian National Army. He was too strong a man to be a puppet in anyone's hands. But even about him and his INA I had my doubts. My communist illusions were blown sky-high when Stalin made his pact with Hitler, and only partly restored when they went to war against each other. I did not approve of Gandhi's 'Quit India' Movement. I supported the Muslim demand for a separate state in areas where they were in a majority, believing that India would continue to remain one country with two autonomous Muslim-majority states at either end. I did not share any of the Hindu-Sikh suspicions or animosity against Muslims.

Not many Indians believed that the British would willingly relinquish their Empire in India. They regarded the Cripps and Cabinet Missions as eye-wash. They did not know the English. Young British officers who did their war service in India were a new breed. They refused to join exclusively white clubs, went out of their way to befriend Indians, expressed regret over what some English rulers had done in India, and sympathized with the Congress-led freedom movement. One event which re-assured me that independence was round the corner took place in the summer of 1946. I happened to be with my parents in Mashobra. I had to return to Lahore, so I took the evening railcar to Kalka. There was only one other Indian besides me in the car, the rest were British officers in uniform and English civilians. After a brief halt at Barog for dinner we proceeded on our downhill journey. It was a beautiful full-moon night. At a bend near Dharampur, a wheel of the car came off the rails. The driver told us to wait till he got to the next station to order a relief car to be sent up from Kalka. We sat among the pines on a hillside bathed in moonlight. The English were understandably nervous as some months earlier a railcar had been ambushed by two robbers who had shot six English passengers and then run away without taking anything. It was suspected to be the handiwork of Indian terrorists. Somebody switched on the radio of the derailed car and tuned in to the BBC Overseas Service. Election results were being announced. The Labour Party had won a landslide victory and Clement Attlee was named Prime Minister of England. The English passengers heard the news in grave silence. The other Indian, whom I did not know, and I leapt up and embraced each other. We knew that with the Socialists in power in England, independence for India was indeed round the corner.

I had no illusions about the Muslim-Hindu/Sikh social divide. Even in the High Court Bar Association and Library, Muslim lawyers occupied different corners of the lounge and the library from Hindus and Sikhs. There was a certain amount of superficial mixing at weddings and funerals, but this was only to keep up appearances. After the Muslim League resolution demanding Pakistan, the cleavage became wide and continued to grow wider. The demand for Pakistan assumed the proportions of an avalanche gathering force as it went along. Every other afternoon huge processions of Muslims marched down The Mall chanting in unison:

Pakistan ka naarah kya?

La illaha illallah

(What is the slogan of Pakistan?

There is but one God. He is Allah.)

An instance of how deep the poison had spread case in which I appeared as Manzur's junior. It concerned a Sikh widow of considerable wealth and beauty named Sardarni Prem Prakash Kaur. She had been married to the only son of a wealthy contractor of Ludhiana. Her husband was a debauchee. He contracted syphilis and died without consummating his marriage. The entire estate came to the young widow. One day, while holidaying in Simla, she happened to be having tea at Davico's. A young Muslim strolling down The Mall saw her sitting alone by the window. Their eyes met and her smile assured him that he would not be unwelcome. He joined her for tea. They became lovers. The young man was handsome, but the good-for nothing son of a barber. He began to live off Prem

Prakash Kaur. They had two sons. Then Prem Prakash Kaur tired of her uncouth lover. Her cousin Gurnam Singh, as handsome as he was cultured, a Barrister-at-law with a large practice in Lyallpur (he was a close friend of Manzur Qadir) decided to rescue Prem Prakash from the clutches of the barber's son. Prem Prakash moved in with Gurnam. Her Muslim lover took her to court over the custody of the two boys. He claimed she had converted to Islam, married him by Islamic rites, and their boys were circumcised and given Muslim names. Besides marriage and custody of children, there were criminal cases of trespass and forcible seizure of property. As these cases moved from the lower courts to the appellate, the pattern became evident; if the presiding officer was Muslim, it went in favour of the barber's son; if Hindu or Sikh, in favour of the Sikh widow. I came in on the scene when the case of marriage and custody came up for hearing before Donald Falshaw, then a District and Sessions Judge. I was engaged in order to give the case a non-communal flavour, as I was known to be friendly with Donald and his wife Joan.

But for the partition of India in August 1947, the case might still be going on. Prem Prakash Kaur and all her property were in East Punjab, which came to India. The barber's son was left in Pakistan. Gurnam migrated to East Punjab, became its Chief Minister, and resumed his liaison with Prem Prakash. He was later appointed Indian High Commissioner to Australia. A few days thereafter, returning home to collect his belongings, he was killed in an air crash.

*****

The atmosphere became so charged with hate that it needed only a spark to set the Punjab ablaze. The yearlong

191

Hindu-Muslim riots in Calcutta led to massacres of Muslims in Bihar, then to massacres of Hindus in Noakhali in East Bengal. Then Muslims of the NWFP raided and scattered Sikh and Hindu villagers and slew as many as they could lay their hands on. Others fled their homes to safety in Lahore, Amritsar, and East Punjab.

While the killings of Hindus and Sikhs were going on in the NWFP, I happened to go to Abbottabad to appear as defence counsel in a murder case involving two branches of a Hindu family. The case was finished in one day. The next morning, instead of driving down to Taxila to catch my train, I decided to walk the distance of about eight to ten miles. It was balmy weather. I found the road absolutely deserted. Even villages through which I passed showed no signs of life. Men and women peeped out of their doorways to see me stride along. It was eerie. A couple of miles short of Taxila a lorry-load of Sikh soldiers pulled up beside me. A young Captain spoke harshly to me, 'Sardarji, are you out of your senses? They've killed every Sikh in these villages and you are out as if on an evening stroll. Get in.'

I obeyed and was dropped off at Taxila station. The railway station was also deserted except for the Station Master and a couple of ticket collectors. I saw the train I was to board come along and stop at the outer signal, I heard some shouting but could not make out what it was about. When the train pulled up on the platform, I got into a first class compartment. I was the only passenger. I bolted the door from the inside. There was no sign of life at any of the stations we passed through. When I got off the train at Lahore, the platform was deserted. There was not a porter in sight. Manzur Qadir had come to fetch me. He told me that communal riots had broken out in Lahore. The next morning I learnt from the papers that a train, the one on which I had travelled, had been held up at a signal near

Taxila and all Sikh passengers had been dragged out and murdered.

A few days later, it was my turn to pick up Manzur Qadir. He had gone to do a case at Gujranwala. On his way back, when his train stopped at Badami Bagh, it was attacked by a Muslim mob and its Sikh passengers hauled out and hacked to death. He had seen the massacre with his own eyes. He looked bloodless and was still unsteady on his legs.

The last time I left Lahore before being forced to quit was to defend three men charged with robbery and murder in the court of the Sessions Judge at Gujranwala. Two of the accused had been members of the INA; I was engaged by an organization set up to defend them. This was not a political crime but a case of homicide. The men had boarded the night train from Lahore to Rawalpindi and forced their way into a first-class coupe occupied by two young English Army nurses. The girls put up resistance; one of them bit the man who tried to pull her down from the upper berth. The other fought back with her hands. The men threw her out of the fast-moving train. When the train stopped at Gujranwala, the three robbers disappeared in the darkness. The surviving girl ran up the platform screaming hysterically. Railway police came on the scene. They found the body of the other English girl lying along the track. The survivor was taken to Gujranwala hospital and treated for shock. The three accused were arrested the next day. They were Sikhs. They had woken up a barber at night and had him cut off their long hair and beards to escape detection. The surviving English girl was flown to England for treatment and was brought back after some months when the prosecution was ready to present its case. It felt it had a water-tight case based on the testimony of the barber and the recovery of stolen goods including a handbag with a compact, lipstick, comb, and other items of a lady's make-up from the accused. When I arrived in the Sessions Court it was clear that the Sessions Judge, a Muslim, had made up his mind to hang the three men. I pinned my hopes on the honesty of the English girl. I did not bother to cross-examine the barber at any length, nor the police over the recoveries made from the accused; village barbers could be made to say whatever the police wanted them to say; and planting incriminating articles on innocent people was a common practice. I concentrated entirely on the English girl. She was still in a state of shock and broke down many times while narrating the incidents of the fateful train journey. As I stood up to cross-examine her, the judge said to me very firmly: 'Be brief! She has been through a lot. I will not allow you to harass her.'

I protested equally firmly that I had to do my duty, or be allowed to withdraw from the case. He relented and allowed me to proceed. I asked the girl whether she could tell the difference between one Sikh and another if they happened to be of roughly the same age. She admitted that she could not. How then could she be sure if these were the three men who had robbed them, which one she had bitten, and which one threw her companion out of the train? She admitted that she could not be sure but these men had been arrested by the police and she had been asked to identity them. Did she know that the accused, who had had themselves shaved, had been forced by the police to grow their beards before she was asked to identify them? No, she was not aware of that. The identification parade had been a very shoddy affair. Of the twelve men lined up before her, only three were bearded Sikhs; she had pointed them out. She readily admitted that if all of them had been bearded and turbanned she would have found it very difficult to spot the guilty. She also admitted that a police officer had offered to help her identify the accused, but she had refused his offer. I asked her to look at the three accused in handcuffs in the dock and point out the one she had bitten and the two who had thrown her companion out of the compartment. She would not look at the accused men. The prosecution counsel and the Judge tried to shout me down. I stood my ground and insisted that my question be put on record before the judge decided to rule it out. The question was recorded. The judge had second thoughts about ruling it out and very gently asked the witness if she would care to answer it. The girl broke down crying, 'No, no, no. I don't want to look at these bloody villains. Please let me go.' All this was recorded and the girl was helped out of the court room by two British soldiers. I made my defence speech to a very irate judge who looked as if he would have liked to hang me. I left for Lahore, and a few days later for Kasauli. I learned later that the Sessions Judge had acquitted all the three accused for lack of convincing evidence. I had little doubt in my mind that the three men I had got scot free were guilty of robbery and murder. That was the sort of thing that nauseated me about the legal profession. It had very little to do with justice.

*****

Suddenly riots broke out in Lahore. They were sparked off by the Sikh leader Master Tara Singh making a melodramatic gesture outside the Punjab Legislative Assembly building. Inside the Chamber, the Chief Minister, Khizar Hayat Tiwana, had succumbed to pressure from the Muslim League and resigned. It was now clear that the Muslims of the Punjab had also opted for Pakistan. As soon as the session was over, Master Tara Singh drew his *kirpan* out of its sheath and yelled 'Pakistan murdabad' (death to Pakistan). It was like hurling a lighted matchstick into a room full of explosive gas. Communal riots broke out all over the province. M█████s had the upper hand in the killings. They were in the majority, better organized and better motivated than Hindus or Sikhs. The Punjab police was largely Muslim and shamelessly prejudiced in favour

195

of their co-religionists. The only organized group to offer resistance to Muslim gangs was the RSS, but all it could do was to explode a few bombs, killing perhaps one or two people. Then it disappeared from the scene. Urban Sikhs were a pathetic lot. They boasted of their martial prowess (they had none) and waved long *kirpans* they had never wielded before.

One day a Bihari working at a petrol station which I used was knifed to death in broad daylight by two Muslim boys aged eleven and twelve. Unsuspecting Sikhs, riding bicycles, were toppled over by ropes stretched across roads being suddenly raised from either side, and stabbed. Our nights were disturbed by sudden outbursts of cries of 'Allaho-Akbar' from one side replied to by 'Sat Sri Akal' and 'Har Har Mahadev' from the other. Muslims had more confidence. They would come close to Hindu and Sikh localities and shout 'Hoshiyaar! Shikar ka hai intezaar!' (Beware, we await our quarry.)

Whatever little resistance Hindus and Sikhs put up against Muslim goondaism collapsed one hot afternoon in June 1947. We heard no sounds of gunfire or yelling; we saw only black clouds of smoke billowing out of the city. The entirely Hindu *mohalla* of Shahalmi had been set on fire. Hindus and Sikhs began to leave Lahore, taking whatever they could with them. A few days later, they were forced out without being allowed to take anything. Their homes and belongings were taken over by their Muslim neighbours.

I did not know how long I would be able to stay on in Lahore. I had sent my two small children to their maternal grandparents in Kasauli. My next-door neighbours on either side proclaimed their religious identity on their walls; a large cross on the one side to indicate they were Christians; on the other, big letters in Urdu stating *Parsee ka Makaan* (this is a Parsee home) . Close by lived Justice

Taja Singh. He had often exhorted me and other Sikhs to stick it out. One morning early in August when I drove up to his house, I found it padlocked. The *chowkidar* told me that his master had left for Delhi. It was my college friend from London days, C. H. Everette, then head of the CID, who advised me to leave Lahore for a few days till the situation returned to normal. 'Leave your home and things in the care of some Muslim friend,' he advised. Manzur was at the time doing some case in Simla. I rang him up and we arranged to meet at Dharampur on the Kalka-Simla road, near where the road to Kasauli branches off. The following night my wife and I and our Hindu cook were escorted by a posse of Baloch policemen provided by Everette to the railway station. We left our young Sikh servant, Dalip Singh, in charge of our house till the Qadirs moved in to look after it. We arrived next morning at Kalka without any untoward incident. I had sent my car ahead to meet us there. We drove up to Dharampur. A few minutes later Manzur arrived by taxi from Simla. He told me that some Kashmiri Muslim labourers had been stabbed in Simla and Muslims were pulling out of Himachal hill resorts. I handed him the keys of my house. We embraced each other. I promised to get back as soon as things were more settled.

We spent some days at Kasauli. By then the mass exodus of Hindus and Sikhs from Pakistan and Muslims from East Punjab had begun. There were gory tales of attacks on trains and road convoys in which thousands were massacred in cold blood. Sikhs who had taken a terrible beating in West Punjab were out seeking bloody revenge on innocent Muslims of East Punjab, mopping up one Muslim village after another. I decided to run the gauntlet and get to Delhi. I had to make up my mind about what to do. I left my wife and children at Kasauli. I took a motor mechanic with me in the event of the car giving trouble. Some miles beyond Kalka I discovered that petrol stations along the road were closed. I returned to Kalka to fill up the tank and take a spare can of petrol. On the way I found our servant Dalip Singh walking along the road. He told me that Muslim mobs had come to the house. The Qadirs and their servants had hidden him in an attic for several days. Manzur had removed my name from the gate and put up his own in its place. However, word had leaked out that a Sikh was being given shelter and goondas wanted to search the house. Manzur was able to get the police just in time to prevent them breaking in. That night he put Dalip Singh in the boot of his car and drove him to the new Indo-Pak border. He gave him money and instructed him to board a train going from Amritsar to Kalka. That is how he came to be there. Not having heard of Kasauli, the fellow had taken the road to Delhi hoping to catch a bus somewhere on the way.

I put Dalip Singh in the car, took enough petrol to get us to Delhi, and proceeded on my way. There was not a soul on the road, no sign of life in any of the towns or villages through which we passed. It was only after I had passed Karnal, some sixty miles short of Delhi, that I saw a jeep coming towards me. I pulled up. So did the jeep, about a hundred yards from me. I took out my pistol and waited. After an agonizing five minutes of staring at the jeep, I noticed that its occupants were Sikhs. Two men stepped out on the road with rifles in their hands. I felt reassured and drove up to the jeep. I asked them if it was safe to proceed to Delhi. 'Quite safe,' they assured me. 'We have killed the lot in villages along the road.' They used the word *sooar* (pig) for Muslims. It churned my stomach. This was no place to argue with them.

I arrived safely in Delhi, a few days before India was to be declared independent. I had my father's home to go to. Hundreds of thousands of others who like me had fled Pakistan had nowhere to go. Some were housed in refugee camps; others occupied old monuments, railway

198

station platforms, or verandas outside shops and offices, or made their homes on pavements.

The magnitude of the tragedy that had taken place was temporarily drowned in the euphoria of the Independence to come. It was like a person who feels no hurt when his arm or leg is suddenly cut off: the pain comes after some time.

On the night of 14 August, I joined the stream of humanity moving towards Parliament House. With me was my wife's cousin, Harji Malik. We managed to get to the Parliament by 11 p.m. The throng was immense disciplined, and full of enthusiasm. Periodically it burs into cries of 'Mahatma Gandhi ki jai' and 'Inqilab zindabad.' A minute before the midnight hour a hush of silence spread over the crowd. The voice of Sucheta Kripalam singing 'Bande Mataram' came over the loud-speakers. I was followed by Pandit Nehru making his memorable speech: 'Long years ago we made a tryst with destiny...Now comes the time to redeem that pledge...' and so on. As the speech ended, the crowd burst into cheers and yelling of slogans. We embraced strangers and congratulated each other for having gained our freedom. We did not get home till after 2 a.m.

I was up early to be able to get to the Red Fort to see the Union Jack come down and the Indian tricolour go up. Once again the whole route was crowded with people going on foot. Lord and Lady Mountbatten drove up in their six-horsed Viceregal carriage. The horses were unharnessed. The people decided to pull the carriage with their own hands. Many British officers were picked up and carried by the crowd on their shoulders. Almost overnight the much hated English had become the Indians' most-loved foreigners.

I stood about fifty yards away from the ramparts of the Red Fort. I heard the buglers sound the 'Last Post' as Lord Mountbatten lowered the Union Jack. I heard the band play the National Anthem 'Jana Gana Mana' as Pandit Nehru hoisted the Indian tricolour. I heard the canons roar to salute the new President of the Republic. I heard all but saw very little because tears of joy blurred my vision. And my heart was full of pride.

10

THROUGH SMOKING TOWNS.......

PARKASH TANDON

While the fading paper flags of the independence celebrations were still waving, the horror of Partition broke on us suddenly one day when a post-card arrived from Uncle Dwarka Prashad. It contained this single line.

With my younger brother, who was also settled in Bombay, I had discounted the first rumours, while Government tried to tone down the press hand-outs . No one wanted to spoil the music of freedom still in the air. But every day the news became graver, and uncle's post-card told us that the end had come.

In June of 1947, when Partition was announced, most Hindus and Sikhs had accepted it fatalistically. 'We have lived under the Muslims before, then under the Sikhs and the British, and if we are now back under Muslim rule, so what? We shall manage somehow, as we have managed before. Nowadays governments are different, they give you some rights, they have to listen to the people ! ' Fortified by such arguments, people decided to stay where they were and face the change.

In July things began to look menacing, but few thought of leaving. There were sporadic attacks on Hindus and Sikhs, but they were mostly looked upon as signs of another riot. The turn had come of the Punjab, where people during the war years had prided themselves on living in peace while the rest of the country shook with the ugly outburst of Hindu-Muslim violence. As things worsened, father wrote to say that he considered it pointless to leave the house. Even if there was real trouble he would be safe, because he had so many Muslim friends and neighbours. Who would want to harm an old man, semi--paralysed by a stroke? Besides, he was so comfortable with his faithful Chattar Singh, who was on such good terms with everybody, Hindus, Muslims and Sikhs alike, to look after him.

In August law and order of ninety years came to an end. Elementary civil protection, taken for granted the week before, ceased . Chatter Singh felt that his own family would prove a burden if he suddenly had to leave; and to take care of father would be an added problem. So he appealed frantically to our neighbours to persuade father to go away for a while, till things improved. He was going to move his wife and children to the safety of Amritsar, now across the border. My older brother wired from Bihar that father must leave and reluctantly he agreed, whereupon Chatter Singh hurriedly packed him off. Many others were sending their women and children and old people away. Like everyone else, father thought he was only going for a short time, till the riots subsided.

Uncle Dwarka Prashad had remarried some years after Savitri's death and had permanently settled in Gujrat. My second aunt was a very handsome woman in her youth, with long brown hair and a melodious voice. After quite a struggle she had slowly managed to tame uncle. He worked hard, and with his natural ability he soon prospered. He built his own house outside the city wall, conveniently near the law courts, where he had built up a lucrative practice. She gave him two sons and two daughters. The eldest, a girl, urged by my father, had studied medicine. She then married a dentist, and they were both s[c]ttled in practice in Amritsar. The elder boy had just finished his law studies at Lahore, while the younger children were still at school.

Uncle had always been tough and fearless, and easily persuaded to fight. He had mellowed with the years as he became an elder of the *biradari*, a senior member of the bar and influential in municipal affairs. He was greatly respected by all communities, and most of his practice came from Muslim litigants in the district. Everyone assured him that h[c] could safely stay, no one would touch him and his family. He wanted to believe in their assurances even as he saw the trickle of exodus gather volume. These others thought it wise to go away for a while; they would all return when everything was calm again. The thought that this was a going away for ever never crossed anybody's mind. A calamity might cause temporary uprooting, but afterwards you came back to what had always been your home.

One day, a train crammed with two thousand refugees came from the more predominantly Muslim areas of Jhelum and beyond. At Gujrat station the train was stopped, and Muslims from the neighbourhood, excited by the news of violence in East Punjab, began to attack and loot. There was indescribable carnage. Several hours later the train moved on, filled with a bloody mess of corpses, without a soul alive. At Amritsar, when the train with its load of dead arrived, they took revenge on a trainload of Muslim refugees. There was also great killing at Sheikhupura, and on the other side in Jullundur. The whole Punjab was in conflagration. Six million Hindus and Sikhs from the West Punjab began to move in one dense mass towards safety, and from the east of the border a similar mass movement was under way in the opposite direction.

Muslim friends came to uncle late one night and said with tears in their eyes that they were unable to offer him protection any longer. The family must move at once, before dawn! Dwarka Prashad now saw it only too well that they had to go away, not for a few days, but for ever. He had in fact been expecting it since the day of the massacre at the station, but the problem had been how to get out; and it was then that he had sent the post-card.

His friends rushed to an Indian military evacuation convoy that had arrived the same evening, and brought a truck. They heaved a sigh of relief as uncle and his family, with two suitcases and a few blankets, drove away. On the Grand Trunk Road their truck joined an unending line of military and civil trucks and cars, bullock carts and *tongas*, people on horseback, and carried on shoulders. In its long history of over a thousand years this road had never seen such a migration.

As dawn was breaking, they caught the last view of Gujrat through the shisham trees by the road; a view they had so often seen when going to the river Chenab at Besakhi. They looked at the weathered dark brown mass of the city rising as a flat-top cone. My aunt's ancestral house was in the highest *mohalla* inside the fortress, and she could see almost the spot from where twenty seven years ago her palanquin had descended the narrow lanes to our old house inside the Kalri Gate. She wondered what would happen to her house, to her cupboards and trunks full of clothes, linen and utensils, and above all to the buffalo and its calf that she had left tied in the yard. She suspected that in a few hours their home would be swept bare, but she was too numbed to care. Through smoking towns and charred villages the convoy moved like a long dark snake. At one time over the narrow bridge of the Bullokee headworks, where I was born, there was a convoy of over two million people seeking its way out . Through Kharian, Wazirabad, Gujranwala, Emnabad, Gakhar, it heaved forward, swelled by other convoys joining it from the side roads. After delays, alarms and rumours of attack, it reached the Ravi and crossed into Lahore. They were put up at uncle's old D.A.V. college, which had become a vast temporary camp. From here they moved on in smaller convoys, and uncle's party eventually arrived at the new frontier post of Wagah, a tiny hamlet which was now in the limelight as a scene of dramatic activity. As the truck passed the barrier into 'India', they looked back at Pakistan, their homeland which did not want them.

(Excerpt from his autobiography *Punjabi Saga*)

11

An Unforgettable August

SOM ANAND

During my school days, August had always been a month of new prospects. It was a time when the leisure and freedom of summer vacations neared their end. We all made hectic efforts to complete the homework set us by our stern teachers. It was a period of excitement too, for the reopening of classes meant meeting our classmates again, hearing their adventures and having a lot of fun.

But in '47, all this excitement evaporated. In its place came fear of approaching holocaust. The schools had been closed since March and there were no prospects of classes starting again. For me there was no homework and no meetings with my friends. Berinder had gone to Jalundhar with his aunt. Father came home from the office every evening with a sullen face. He was a man who followed his daily routine religiously; but though the routine remained, the zest had vanished. As the situation worsened, most of his friends and neighbours left the city. With hardly any one to talk to, the before-dinner sessions of chit-chat came to an end. In his bank office too, there was little to be done, for in the disturbed conditions that prevailed, few went to banks to operate their accounts. Lahore was rife with all sorts of rumours but father never told me anything. My only source of information was our chauffeur, Gulzara Singh, who would exaggerate everything he heard or witnessed. Hearing the grisly stories of killing and arson, a gnawing fear, which I had never felt before, took hold of me. Every evening I had dinner with father without even exchanging a single word. His silence and a strange expression of sorrow stamped on his countenance disconcerted me greatly. I tossed in my bed at night, wondering what independence would bring for us.

Model Town, fortunately, was not touched by the massacres in the city. There were several Muslim villages near Model Town and the nearest was not more than a mile from our house. It was named Jeun Hana. Strangely enough, no one ever felt any danger from the Gujjars of that village. I cannot say what prevented them from coming to loot our locality of well-to-do people. One probable reason was that they got much of their business from the inhabitants of Model Town. Our milkman Imam Din, continued to visit us twice a day with his usual supplies. His only regret was that with so many people leaving the place, the number of customers had gone down considerably. Like other Muslims of the area, Imam din was tall, robust and without education. He had voted for the Muslim League but he did not understand politics. He was a mild and friendly man and I could not imagine him coming to Model Town bent on killing any one. Another reason why the people of Imam Din's village remained immune to the communal frenzy was that no one came there to instigate it. Jeun Hana was far away from the city, and the organised groups were too busy in their own localities to care for such a far-flung area. In any case we escaped the orgy of the riots except the last incident which forced us to leave.

During those days, my going to the city was strictly prohibited and with nothing to occupy my days, I used to roam aimlessly on the roads. It saddened me to see people packing up or leaving with their luggage in cars, trucks or *tongas*. The sight of empty houses with cattle grazing on their lawns depressed me even more. Model Town was fast becoming a deserted place--shops closed, gates locked and no one to talk to--exactly like a ghost town in a story book. Then for several nights from the roof of our house, I saw the glow of that big fire which had burnt down the Shahalami Gate area in the city. It horrified me and one day I timidly suggested to my father that we should also go to Delhi, at least for some days. But as I had expected, he brusquely rejected the idea saying "All these fools will be coming back after a few months."

August had entered its second week. Weary of the boredom, father decided to go away at last, but only for a few days. The choice fell on Kapurthala, the town where his old friend Aziz Bakhsh lived. On the 12th evening, Gulzara Singh was asked to get ready to leave the next morning. The prospect of an outing after so many weeks of immobility excited me. When we started out the next day, I was surprised to see that our chauffeur's wife and child were also accompanying us. Little did I realise at that time how disturbed at heart Gulzara Singh was feeling. Being a Sikh, his life was in greater danger than ours. It did not strike me then that if we were trapped by the fury of the mob, he would be the first target of attack. But the drive to Kapurthala proved uneventful. It rained all the way and in that heavy downpour the roads were clear of the threatening mobs which he feared. When at noon we reached the beautiful town of Kapurthala, Gulzara Singh heaved a sigh of relief. "We're safe", he said with a dry smile on his face.

In the middle of August, Kapurthala was peaceful. The riots had yet to start in that princely state with its Muslim majority and Sikh ruler. Our first two days there were spent without anxiety. The third day was 15th August, the dawn of India's freedom. In the morning I went to see the flag hoisting ceremony with our host's children. It was a drab function and the few hundred who had gathered there did not seem too enthusiastic. One reason for this could have been that at that time the people of Punjab were in the grip of a fever, the fever of communal hatred, which overshadowed all other feelings. Seeing the national flag going up the mast for the first time, my thoughts went back to our home in Model Town, my school and my friends and the life I had spent there which at that moment seemed to be a dream. I returned from the function depressed and dejected.

By evening it became clear that going back to Lahore would not be easy. The bazaar rumours, which Gulzara Singh related to me, were really disconcerting. He said that large-scale killings had taken place at the Lahore railway station and that people were pouring into Amritsar from Lahore. Such stories were very disquieting; and Aziz Bakhsh and his family now started pleading with father to give up the idea of going back to Lahore. But my father rejected this proposal firmly.

The question now was who would drive the car back to Lahore. To take Gulzara Singh with us would mean that he would be easily identified as a non-Muslim. But father was adamant on this point too. Two days were spent in discussing various proposals. Then on the 17th evening, we heard on the radio of the Boundary Commission's Award. Giving details of India's frontier through the Punjab, the announcement referred to a canal and to the village of Wagah. We had never heard of Wagah before. It was all confusing to me but in the end we clearly understood that Lahore was to be on the other side. So whatever little hope that was left had now gone. Our fate had been sealed and to me the future looked bleak. Lahore was now in another country and even if we succeeded in getting back, it was not certain how long circumstances would allow us to stay.

The next evening father summoned his chauffeur to announce that we would be leaving early next morning. For a few moments Gulzara Singh was silent. From his face I could guess the mental agony he was passing through. Gulzara Singh had been with us for the last twenty years and he had become almost a member of the family. I had never heard him say "No" to father. Now he was caught in a dilemma. Driving to Lahore when the city was running with blood was like going into the den of hungry lion. Yet he did not have the heart to refuse. In his anxiety to get back home as soon as he could, father had overlooked the danger of taking a turbaned Sikh along and Gulzara Singh had become such an integral part of our household that it had never occurred to him that he would need a new chauffeur in a Lahore which was no more part of India.

Gulzara Singh stood there silent and grim, not knowing how to express what he felt. Then he suddenly took off his turban and placed it at father's feet. "Lalaji", he said in a choked voice, "all my youth has been spent in your service; you are like a father to me. But they do not spare any Sikh in Lahore these days. I am sure to be caught and killed. Your life too will be in danger. If you want me to die, kill me here." Father was silent. He understood the gravity of the situation. At that moment, Aziz Bakhsh suggested that one of his cousins (I forget his name), could drive the car instead of Gulzara Singh. After some hesitation this proposal was accepted and early next morning we were ready to go. The whole of Aziz Bakhsh's family came out on to the road to say "Khuda Hafiz" to us. Gulzara Singh too was there with tears in his eyes. The car started and we felt a little relief from the tension. For a moment it seemed to me that it was the same old journey. But the next moment my eyes saw the new man at the steering wheel. Gulzara Singh's departure was our first loss, and much more was to follow.

We drove fast and at that early hour the Grand Trunk Road was empty of traffic. Our new companion was given a Gandhi cap to wear and it was decided that it would be replaced by a Jinnah cap after we crossed into Pakistan. The sun rose high and we left India's border town of Attari well behind us; but the border was nowhere to be seen. After a drive of about fifteen or twenty minutes from the border town, we crossed a canal and father remarked that the frontier would lie somewhere near this place. "So we have crossed the dividing line", I thought and felt a pang in my heart. But there was yet nothing to indicate the international border. My eyes were looking around to see if there were any signs of the new-born country. There were only vast, empty stretches of land on both sides of the road. Caravans of uprooted people had yet to pass through this unhappy land. Then just after we crossed into Pakistan, two men were seen standing on the road. As the car neared them they raised their hands and signalled us to stop. The car screeched to a halt. I was a little scared to see hefty villagers standing on the lonely road with dagger-like weapons in their hands. They too seemed to be in a panic. One of them said: "Sir, the village next to ours in district Amritsar was attacked last night by the Sikhs. They say that today it is the turn of our village. Will you be kind enough to take us to Shalamar Bagh? We want to get a truck to take our families somewhere safe." Before father could say anything, the driver signalled them to get in. They got into the front seat and the car started off again. On the way they said little except to give more details of the attack on the village next to theirs. Listening to their tale of woe, I felt for the first time that the riots were really spreading fast in the Punjab. After they got out of the car near the Shalamar Bagh, our new driver explained that it would have been dangerous to refuse these people a lift. They were armed and desperate so anything could have happened if we had refused. Father agreed with him and we decided to take the shortest possible route to Model Town. This meant avoiding the congested areas of Lahore. Though calm seemed to prevail, we were not sure what was happening in the city. Passing through the outskirts, I saw Pakistani flags fluttering on the housetops. The sight was not altogether unfamiliar to my eyes. I had seen the League's green banner several times in the Muslim localities of Lahore. But that was the first time that the star and crescent standard, with a white band at the end, was seen hoisted on the buildings. The indication was clear. We were in Pakistan and Lahore was part of it. India's partition had become an established fact. My mind went back to the discussions our elders used to have on the future prospects. Even two years ago, no one had imagined that independence and partition would come with such anarchy and bloodshed.

We reached home at noon to find our cook in a very sullen mood. He had probably given up hope of our coming back. The house had been left in his charge with strict instructions that he was not to leave it. After a few days when the riots had grown in intensity, he naturally felt that we might not come back, and it became difficult then for him to keep his vigil. The neighbours had to persuade him to stay at his post. By that time, only one non-Muslim family was left in our area. Like my father, Mr. Bhatia had also been hoping that events would take a turn for the better. But unlike us, they were a large family and when we left for Kapurthala, all of them felt as if they were stranded passengers on a sinking ship. Our return revived their hopes. That afternoon when I entered Mr. Bhatia's house, there was a cry of joy. The younger ones showed a brave face and taunted me, "You coward, where did you go?" To celebrate the occasion, a game of cards was arranged at once. In those listless days this was our favourite pastime to ward off worry and fear. But I was to lose their company very soon. Before long Mr. Bhatia decided to leave Lahore for some place in East Punjab. There was no sign that the university would open in the near future (he was a lecturer in the Forman Christian College) and the situation was becoming more dangerous for non-Muslims every day. Thus, within a fortnight, the Bhatias left in a military truck for Ferozepur. Bidding them good-bye proved to be really painful for me and father. They had drawn nearer to us in the days of strain and their continued stay gave me the hope that one day everything would be the same again. At a time when the neighbourhood was full of unfamiliar faces, the company of Mr. Bhatia's family provided the much needed moral support to both of us. But their house was not left vacant. Mr. Ata Muhammad, a family friend of the Bhatias, was asked to stay there until they returned. (Even at that stage the hope of coming back to Lahore was not completely lost.) He was a pleasant young man, soft spoken and mild mannered. I soon established a friendship with him. Later on this friendship was instrumental in saving my life.

With Mr. Bhatia's departure, only one non-Muslim was left in our area. Sardar Kartar Singh was an old man, emotionally tied to his house, buffalo and other worldly belongings. The rest of his family had gone and he was living alone, keeping watch on his property and hoping for better times to come. His position was that of a lonely soldier who keeps to his post, ready to face a massive attack. I had always thought him a crazy old man, but his lonely existence evoked a feeling of pity in my mind. Father also thought he would be better off living with his children in East Punjab. But we had never imagined that there was any danger to his life. Yet in the end the poor man did fall victim to the frenzy of a band of marauders. Before describing this tragic drama, which involved all of us, I must relate how Aziz Bakhsh and his family were brought from Kapurthala. The riots spread in East Punjab with much greater fury after Partition. The princely state of Kapurthala was also engulfed. Aziz Bakhsh's cousin, our new driver, was greatly perturbed to hear this. Father was getting frantic letters from Kapurthala asking him to rescue them from the hell in which they were trapped. The state's capital was so far free from bloodshed but there could be no guarantee that it would remain so. In the end the young man decided to go there himself and see what could be done to bring the family to Lahore. He set out with a lot of encouragement from all of us. But the next day he was back in our kitchen, weeping bitterly. He had never reached Kapurthala. At Jalundhar he had decided to walk to his town, a distance of 7 miles, as there was no transport available in those disturbed days. But hardly had he gone two or three miles when a ghastly scene made him stop and turn back. Near the railway line, dead bodies were lying scattered over a large area. It was apparent that a caravan of people had been massacred there. So great was the slaughter that a nearby rivulet's water had turned pink with blood and human limbs could be seen floating in it. He learnt that a train carrying Muslims from Kapurthala to Pakistan had been stopped at that spot the previous night and a horde of villagers had fallen upon their hapless victims. The killing and looting which followed had lasted several hours. And in the early hours of the morning this trainload of dead and half-dead people reached Jalundhar. Fearing that worse might be happening in Kapurthala town, he turned back and got back to Lahore without contacting his relatives.

It was clear from this account that the situation had become grave. Though it was very unlikely that Aziz Bakhsh had boarded the ill-fated train, the problem of rescuing him from the beleaguered town of Kapurthala had become much more difficult. But there was no time to lose, and something had to be done immediately. Father could think of nothing else than to make a dash to Kapurthala in his car and bring his friend's family to Lahore. At that time East Punjab was completely in the grip of rioters and there was great risk involved in the plan. It meant jumping into a cauldron. Though I tried to dissuade him, he was determined to go. It was decided that I would not accompany him because my presence could not be of any help. I was very keen to go and stay for some days with Berinder who was in Jalundhar at that time. But this was not thought advisable and my hopes of getting out of that lonely and listless atmosphere were dashed. In those days even going out of the house was discouraged, and it seemed to me that the boredom of staying indoors all the time would never end.

Father left for Kapurthala early in the morning. His only escort was Mr. B.P.L. Bedi and the Communist leader's hefty frame, composure and gift of oratory proved to be real assets in that situation. Moreover, Mr. Bedi was well-acquainted with Kapurthala and its inhabitants. He had spent many years there with his maternal uncle, Dewan Harnam Dass, who was well-connected and an influential dignitary of the town. In view of this background, there could be no one more suitable to provide moral support for father on that occasion. The plan was to reach Kapurthala and then make arrangements for moving the family to Lahore. I thought this would take several days, but to my great surprise, the big black limousine entered our gate after dusk the same night. "What's happened?", I wondered. The next moment the car stopped and Mr. Bedi stepped down followed by father, tired and cheerful. Then a host of children and women got out. All of them were packed in the car like chicks in a chicken-coop. It was really a great relief to see Aziz Bakhsh's family safe in Lahore.

What I heard later about the journey proved to me how courage eases a difficult job. The car moved towards Kapurthala at a good speed. At several places, there were

215

mobs of rioters blocking the road. (There were also heaps of dead bodies on both sides of the road -- unfortunate people who had fallen victim to rioters.) But seeing a big limousine running at that speed, they made way for it, probably under the impression that a government dignitary was travelling in it. The rioters were in fact waiting for the refugee caravans. At Kapurthala it was decided that Aziz Bakhsh's family should come out through the main door of Dewan Harnam Dass's house onto the main road to get into the car. This was done so that it would not be obvious that a Muslim family was leaving with its valuables. But as the women and children trooped out with little bundles in their hands, a group of passers-by collected around the car. In a few minutes it became a crowd, and when the news got around, it turned into a menacing mob. The situation could have become dangerous but for Mr. Bedi's deft handling. His political training, knowledge of the art of public speaking and crowd psychology came in handy at that moment. He addressed the young men of Kapurthala in his characteristic Punjabi idiom, told them of his relationship with Dewan Harnam Dass, the days of his boyhood in the town, the Kapuria *halwai's* delicious sweets which he had consumed in abundance and Kapurthala's fame as a place of communal amity. This short speech had the desired effect and the crowd.

THEN CAME THE PATHANS

Our house was now full of people, victims of India's Partition. The women and children were very depressed because the unfamiliar surroundings made them miss their own town. As for me, the boredom of empty, listless days had gone; now there was plenty of activity, but seeing so many unhappy faces' around, gave me little consolation. Meanwhile I had interesting company in the person of Pran, a distant relation who had come to Lahore from Delhi to

216

collect his father's baggage. (He is now Dr. G.P.Talwar of the All-India Institute of Medical Science.) The stories he told me of large scale rioting in East Punjab were really nightmarish. Once, while walking in the countryside, he was caught by a group of villagers who mistook him for a Muslim. All his arguments to convince them that he was a Hindu were of little use, and they were bent upon killing him until in the end he took down his trousers to prove that he was a Hindu. Later I heard innumerable stories of people who were killed because of mistaken identity. A somewhat different story was one I heard from Berinder about Dr. Zakir Hussain's escape at Jalundhar railway station.

Our escape in Model Town was equally providential. The month of September was in its fourth week. It was a quiet and listless Sunday and we were not expecting any change in the day's routine. At about noon, Mr B.P.L. Bedi came to our house. He asked father to accompany him to the city for some purpose. After a little discussion, both of them left in the car. Not knowing how to fill our empty hours, Pran and I went to have a chat with Ata Muhammad. He was a real gentleman and seemed to have no communal prejudices, a rare quality in that hate-infested atmosphere. We had been sitting there for the better part of an hour when suddenly a shot was heard from the direction of our house. I was too engrossed in the conversation to pay any attention to it but Mr Ata Muhammad immediately sent his servant to see what had happened. He returned after some time and whispered something to him. Our host immediately jumped up telling us to come in from the verandah into his sitting room. "What has happened?", I asked in surprise. "Your house has been attacked", he replied with anxiety and panic writ large on his face. For me this was incredible. There had been no person in Model Town who had taken part in the rioting; even during the worst days the place had remained peaceful.

But now there was no time to waste. Something had to be done to get help. Pran said that he would go to the Club House to fetch Gorkha soldiers stationed there. He rushed out and I was left alone with Mr. Ata Muhammad in his sitting room. In a few minutes his wife came in and tried to assure me that my life was not in danger in their house. But I still had not realised the gravity of the situation. After about half an hour, we heard the sound of an army truck passing that way. "Now you can go", Mr. Ata Muhamrnad said, feeling a little relieved. I went out and he accompanied me to the turning where our lane led off from the road. There he said goodbye to me and went back to his own house. I could see the army truck standing in front of our main gate and I ran towards it wondering what could have happened. There was a large crowd gathered outside our house, but I paid no attention to it and went in by a side entrance. There was not a soul inside. I rushed from room to room and it looked as if burglars had visited the place. The wardrobes were open and everything was in heaps on the floor. Then I crossed into the inner compound, and saw Sardar Kartar Singh's body lying in a pool of blood. Terror stricken I ran outside and saw our next door neighbour, Maulvi Muhammad Ahmad Khan, talking agitatedly. I stood at the gate trembling with fear. By this time, the army truck had gone and the crowd was dispersing. Maulvi Sahib caught hold of me and shouted at the top of his voice: "Where have you been? We were all worried about you." Then he took me by the arm, led me into his own house and put me in the care of his wife.

His house looked like a refugee camp. Uncles, aunts, cousins had all come to him from their villages in East Punjab. Besides, members of Aziz Bakhsh's family had also crowded into the compound. Our cook was there too. There was no need to ask any questions. He came out with the story the moment I stepped in. "Babuji", he said with some relief in his voice, "you were fortunate to escape those cruel Pathans. Another ten minutes, and it would have been much worse. I would have been finished too but Maulvi Sahib's arrival created such confusion that I got the chance to run by the back door." This blood-chilling tale gave me the shivers. There was no doubt that father and I had a narrow escape on that fateful day. I was told the story piecemeal because all who had been in the house that afternoon, had yet to recover from that traumatic shock.

Piecing things together, I learnt that the Pathans came to our house shortly after Pran and I had left for Ata Muhammad's house. They came in *tongas* and were armed. There were a lot of Pathans in Lahore in those days; they had probably come to get their share if the loot which was going on in the city. This particular group had established its headquarters in a refugee camp not very far from Model Town. (The refugee camp was meant for those Muslims who were coming in from East Punjab.) They had their intelligence to tell them about non-Muslims still remaining in nearby areas. Our cook told me that after entering the house, one of them brought out a piece of paper from his pocket and shouted father's name, then mine and then asked about the car. They said they were police officers but the poor cook had never seen such policemen in his life. Not having the courage to put any questions to them, he asked them to wait for father in the verandah. But they had come to look and kill and did not have the patience to wait long.

After about ten minutes, one of them said in an imperious tone: "Where is Lala's wife?" (Fortunately mother was with my brother in Delhi those days.) The servant took them into the inner compound and to get himself out of the difficult situation, pointed to the ladies of Aziz Bakhsh's family. They told the women to remove their jewellery and seized everything of value that they could see there. The ladies cried, shouted and swore that they were Muslims, but the Pathans would not believe that a Muslim family was living in a Hindu's house. When they had finished, their leader said: "Show us where Lala sleeps." They were led to father's bedroom. They broke the locks and brought out every single piece of clothing from the wardrobe. Interestingly enough, they took only the coats; trousers did not interest them. But there was not much in our rooms that they wanted, for heavy furniture was of no use to them. Even the radio set was left behind. They were tribesmen, and did not know the purpose of the strange contraption.

While they were busy tying up their loot in bundles, our next door neighbour, Maulvi Muhammad Ahmad, arrived in his car from the city. Hearing the noise of his engine they rushed out thinking it was father's car. Maulvi Sahib shouted at them; by that time the ladies of his house had also gathered on their roof to call the people in the neighbourhood for help. The Pathans pointed their guns towards them with the threat: "We will shoot you if you help *kafirs*". The threat was effective, and they fell silent. As ill luck would have it, the only person in the neighbourhood to hear the shouts was Sardar Kartar Singh, who lived just opposite our house. He came out to see what was wrong. As he came forward, Maulvi Sahib and others made signs for him to go back. But the old man was short-sighted, and in any case it was too late. The blood-thirsty Pathan marauders had seen a Sikh and they immediately caught hold of him. Without delay he was taken to our compound and bound hand and foot with a rope. Leaving the poor old man in that state, they went into father's bedroom to tie up their bundles. When they had done this, one of the Pathans shot him dead and then said, "We have wasted a bullet on this old *kafir*; he should have been killed with a knife." With this parting message, they left with the booty.

We spent that night at Hafeez Jalundhari's house. Father returned in the evening and when he was told of the raid, he sent a message to Hafeez Sahib. He came with Mr. Bedi and after hearing what had happened, they both advised us not to stay there as they felt that the house could be raided again during the night. I was told to pack some clothes but in the confusion and panic I could only find a couple of my shirts and trousers. It was a terrible night for me. Hafeez Sahib and his family tried their best to make us feel at home, but the day's happening had shattered our peace of mind. Lying there in unfamiliar surroundings, I wondered all night what the future had in store for us and whether it would be possible for me to go back to our house again. All these months I had been hoping that we would move to Delhi for some time. And now when circumstances had forced us to leave our house, I felt sad and dejected.

The next morning was taken up in consultations between father and Hafeez Sahib. I was forbidden to go out for fear of the Pathans. In those days, my *kurta-pyjama* would easily betray my identity as a Hindu and after what had happened no one wanted to take any risks. Confined to a room, I waited sullenly to see what would be our course of action. Hafeez Sahib made a hurried trip to our house to see the situation. He came back with the news that it was still dangerous for us to go back. Someone in the neighbourhood had told him that the Pathans were still keeping a watch on the area. What then was to be done? Mr. Bedi suggested that we should go to Delhi by air, leaving everything in Hafeez Sahib's charge. There seemed to be no other way, and father agreed to it. By the afternoon of that day, we were in Delhi telling my brother the story of our narrow escape.

Thus Delhi became my home, but even after more than four decades, I have not reconciled myself to the situation. Emotionally drawn to Lahore, I have always returned to see my old haunts whenever an opportunity has arisen. I am not alone in this craving. Lahore's name has been etched in the memory of all those Punjabis who have ever been a part of the pulsating life of that many-splendoured city.

MAULVI SAHIB AND HIS BEGUM

A few months after our coming to Delhi, father again returned to Lahore. The affairs of the bank could not be settled without his presence there and Hafeez Sahib had a tough time with the depositors. In the early post-Partition years, the bigger Indian banks had retained a skeleton non-Muslim staff in Lahore, but the National City Bank was a small institution and its problems could not be solved without the Managing Director's presence. It was fortunate that Aziz Bakhsh's family was still living in our house; otherwise it would have been occupied by some other evacuee. Once the riots ended father's work took him frequently to Lahore, and not surprisingly, he felt quite at home in Model Town. Within a year he decided to end this shuttling between Lahore and Delhi and stay in Lahore until his job was completed. I had to remain in Delhi to continue my studies. This arrangemer worked so well that he never came to India to settle down, and Lahore thus remained my "home town" as long as he lived, and every year I visited it during my vacations.

Model Town was not the same after Partition. There were so many new faces in our neighbourhood that sometime I felt as if it was a new place. This reminds me again of Maulvi Muhammad Ahmad, our next door neighbour. I have already mentioned him and I must now say something more about him. He and his wife provided such a contrast in human behaviour that looking back, I wonder that appearances can be so deceptive.

We all called him 'Maulvi Sahib'. the epithet 'Maulvi' was due less to family connections (his uncle was a professional Imam of their village mosque near Amritsar), than to the beard he sported. It was a well-cut beard and gave a distinguished look to his tall and hefty figure. Maulvi Sahib was a 'pucca' Congressman. His Gandhi cap and immaculately white *khadi* clothes proclaimed his political affiliations. This made him popular with his Hindu and Sikh neighbours. A nationalist Muslim was a rare species those days. We did not know what position he held in the party organisation but it was known that he had close contacts with Dr. Khan Sahib, then Prime Minister of the North-West Frontier Province, and with Maulana Abul Kalam Azad. Probably this was how he got into the business of publishing textbooks for schools in the N.W.F.P.

For me his 'begum' was a more interesting woman. She was a 'purdah' lady and in Maulvi Sahib's house, visitors were generally not admitted beyond the verandah. Therefore, I had no opportunity even to peep inside. The couple were childless and we would see only a black 'burqa' coming in or out of our neighbour's main gate. (And the 'burqa' was of very ample proportions.) For a year or so this was the only contact I had with Maulvi Sahib's 'begum.' Then, as he became more friendly with father, one day I requested him to help me occasionally with my Persian lessons. But he was a busy man and I a mere schoolboy, so he told me to see his wife about it. (Later on I learnt that his knowledge of Persian was rather scanty.)

For me the problem was how to approach the 'begum' sahib. I had never gone inside the house and naturally felt shy about making friendship with an elderly lady. Then one day I picked up courage and entered their main gate which had so far been a prohibited place for me. Seeking me coming in, their servant, Majah, gave a grin in his characteristic style. I felt as if someone had caught me stealing and slowed my pace, but the next moment I heard him saying loudly, "Come in babuji, come in." Those words gave me courage. Then I heard another voice from inside the house: "Majah, who is it?" And as if to announce my arrival he shouted back: "Som Babu has come."

A few moments later I was in the courtyard. A very fat lady was sitting on a bare string-cot with a tray full of vegetables in front of her. She was in the process of peeling potatoes. I could not decide whether to greet her in the Hindu or Muslim way. But her "Come in, come in" ended my dilemma and I sat down on the cot without saying either "aslaam-o-alaikum" or "namaste". She was an engaging conversationalist and in no time at all I forgot that we were almost strangers to each other. As our familiarity increased, I faced the problem of how I should address her. To Majha and other servants, she was 'bibiji', to Maulvi Sahib she was 'Azra' and to her younger sister-in-law she was 'Aapa'. I decided to call her 'Aapa' too and after a little while she became 'Azra Aapa'.

Azra Aapa had no formal education. In her family girls were simply not sent to school. Despite this handicap, she had a fairly good understanding of Urdu and Persian literature, with a smattering of English as well. I was surprised to hear her discussing Marx and Freud. But she had read about these Western authors in Urdu and made no pretensions to scholarship. What I wondered most was how a person who had never gone to any educational institution could gather so much knowledge. Later on when I came to know more of her background, I understood. She had come from a family of poets, writers and journalists; her eldest maternal uncle, Maulana Zafar Ali Khan, was the father of Urdu journalism. He had become a legend in his life-time, and the daily 'Zamindar', which he had founded and edited for many decades, brought Urdu journalism onto a modern footing. Another uncle, Hamid Ali, was also a litterateur of distinction and editor of several literary magazines. Her young brother, Raja Mehdi Ali, is still remembered in India. The songs he wrote for the Indian films (he remained in Bombay after Partition), made him one of the leading song-writers in the industry. Literature was, therefore, the staple diet of the whole family. They breathed it, talked of it and worked for it. Despite a lack of formal education, the ladies were not impervious to this atmosphere. I had the opportunity of meeting Azra Aapa's mother. The old lady spoke in a typical rural Punjabi accent but she was not lacking in grace or sophistication. One-time editor of a woman's journal, she too had made her mark in the field. The daughter had, no doubt, inherited much from her.

As my visits to Maulvi Sahib's house increased in frequency, the Persian lessons were reduced to secondary importance. I went there more for chit-chat than for anything else. The lady had a busy schedule but she also had the remarkable capacity of being able to do many things at the same time. Every day one of her main tasks was to keep Maulvi Sahib's temper in control and quite often she failed in this. When he got angry, he would shout at her, break the crockery, and abuse the servants in the choicest Punjabi epithets. Such noisy quarrels could not possibly be kept a secret and were naturally a spicy subject of gossip in the neighbourhood.

I never understood why Maulvi Sahib lost his temper so often. Probably he found something lacking in the house which made him dissatisfied all the time. This much was certain that husband and wife were poles apart in taste and temperament; he was a businessman and politician, she a lover of poetry and the finer things of life. As an orthodox Muslim, he wanted to keep his wife in 'purdah' but the 'begum' hated to be confined within the four walls of an empty, childless house. She wanted to move amongst men and talk to them as an equal. This was against family traditions and the tenets of Islam, and Maulvi Sahib could not tolerate such license in women.

Besides such differences, their political opinions also kept them apart. As I have said earlier, our neighbour was a 'pucca' Congressman and a follower of Mahatama Gandhi. (For him crockery-breaking in the course of a quarrel or an occasional wife-beating did not violate the principles of non-violence.). His 'begum', on the other hand, was a great admirer of Mr. Jinnah, the Quaid-e-Azam. She believed that the Muslim League was the only party for their community and those Muslims who opposed the creation of Pakistan were no less than traitors.

This clash of two faiths in the same house sometimes resulted in amusing situations for the neighbours. I vividly remember one such occasion when the Interim Government was formed in 1946. It was the first Government at Centre with an Indian at its head. The Congress High Command had, therefore, called upon people to celebrate by hoisting the party flag. Mr. Jinnah, on the other hand, boycotted it, and Muslim Leaguers all over India were asked to demonstrate their anger with black flags.

Our Maulvi Sahib hoisted the tricolour with great enthusiasm early on the morning of that day. But a few hours later we were surprised (and amused) to see a black flag flying beside it. It was great fun for the neighbours, but for Maulvi Sahib, it was a matter of shame and disgrace. What infuriated him more was the fact that his sisters-in-law, who had assembled in strength in his house on the occasion, sang a song in praise of Mr. Jinnah. No doubt the mischief was the doing of those naughty girls, but he suspected that his 'begum' was also a party to the conspiracy. As a result, there was a great row and no one had food that day. "Why make such a fuss", I asked Azra Aapa the next morning. "The man has no sense of humour", she replied calmly.

Such quarrels continued until India was partitioned in 1947. There may have been a more deep-rooted cause to this unhappy situation than mere political differences. I could see that husband and wife had little common ground. They were cast in such different moulds that each became a misfit in the other's company. The contrast became more glaring at the time of riots. As a friend of the non-Muslims, Maulvi Sahib had every sympathy for those who were forced to leave their home. The 'begum', on the other hand, thought the transfer of population would prove good for Pakistan. But during the anarchy which followed the great exodus, Maulvi Sahib grabbed everything that had been left in his custody. His wife, who was considered no friend of the Hindus, was always anxious not to keep anything which belonged to others. This contrast in behaviour proved to us that political and religious convictions does not determine a person's norms of morality.

Looking back on those years, I ask myself why an educated and enlightened lady like Azra Aapa believed in the philosophy of communal hatred. She was not a religious woman; she never said her prayers and sometimes even questioned the belief that the Quran was the word of Allah. Then why this faith in the two nation theory? One can say that there was nothing puzzling about it. There were hundreds and thousands like her who were not religious but who passionately believed in what Mr. Jinnah was advocating. And she belonged to a family where almost all of the elders had implicit faith in him. Going a little deeper into the causes, I find that education had made the Muslims communal in outlook. This may seem strange, for education is supposed to widen mental horizons. But in the

227

case of Indian Muslims, education made them aware of the Hindu's nauseating prejudices. And along with this they also started questioning economic disparities between the two communities. For centuries, the rich Hindu had equated his Muslim neighbours with the untouchables, and this could no longer be tolerated by the new crop of educated Muslims.

These factors must have operated for decades and, as I saw during my school days, the Urdu press had now become a powerful instrument for fanning the fire of communal hatred. Maulvi Sahib's 'begum' picked up her arguments form the editorials of 'Nawa-i-Waqt' or 'Zamindar' and brought them out in discussions with her nationalist husband. Interestingly, she had great respect for Gandhi and Nehru but not for Maulana Abul Kalam Azad who was a traitor in her eyes. On the other hand our milk man, Imam Din, who never read newspapers, was blissfully ignorant of the two-nation theory.

JEWELS AND COCUMBERS

It was all excitement as I walked down Anarkali; it was my first visit to Lahore after Partition. In those early post-Partition days, the atmosphere was still charged with hatred for the non-Muslims who had left the troubled city. For me, setting foot on that soil again was an experience I had never known before. In fact 'excitement' is not the right word for that vortex of emotions. When I left our home after that horror-filled experience of the Pathan's raid, I had not expected to set my eyes on these places again. Now as I looked at the familiar sights, I felt as if I was looking at a place associated with some previous life.

Lahore was in a sullen mood those days. The influx of refugees from India and the mass exodus of those who had lived there for centuries had rent the whole fabric of life. Despite the bitterness which the riots had produced, the older residents felt the void created by the departure of the non-Muslims. For me, the crowning irony of this love-hate relationship was the reaction of our Maulvi Sahib's 'begum'. The unsettled conditions of life had brought swarms of newcomers to Model Town who were, strictly speaking, not white-collar people. Despite her enthusiasm for Pakistan, our neighbour was somewhat irritated to see all those uncouth people, speaking in unfamiliar accents around her. She particularly missed those Hindu gentlemen who would give up their seat to her in a crowded bus. She was class conscious, and Pakistan or no Pakistan, her middle class culture was not to be discarded.

The refugees were even more unhappy in their new situation. They were dismayed to find themselves in an inhospitable land. Everything was foreign and unfamiliar to them. Their feelings of having been forced to come to an alien land was heightened by their economic plight. To complete the irony, many of them spoke with a touch of nostalgia of their non-Muslim neighbours and friends whom they had left behind. Talking of those early post-Partition days, I cannot fail to mention our vegetable-seller. He had been coming to Model Town since my childhood; every morning his resounding voice filled the air, telling us the price of potatoes, onions, brinjals, mangoes and all the things he had brought from the market. I heard him again on my first visit to Lahore after Partition. I recognised his voice but he was shouting something else besides the price of his vegetables. Previously I had never taken any notice of his announcements, but this time curiosity prompted me to ask our cook what the old 'sabziwala' was shouting. "Babuji", he replied, smiling as he said, "the bastard is shouting 'The jewels have gone, and the cucumbers have come." *(Chalay gaey heeray, aa gaey kheeray.).* All this was, of course, said in a humorous vein but behind it lay the vegetable seller's bitterness at having lost his affluent customers. In those days, when Model Town was swarming with uprooted people, there were very few left who had enough money to buy fruit and vegetables. (Even otherwise, Hindus and Sikhs use vegetables in their daily food more than the Muslims do.).

As a matter of fact, the dawn of freedom had seen a new Lahore which was quite different from the old one. And the pangs of transition were felt by all classes. The city's clubs, where the elite had assembled every evening, presented a deserted look. Despite the bitterness of Partition, there were many who mourned the absence of their non-Muslim friends. In those days one of our neighbours, Raja Farooq Ali Khan, complained that Lahore looked monotonous now. "There are no Sikhs", he said, "with their beards and turbans. *Sarees* also seem to have gone out of fashion. Instead we see only *burqas* and Jinnah caps." Lahore, it must be said, had always had the atmosphere of a cosmopolitan city. The Punjabis with their zest for all the good things of life had made it a glamorous place. Lahore had been the place where one came to see the latest fashions. After Partition that glamour and colour disappeared and the change came about so quickly that Lahorites who had lived the old life could find no words to express their sorrow. Of course, patriotism demanded that they welcome the transformation through which the city was passing and there was much fervour for the new-born Pakistan. But accompanying this enthusiasm was the misery of the refugees. And Lahore's residents, who were used to the presence of their non-Muslim neighbours, felt that the affluent "kafirs" had not been such bad people after all. A few brave souls mourned their loss loudly and openly. One of them was Abdullah Malik, a writer and journalist who was on the staff of the daily 'Imroze', Lahore's leading Urdu paper. He wrote an article in his paper which was an elegy for the old Lahore. The authorities reprimanded the paper and gave a warning that if such things appeared in the future, strong action would be taken against them.

In the post-Partition days there was nothing more offensive to the Pakistani establishment than to say that Lahore had lost something valuable with the departure of the non-Muslims. Despite these constraints, there were lots of people in the city who felt that something was lacking in their lives. Father had many stories to tell of how people reacted to a Hindu presence in their midst. Once the owner of our locality's ration-shop refused to supply the provisions due to us on our ration card. The servant who had gone there thrice to get the monthly ration was sent back with some excuse. Ultimately, the shopkeeper told him bluntly not to come to him for a *kafir's* rations. Father did not know what to do. In those days the atmosphere was still clouded with the hatred engendered at Partition; the wounds inflicted by the riots were still fresh and life in the city had not settled back into its normal routine. In view of the general mood of the people, what the shopkeeper told our servant was not at all surprising. After giving some thought to the matter, father went to the rationing officer of the area. He presented his ration-card and told him straight away that because he was a non-Muslim, he could not get his provisions. "You are a Hindu, Sir?", the rationing officer said; and he almost jumped out of his seat in surprise. He found it incredible that a Hindu was still living there and was courageous enough to come to his office with a complaint.

After his initial surprise, he gave quite a speech to the effect that his Hindu and Sikh neighbours had gone and lamented that he could see them no longer. Father was not prepared for such a reaction and he wondered how unexpectedly some people had reacted to the mass migration of non-Muslims from Pakistan. The drama ended that same morning with a reproof from the rationing officer

231

to the shopkeeper. Needless to say, after this incident we had no difficulty in getting provisions from his shop.

In those days while I walked the streets of Lahore, I too met acquaintances and friends who showed great surprise at my being there at such a time. "What are you doing here?", was a sentence that I heard several times a day. It amused me how all those whom I had known in the past reacted to my presence in their midst. Their reactions, as a matter of fact, became a study in human psychology for me. Some friends whom I had thought were close to me, did not seem to be at all happy to see me again. All the old friendly warmth had gone. I was somewhat bewildered by their cold cordiality. As far as I could remember, they had never been communally prejudiced and I could not understand the change that had come about them. Had they been swept off their feet by the "Hate the Hindu" wind which had been blowing in the days of Partition? This question puzzled me every time I met them in the post-'47 period.

Equally puzzling was the reaction of some people who had not been close to me. One of them was Habib, who had been in my class at the high school. We were poles apart in taste, temperament and political views. Habib was an ardent supporter of Jinnah and the Muslim League and our heated discussions in school had not left a particularly pleasant memory. In my view, he was a narrow-minded communalist. Therefore, I had little desire to meet him again. But after Partition, I was cycling in Model Town one day when he saw me. He raised his hand to stop me. Later as we talked, I could sense a change in him. He seemed very friendly and all his gestures indicated the joy he felt at seeing me again. This was very surprising for me. Afterwards we had other occasions to meet and these meetings developed into a friendship.

As I discarded some of the prejudices of my adolescent years, it became a pleasure to hear Habib talking. He was a simple-hearted person who did not mince words in giving his opinions. He would, for example, remark while passing through a bazaar: "See all these shopkeepers are Muslims. Before Partition there were hardly one or two Muslims who owned shops here. This is the advantage of having a separate homeland." Habib's attitude was strikingly different from that of other old friends in Lahore who never liked to discuss politics with me. But I did not take his views very seriously. We knew that it was not possible for us to convince each other and, therefore, we never took the discussion too far.

Unlike Habib, Abdul Rauf had held almost the same views as I had on India's communal problem. I need not say that he was a Communist. He was senior to me and in student gatherings we had never gone beyond saying "hello" to each other during my wanderings in Lahore in post-Partition days. I wondered if the Muslim Communists had all gone over to India along with their Hindu and Sikh comrades. None of them was to be seen in the Coffee House or in their usual haunts. One day as I was walking along The Mall, I noticed that the bookshop run by the Peoples' Publishing House was still there in the Y.M.C.A. building. Their signboard indicated that the Communist Party's establishment had not completely closed down. I went in expecting to see some old acquaintance there. Abdul Rauf was sitting in the manager's seat. He looked at me and his face became a big question mark. "What are you doing here?", he said in a voice which was hardly audible. Then getting up from his seat, he came forward

233

and embraced me in the true Indian fashion as if we had been old friends. I had to tell him briefly how it was that I was back in Lahore. Abdul Rauf thought it strange that a Hindu should choose to come back to Lahore after all the nightmare and turmoil of 1947. But I could understand his joy at seeing me again. Anyone in Pakistan who had had a large circle of non-Muslim friends before Partition could not help feeling a little emotional at meeting a Hindu acquaintance from old times.

(Excerpts from his autobiography *Lahore: Portrait of a Lost City*)

12

I Still Remember Lahore Burning

PRAN NEVILE

A former diplomat recalls the events that erupted in the historical city of Lahore and calls for greater movement of people across the border between Pakistan and India today.

I have vivid memories of those terrible days when Lahore, the city of my birth and upbringing, was burning and dying, while the British were engaged in the momentous task of the partition of the subcontinent and transfer of power to Indians. To Nehru, the first Prime Minister of India, independence meant to use his memorable phrase, 'a tryst with destiny'. To Jinnah, it was the fulfillment of his dream of a separate homeland for the Muslims, Pakistan.

Lahore has a long and ancient past. No other city in the subcontinent can perhaps be said to have a more checkered history than Lahore, a city ruled by Hindu kings, Mughal emperors, Sikh monarchs and British sovereigns. As the capital of British province and center of a modern system of administration, Lahore emerged as the fortress of the Indian empire that watched over the troublesome Afghans and the Russian borders. With its chain of colleges and professional institutions, Lahore was the leading center of education in North India. So much so that students from

Delhi came to Lahore for higher education. The city had acquired the reputation of being the Paris of the East. Fashion ruled the life of its people whose lifestyles, habits, and customs were considered to be most admirable. It had also become the nucleus of commerce and politics.

The interplay of historical forces had made the Muslims of the Punjab less fanatic and the Hindus and Sikhs less orthodox and ritual-conscious than elsewhere in the country. The three communities mixed freely and had cordial and friendly relations, subscribing as they did to a composite Punjabi culture which blossomed from the early decade of the century. Muslim influence of nearly a thousand years had left its impact on the citizens' dress, customs and manners, food and language, and even their names.

The British announcement of the decision to quit India by June 1946 had a disastrous effect on the situation in Punjab. The Muslim League launched a campaign of direct action against Unionist Party leader, Khizr, for banning the paramilitary Muslim League National Guards Organization along with the Hindu RSS (Rashtriya Swayamsevak Sangh). Muslim League leaders defied government orders and courted arrests and there were strikes in Lahore. Khizr was forced to come to terms with the League by lifting his ban but in his exasperation, he gave his resignation on March 3, 1947. The Punjab Governor, Evan Jenkins, explored the formation of the Muslim League Ministry and while he was holding a meeting with the Nawab of Mamdot, the Akali leader Master Tara Singh appeared outside the Legislative Assembly brandishing a sword and shouting *Pakistan Murdabad* (Death to Pakistan). This led to anti-Pakistan demonstrations by Hindus and Sikhs which sparked off widespread rioting that spread from Lahore and other towns and also the rural areas. The riots left a legacy of hatred and mistrust and even the police force was communalised. Whole villages were put to sword which were followed by revenge and retaliatory massacres by the other community.

According to the British Plan of June 3, 1947, it was decided to partition both Bengal and the Punjab and the date of transfer of power was brought forward to August 15, 1947. The advancing of the date was an ill-judged decision which contributed considerably to the communal massacres which accompanied partition. There was active growth of paramilitary organizations and by June 1947, the Muslim League National Guards were reported to have 39,000 members, the RSS over 58,000 and the Sikh Akali Fauj 8,000. By mid-July, hundreds of non-Muslim houses had been burnt down. The Hindus and Sikhs retaliated by throwing bombs into the crowded Muslim localities. The exodus of Hindus and Sikhs, which had begun from April, was now in full scale. They locked-up their properties and believed that they would return when things settled down with the restoration of peace and good-will. That was not to be. The British divided and quit India on August 15, 1947. The Boundary Commission, under the chairmanship of Sir Cyril Radcliffe entrusted with the task of demarcating the boundary lines, submitted its award to the Viceroy on August 12 and it was made public only on August 16 so as not to disturb the Independence Day celebrations in the two dominions of India and Pakistan.

I was a witness to the chain of events. The specter of partition was there but we did not think of leaving Lahore even if it became part of Pakistan. Hindus were hoping that Lahore might be included in India. I left Lahore in the first week of March when rioting broke out in some parts of the city. I vividly recall how the train to Delhi was overcrowded though there was no incident. I could never imagine that this would be my last visit to Lahore. As the situation worsened in April and May 1947, and educational institutions closed down for the summer vacations my brothers and sisters joined me in Delhi in my one room studio. My father in the Government service had opted for Pakistan since he had no intention of leaving Lahore. He had a narrow escape once while returning in a *tonga* from his office when a mob attacked him. Luckily someone in the crowd recognized him and escorted him back home. He stuck on with my mother in Lahore until the middle of August but on the 14, some Muslim friends came to warn my father and strongly advised him to leave Lahore for a few days and return when the situation improved. They escorted my parents to the railway station and somehow managed to put them in a rail compartment occupied by some English army officers who provided them with a hiding place under their seats. This was the last train to steam out of Lahore station as the train services were suspended thereafter.

Fifty years have passed but the memories are still fresh in mind and most of us consider ourselves rootless. We are still groping for an identity. We had to make linguistic and social adjustments. We cannot help expressing our disgust with the political leaders of the time and their responsibilities for the sufferings. It is ironical to recall that Mahatma Gandhi advised non-Muslims in Lahore in the first week of August 1947 to remain when more than half of the non-Muslim population had already left the city. The massive destruction of life and property that accompanied Partition and subsequent fifty years of cold war in the subcontinent were not anticipated by the political leaders.

Unfortunately, India and Pakistan, with age-old common heritage, and social and cultural traditions, are still distant neighbours. I recall the enthusiasm with which we welcomed the participants from Pakistan at the annual Indo-Pakistan Mushairas held in Delhi. I remember how once the celebrated poet of Pakistan, Hafiz Julundhari, dubbed the politicians of the two countries as quail fighters and exhorted the poets and writers to ignore them and recreate bonds of friendship between the common people.

It is important to give due recognition to the ethnic ties and common cultural heritage of the Punjabis across the borders. Though there are practically no divided families in the two Punjabs, yet there is a burning desire among the aging and fading generations of both Hindus, Sikhs and Muslims of the Punjab to visit the places of their birth and upbringing.

For decades, the post-Partition generations have been fed on tales and anecdotes by their elders about the towns and villages across the borders from where they were forced to flee for no fault of theirs. So even the young Punjabis are keen to visit these places not only to satisfy their curiosity but also interact with their ethnic counterparts on the other side. I wish both the Governments of India and Pakistan would pay heed to this aspect and take suitable steps to facilitate such visits on either side. We, in this regard, have the example of France and Germany which created more destruction through wars in Europe than any other countries in the world, and yet today, they are part of the European Community with free movement of people and no custom barriers.

Let us wish and hope that one day, in not too a distant future, India and Pakistan will likewise come together not politically in the old conventional sense but economically, socially and culturally with free movement of people and goods through agreements and understanding.

4

Oranges and Apples

13

Oranges and Apples

KAMLABEHN PATEL

The loss of lives and property, and the widespread violence that accompanied Partition have been well documented by historians and scholars of Independence. Less well-known is the incidence of the largescale abduction of women of all three communities, Hindu, Muslim and Sikh, during that period. No official estimates exist of the exact number of such abductions, but it is safe to assume that there would have been well over 10,00,000 or more. In the aftermath of Partition, the governments of India and Pakistan were swamped with complaints by the relatives of 'missing' women, seeking to recover them either through government, military or voluntary efforts. Recognizing the enormity of the problem, the two governments entered into an Inter-Dominion Agreement in November 1947, to recover as many women as possible, as speedily as possible, from each country and restore them to their families.

In all, approximately 30,000 women--12,000 Muslim and 18,000 non-Muslim--were recovered by the police and social workers of both countries, primarily between 1947 and 1952. Kamlabehn Patel, an Indian social worker, was stationed in Lahore for a few years and was actively involved in recovering Hindu and Sikh women from Pakistan. Recovery work had been entrusted to the Women's Section, Ministry of Relief and Rehabilitation, under the direction of two principal honorary advisers, Rameshwan Nehru and Mridula Sarabhai. Kamlabehn Patel, a Gandhian, was Mridula Sarabhai's right-hand woman in Lahore till 1952, and represented both India and Pakistan on the Special Tribunals set up by both governments, to resolve disputed cases.

How I got involved in recovery work was by accident. Actually, I was supposed to go and work with Bapu at Sabarmati Ashram but I didn't really want to go there. Mridulabehn came to my rescue. She told Bapu there are other things she can do as her health is fragile. I will find something else for her. So she asked me to work with her. I said, but what can I do? She said, you be my personal secretary. But I can't type, I said, I don't speak English, how can I be your secretary? She said, look all these skills can be bought, I don't need those from you--I'll give you a typist, you don't worry about all that. What I want from you is that you should be able to take decisions on important matters if I'm not around, so that I know, Kamla is there, I don't need to worry.

I thought about it for a while and then she said I would go on six months' probation! I first went to Pakistan in November 1947. Mridulabehn sent me a telegram asking me to come to Delhi. When I reached there, she wasn't around, but I was handed a ticket to go to Lahore. I didn't know why I was being sent there, I was just told, you have to reach there immediately.

Shiv Prakashji, our first High Commissioner, was already there. He was quite adamant that proper arrangements should be made before we went--he thought Bimlabehn was crazy not to have insisted on it. However, we went. We had to establish a camp in Lahore, meet government officials and start a dialogue. We had not attended any conclave regarding this work and so at times were quite at sea about it, and yet went ahead.

Gradually, we learnt how to handle the work and situations as they arose. We made mistakes, small as well as big ones. For instance, one day a peon came and said to me that Kapur Saheb (an ICS officer) sends his salaams. I did not understand the meaning of this 'salaam', so I said please give him my salaams too! At night, when all gathered, I mentioned this episode to everyone. Then I understood that this was his way of calling for me and that I should have gone to see him. The next day I went to see Kapur Saheb and apologized for not understanding his message!

There were approximately 22,000 women who were in my charge. Thousands of women who came from various districts of Pakistan and so many others from several places in India, all had to be rescued. Now when I look back at all that I was able to accomplish, I myself marvel at my own courage and the circumstances that pushed me into this work.

There was an ICS officer, Mr. K. L. Punjabi, who felt that we had not recovered enough women in proportion to the money spent on this work. But I said to him: 'When you see a family reunited, you see father meet his daughter and the joy on their faces, you don't remember the lakhs that have been spent. When you see their happiness, you realize it is worth it.'

Let me tell you about Sialkot. I went to Sialkot which was a closed district. I had no intention of going there because of the whole Azad Kashmir business. It was an anxious time since there was no agreement on Kashmir. I was instructed to go with the SP wearing a *shalwar-kameez*. No *sari*, under any circumstances. This SP was a complete rogue. He used to worm out all the information

from us by being on his best behaviour. Often I told
Mridulabehn that I was afraid of dealing directly with him
and because he was waiting to catch me out, I would make
a mistake. And my mistake would be India's mistake. She
said, don't worry, only you can do this work, and I'm as
capable of making a mistake as you are.

You can imagine how I felt, an Indian woman
entering a closed district at that time.... We were fighting
about Kashmir.... But they were so excited that an Indian
woman was coming! People came to see me, cried while
asking about their relatives on this side. They asked about
the situation obtaining on the other side. In their anxiety
they asked questions which seemed foolish, like: 'My
mother's relative went that side, would you know where he
went? Did you ever meet him?' They were very hospitable
towards me---a woman had come from Hindustan to see
them---in spite of the fact that we were within five miles of
the fighting.

I was still afraid because I was an Indian. Suppose a
crowd had gathered to throw stones, attack? But the
opposite happened. On the way nothing happened because
the SP was in his uniform, but I was afraid that he himself
might start something.

You see, the Hindus never did accept the Muslims
because if they had, these things would have been avoided.
If they had looked upon them as one does on a younger or
older brother, then they would not have developed this
complex. Even the common people treated them like
untouchables, never let them get close. Look, I am a
Gujarati. Among us, there was not much warmth for them.
In Gujarat, there were no Muslim *zaminzdars* or highly
educated people, only farmers or artisans. They could not
equal either the money or education of the Muslims of the
Punjab or UP. At the time of Partition, when I went to
Punjab for the first time, I realized that there was a lot of

socializing and warmth among the two communities. They used to embrace each other and when they were forced to separate, they longed to see each other again. If they were together alone, they would embrace, but in public they would shout slogans against each other!

When the recovery work started progressing, this antagonism became much sharper. Of course, it became an issue between two countries then. There was this young Pathan girl--she must have been about 15 or 16, whose family used to go to Kashmir every year for the summer. They were from Rawalpindi. There she used to meet a young boy from Amritsar, a Hindu, whose family also used to go to Srinagar.

When the trouble after Partition began, and she saw all the camps being set up around Rawalpindi she realized something was going on and that she wouldn't be able to meet young Jeetu any more. Her name was Kismet. So what did she do? She ran away to Amritsar. She had no idea where Jeetu's house was, but all she knew was that he lived there. How she got there is a story by itself.

She arrived at the Hindu refugee camp in Rawalpindi--she had taken a few belongings with her in a small bag--went to the camp commander (the Indian Army was in charge of this camp) and said, 'I am a Hindu girl separated from my parents--please help me reach India.' Because she was so young, he took her himself in his jeep to an Amritsar-bound train and saw her off.

When Kismet got down at Amritsar--she was not at all anxious because she had succeeded in running away-- she waited patiently in one corner of the platform. A volunteer saw her--those days Bhimsen Sachar (later Chief Minister of Punjab) sometimes used to be at the station to receive incoming trains. He was there that day, and the volunteer took Kismet to him. She told him her story--that

245

she was from a village in Rawalpindi, had been with her maternal aunt when the riots broke out. After some days, when she finally reached the safety of a camp, she was told that her parents had already started out for India. Now she was quite alone. Bhimsen Sachar instructed one of the local workers to take special care of her and she managed to find Jeetu's parents' address from this worker, in the course of conversation. She then sent him a message to come and fetch her from the camp! No one doubted her story or the fact that she was a Hindu refugee! But because she was a minor she wasn't allowed to leave the camp with Jeetu. Somehow, he and his parents managed to get permission from the deputy commissioner to take her away from the camp, and before anyone knew anything, they had got married in the Golden Temple.

Now this case became a prestige issue between India and Pakistan. Her parents reported her missing, the Pakistan Rehabilitation Minister requested Gopalaswamy Iyengar to look for Kismet and send her back to Rawalpindi. Gopalaswamy Iyengar called Mridulabehn and me and asked us to make a special effort to find her.

Now, Jeetu knew that something was going on. So when I next came to Amritsar from Lahore, he rushed to my office and told me the whole story. It had been discussed in the Search Service Bureau at Amritsar and was registered as a case of abduction, so he knew about it. He pleaded with me, saying it was not an abduction at all, that Kismet had come on her own, that they had been properly married. But by now it was an inter-dominion issue: K. L. Punjabi and another senior officer, Nagpal, and myself, discussed the case. I was not at all inclined to hand her back to Pakistan. How could we consider it an abduction when the girl had travelled all the way from Rawalpindi herself, taking such a risk? And how could the Government of India force her to return against her will? But Punjabi did not agree with me. He said, 'If we don't honour the agreement, how can we expect Pakistan to enforce it---we have to consider the wider interests of the country.'

Well, we managed to persuade Jeetu and Kismet to meet Mridulabehn at Hotel Amritsar--that was where she camped when she came there--but it was a difficult meeting. Mridulabehn offered to accompany Kismet up to Wagah to meet her parents, but she refused. She told me afterwards, 'If God himself came with me, I wouldn't go! My parents will kill me as soon as they see me . '

Now, Jeetu was very worried because he thought the police might come and take her away forcibly. So both of them ran away to Calcutta! Nobody knew where they were, and the Pakistan government was putting great pressure on India to recover her.

It's a long story, but ultimately Jeetu and Kismet returned to Amritsar and a message was sent to Kismet's uncle, in the External Affairs Ministry of Pakistan, to come to Delhi to discuss the case. We arranged for him to meet Kismet, in our presence, and it took almost five days to persuade her to return to Lahore and meet her parents. She was told she would stay with the IG of Police there, Khan Qurban Ali. She needn't go to Rawalpindi, and after a week she should decide what she wanted to do.

Jeetu, Kismet, her uncle and the Pakistan SP Rizvi, arrived in Lahore by plane--Kismet was loaded with gold jewellery. We went to the Secretariat where we were supposed to hand Kismet over to the IG, but she refused to get out of the car without Jeetu. After a lot of arguing finally Jeetu persuaded her to go in, saying he would come and get her in seven days' time.

From Khan Qurban Ali's place her parents took her home---Khan Saheb should not have allowed it, but he did. We were very upset but what could we do? Mridulabehn and I went to her *Abba's* place where we were made to wait for a long time. Finally Kismet came out from the *zenana* and we got a real shock. She was completely transformed. Her walk, her dress, her behaviour--we thought it must be her sister, not her. Then she turned on us and with an accusing finger pointed at Mridulabehn, said: 'There she is! That woman with short hair is the one who prevented me from coming back! I asked her so many times but she wouldn't listen. And let that Jeetu come near me--I'll tear him to bits and feed him to the dogs!'

We couldn't believe our ears. Could this be the same Kismet who had refused to come? But there was no point in staying there any longer, so we left. I was both shocked and dismayed: what would I say to Jeetu? How could I explain this turn of events to him? When he came to see me in Amritsar, he was very angry and very sad, and he said I had betrayed him. 'You should have taken me with you,' he shouted. 'Why didn't you take me? She would never have stayed back if I had been with you.' He never recovered from Kismet's action, and tried many times to find her in Lahore. I tried to dissuade him, but he wouldn't listen. He was like a man possessed. He never did find her, of course.

Even today, I tremble a little when I remember this incident. We were hundred per cent sure she would come back. Kismet said all those things to rehabilitate herself in her parents' eyes, out of fear, that is why she changed. I met her mother, father and sister---they were so happy that their daughter had come back. Jeetu's family were banias--he was the only son and they were all very happy with Kismet---what was special was that she was a friend's daughter. And Kismet argued with us for almost an hour. Rizvi, her uncle, Jeetu and I were there. She said to me, I will not leave Jeetu behind, I will take him with me. I understand that she was only a 14-year old girl and that after the thrill of eloping passed, she was afraid that her parents would kill her, would not keep her. She was very young, if she had been older, it may have been different. Now, Sudarshan was older, about 23 years old, very strong-willed, but she melted when she saw her brother and father crying. So, she went with them, but then she thought it was wrong to do so and she came back.

It was such a difficult time, so many people leaving their homes, so much violence.

But I think there were economic reasons, too. The number of Hindus in the Punjab was greater than the number of Muslims in India. Another reason could be that wherever the Hindus went, they exploited the Muslims. There were quite a few bania moneylenders who lent money at such exorbitant rates of interest that they were like blood suckers. When an opportunity offered itself, they took their revenge. So many factors were involved, it was not only one factor that brought about Partition. One cannot only blame the Muslims for subjecting Hindu women to violence, the Hindus also did it. In the Golden Temple 200 women were made to dance naked for the whole night.

Yes, in 1947, not in the Durbar Sahib, but in its compound. And so many people enjoyed this unholy show. If I tell this to anyone, they don't like it, but these are facts. I will talk on behalf of women. I was not a politician. If I had been one, I would have said that the Muslims did everything, but we never did anything. But we were no less--how many we kept back, how many women we sold in the same way that baskets of oranges or grapes are sold or gifted. Women were distributed in the same way. You may ask why we uprooted these women again, but in my view, they were never ever secure, had never put down roots.

The Muslim women we recovered in India were mostly sent back; there were approximately 12,000 women. Ours were about 9,000. Most of the Muslim women were recovered from the Punjab, from the villages and towns.

But more from the villages. That is because economic factors played a great part. Those nine or ten thousand women who were brought back from Pakistan were accepted by the Hindus. Why? Because of economic factors. People had come from there as refugees and so they did not have money. They did not have a woman to do the housework--a housewife. But here, there was a woman available. So forgetting everything, they took her. They accepted them out of helplessness, not out of broad-mindedness. It was not so important for the Muslims because they did not think of the women as impure, and they hesitated much less when taking them back. But not the Hindus.

This was my experience. A Hindu woman felt that she had been rendered impure, had become sullied, was no longer *pativarta*. A Muslim woman did not feel like this. It was not in her blood; it is in ours. We feel we have been polluted, we are no longer worthy of showing our faces in public. How can we face our family when we go back? We reassured the women saying, 'See how many times your father has come to fetch you.' Even then they would feel ashamed of themselves, because this tradition is so deeply ingrained in us. And Muslims were not stigmatized by society. While Hindus say that since they (the women) have lived for so long with a Muslim.... Their parents would say that they had left their daughters with one or other of their aunts--they could not say openly that their daughters had been abducted.

This is our psychology. In the upper and middle classes this difficulty was there, but not in the lower classes. A middle class woman might commit suicide.

250

There were some cases like this, of course, but not too many. I have written about a case where the parents thought it was all right to sacrifice the life of a young girl in order to save a whole family. And when we were arguing about her recovery the father said, this is our girl, and the girl denied it because she was terribly hurt by their behaviour. She said, 'I don't want to go back. I have married of my own free will. I don't want anything from my parents.' When she refused to return, it became very awkward. She was in the home of a police inspector. We felt that if we had found an abducted woman in the house of a police inspector, then how could we expect the police to do any recovering? That is why we had to bring her back. Our social worker went to Multan and met her. She said, 'I will not go.' Then we requested the Pakistan authorities to leave her in our camp in the Ganga Ram Hospital (Lahore) for a couple of days. Then if she said that she didn't want to return it was fine, but she would have to report at the camp and confirm that she didn't want to. So, she was brought by force. Her husband said, 'I will take her back at night.' I said, 'She will not return at night, she will stay the night with me.' He said, 'Why should my wife stay with you, what right have you to keep her?' Then I said, 'She is after all, our daughter. When a daughter comes to her mother's place, she stays for a few days. She has no parents.' That girl kept saying that she didn't want to go to her parents, she wouldn't budge an inch. After two or three days, she broke down, she told us that her parents had been told by the police inspector, 'If you leave your daughter, gold and land with me, I will escort you all to the cantonment in India.' That man was already married and had children. He didn't need to marry her. He told her father, 'You give me this girl in exchange for escorting you all to an Indian cantonment.' Then her father gave him his daughter, 30 tolas of gold and his house. One night I called the girl to my bedside and said, 'If you want to go back (to the inspector), then I will send you. If you don't want to go back to your parents, don't go, but please tell me why.' Then she became tearful and said, 'Behenji, what can I tell you? I am not happy at this inspector's place. As long as he is in the house, I am all right, but as soon as he leaves on duty, his wife harasses me, calls me the daughter of a *kafir* and so on. She makes me do all the work as if I were her maid. The man loves me, but he is under pressure from his family. But those parents who sacrificed me--I will never go back to them.' I said, 'All right, don't go back to them, stay with us.' We couldn't let her return to Pakistan. This was a prestige case. If we let it go, we would have to eat humble pie in front of Pakistan. We had to bring her before the Tribunal when it met. Just before that I had thought that I would get her married to a nice boy in India, specially because she was not happy with this man. If she had been happy, I would not have thought this way, but she was unhappy and would have had to spend the rest of her life in this fashion. There was an officer whose private assistant was a very good man. I let the boy and the girl meet once, in secrecy, because it was against our policy. For this Mridulabehn got very angry with me, but I was quite obstinate. I insisted that we had no right to keep a woman in this manner. When everything was settled, I decided that this young woman could now face the Tribunal without flinching. During the cross-examination, the Pakistan SP called for the Inspector (her abductor) as a witness. Imagine that! But we were forced to agree because we were told that as a police inspector he could make trouble for us in our recovery work, later. So he came. Meera (the girl in question) was also called in and asked 'Where do you want to go?' She said that she wanted to go to India. The man glared at her and shouted, 'So you want to go to India, eh?' She said, 'Yes, I want to go to India.' Then he yelled, 'What do you think you are saying? I saved your parents, I have spent so much money on you. Even the bangles you are wearing are mine.' I intervened and told them (the escorting police) that she should be taken in to change into her own clothes. Then I gave him back the clothes, gold and other things he had given her, saying she could do without.

She got married later, but not in Pakistan obviously. We had the marriage in Amritsar afterwards, with the proper arrangements. The boy got a posting to Shimla after a transfer from Pakistan. Her parents also came to the wedding. Five or six of us friends, got together and arranged a tea party for her. Now this fact, after being exaggerated, got to Mridulaji's ears and, of course, she put me on the mat because these kinds of cases were outside our jurisdiction and we should not have been involved in them--they were really Mrs. Thapar's responsibility, because they had to do with rehabilitation, not recovery. Mridulabehn said, you were my representative when you did this, you exceeded your brief. I said well, if you like, I will put in my resignation and go back to Bombay. I felt deep inside me that I had carried out my responsibility faithfully. If, because of me, their policy had been harmed, then I would go back. At that she cooled down. Then, after a year when I was in Amritsar, this girl came to see me with her child. She came to see me specially, all the way from Shimla. They were both very happy, she said. But I can't forget her anger at being sacrificed by her parents.

One of the best things about our recovery work was the fact that all parties--Communist, Socialist and Congress, etc.--sank their differences and worked together. Our social workers used to accompany the police party-- their women never did, they didn't have the motivation to go with the police. The police used to bring the women and leave them in the camp. We had several members of the Congress, Socialists and even Communists among our social workers. One day, Begum Fatima of Lahore said to us, 'I have heard that you have kept a Muslim girl as a prisoner and hidden her in the camp.'

'What are you saying Begum Fatima,' I replied, 'we have hidden four crore people, if you wish you can take them all.' And, in truth,

I had hidden her! She was a disputed case. But one had to do these things because the circumstances demanded it. I said that for one thing, our girls have gone to sleep and for another, you're talking about one girl, when I have four crores here! We were always being accused of keeping Muslim women. I was especially prone to this charge because I had to meet the Collector for sorting out problems relating to the camp--its site, rations and allotment of houses. Urdu newspapers published reports that India had sent out very inexperienced young girls to do recovery work!

Adapted from an interview of Kamlabehn Patel by Ritu Menon and Kamla Bhasin.

14

WHAT WE LOST TO TASTE FREEDOM

B.A.CHOWDHRY

With freedom came tears, pain, despair, and destitution. What we lost to taste freedom.

On September 13, 1947, I set out on a mass evacuation duty across the international boundary of India and Pakistan. The convoy consisted of civilian trucks headed by a military escort and I had under my command a posse of ten soldiers in uniform. The destination we were to reach was Nakodar - Mehatpur refugee camp.

At the starting point from Lahore, the convoy trucks were brimming with non-Muslim refugees to be taken to Amritsar. As we moved along, we saw Lahore wearing a deserted look. Columns of smoke were rising high up in the sky from all around the residential areas, making the atmosphere gloomy, and dull.

We left behind the outskirts of the city and saw roads littered with dead bodies on the one hand, and on the other crowded, wild-looking, maimed, starved mankind clad in torn, dirty rags.

As we proceeded further still, a pile of dead bodies on both sides of the road stretched for miles. There was no time to perform funeral rituals, since deaths were occurring at brief intervals in virtually every family due to the cholera epidemic. The dear departed ones were stacked on road sides heartlessly, with no display of emotion or tears, since these faculties had vanished in the face of utter horror let loose on the fugitives by gangs of Sikh militants. These gangs were assaulting Muslim caravans and convoys, abducting young girls, looting leftover belongings and massacring old and young indiscriminately.

We reached Amritsar in the afternoon and stopped at Company Bagh. Here Muslim refugees constituted a majority of the refugees. The Bagh, once a recreational green spot, had been converted into a plain ground. We were not allowed to continue our journey by the local authorities till the next day because night had fallen and the convoy was scheduled to be reloaded with Sikh refugees to drop on our way.

There were frenzied activities throughout the night in an effort to get on the trucks. We started-off at about 7 a.m. and treaded through the crowd and started the journey at a trotting pace. As far as the eyes could see, dead bodies were lying, their smells making it very hard to breathe. The sky above was overcast with birds, spiralling to feed on dead flesh. Amid this scenario, we kept our onward journey.

We reached Julundar shortly after dusk, which presented an unsettling sight. The Sikhs, flashing their swords, looked aggressive and were rearing to ambush the frightened Muslims who had huddled together to save their lives and honor.

Next morning, we once again resumed our journey with loads of refugees to be dropped enroute. When we came across Partapra camp, a Muslim refugee enclave, news had already spread that an evacuation party from Pakistan was nearby. The entire camp swarmed around and begged an immediate evacuation or at the least requested protection from the bandits. Our final stop was only a few miles away: Nakodar which was equally depressing. But having safely deported the passengers, we decided to return the next day. I was in the grip of a severe headache and was taking a stroll at the outskirts of the camp, when I noticed soft feet following me and I heard a feeble voice pleading me not to go any further since the lurking Sikh bandits will shoot at sight. I stopped to see a sobbing young girl of 18 years with a small bundle in her hand. She addressed me, "Salaam Sahab ji, take me with you."

"Where to ?," I inquired. "Pakistan," she said. "Every one in my family has been murdered by the Sikhs and I am the only one left alive." She pushed the small bundle towards me which carried her family ornaments. She said if she had anything more, she would certainly have offered it; tears coursed down her cheeks throughout our conversation.

I returned the bundle to her and advised her that she should keep it with her in safe custody, since she would need them more in Pakistan and told her that she should see me the next morning just before our departure. She seemed disappointed that I did not accept her offerings, and disappeared in the dying and barely living humanity in the camps.

We left at day break with refugees, seeking safe haven in Pakistan. I was the last person on the convoy to leave. I caught sight of the girl leaning against a sheesham tree, holding her bundle with both her hands. I called her to my truck and she came running, sure in the knowledge now that she will reach her destination.

When we approached Amritsar, a Baloch regiment was stationed to regulate the incoming flow of refugees. The *jawans* of the regiment greeted us with a fistful of *atta* for each one of the refugees. in addition to some hearth and firewood. This was followed by an excited activity

257

specially by the womenfolk. They got down from their respective trucks, and began to prepare bread. The girl I had favored on compassionate grounds was the first one out of the lot to offer a *roti* to me: a gesture to pay back her debt.

We reached the Wagah border post at about dusk time with all the convoy members shouting hoarsely Pakistan Zindabad freedom greeting them on the new land.

15

THE BLOODSHED COULD
HAVE BEEN AVOIDED

MADAN LAL KHURANA

Freedom was a dream for all, but bloodshed was a nightmare that should not have happened. Delhi's former Chief Minister writes about his family's exodus from Lyallpur in 1947.

I owe my life to an unknown Gurkha *jawan* but for whose bravery and presence of mind, I would have never escaped the clutches of death. Whenever I think of that train journey, when there was human carnage all around me during the Partition riots, I cannot but thank this young soldier who jumped in and saved a lot of lives.

I was just about 11-years-old. I had just passed my fourth standard exams, and we were staying near Anarkali Bazaar in Lyallpur, West Punjab when the riots of 1947 broke out. I saw the naked dance of death, the arson and the mindless looting happening right in front of me. Hindus and Muslims were thirsty for each others' blood. On the one side, there were young Hindu boys, armed with swords and pistols, and on the other side, there were the Muslim youngsters, both sides busy inciting people with their slogans and speeches, beseeching their people to kill everybody on the other side. I remember the days when we used to keep a midnight vigil so that our locality was not attacked, so that we did not lose anybody from our locality.

In September, we were taken to a refugee camp in the DAV school nearby. One day, there was an attack on our camp late in the night and many hapless people were killed mercilessly. We were put in a special train from Lyallpur to Amritsar. It was stopping at every place. That day, the train had stopped in the middle of a jungle, there was no station. I was young and in the middle of the night I felt very thirsty. I still remember how all of us were forced to drink the dirty water from a rain clogged pond.

There were about half a dozen Gorkha *jawans* in our train. When it reached Lahore, there was an attack on us. For about half an hour, there was an exchange of fire from both sides and all through this, we were simply remembering our gods. There was nothing much we could do and there was also this realization that the *jawans* on our train could not have held on for a long time.

It was at this point of time that one of those *jawans* jumped out of the train, ran up to the driver's cabin, put his revolver on the driver's forehead and threatened him to start the train immediately. There were more mobs on the way to Amritsar and therefore, they decided to divert the train to Ferozepur via Kasur. We were thus saved, but I can never forget that half an hour in our life when we were literally hanging between life and death. If it was not for that young soldier, none of us would have survived that ghastly attack.

We had a tough time in the refugee camp in the DAV school. Whenever we used to hear the sorry tales of people pouring into the camp from the nearby areas, life became all the more miserable for us. All the women in one village were thrown in the village well to escape the clutches of the rioting mob. So many of our people were killed and all those who escaped the killing mob, thanked their stars only after they reached the camp.

I still remember that when we left our homes, we had gone to the camp with just a couple of things which we needed for our daily routine. It never occurred to us that we were leaving our homes forever. There were many families who did not mind staying back in Pakistan because they had been living there all their life and they did not want to leave their ancestral places. But when they saw that their daughters were no longer safe in the face of the rioting mob, they were forced to come out.

Freedom came but it did not bring anything for us. When the entire nation was rejoicing in this new-found freedom, for us there was death all around us. It was no time for us to feel happy. So many of our people were killed.

I am of the opinion that if Pakistan was inevitable, before it was made, all of us should have been told well in advance that all those who wanted to be in Pakistan should remain there and all those who wanted to go to India should cross over. If only they had made this announcement before it was too late, there would not have been so many deaths. Where were all those assurances that were given? Hundreds and millions of our people stayed back just because of Nehru's assurances. And look what happened to so many of them.

But even after all these years, I am sure that the strong bonds of love are still intact between the people. I give one example. I once appeared in Rajat Sharma's *Aap Ki Adalat* on Zee TV. In his introduction in the beginning of the show, Rajat mentioned that I was born in Lyallpur in 1936. You cannot imagine my happiness when Rajat told me a couple of days later that Zee TV had received hundreds of letters from Lyallpur congratulating me for attaining such a high position in India. They were all very proud of me. The sentiments of the people across the border is still there and this is the only encouraging thing in these days of tension and hatred.

It is unfortunate that even after 50 years of Independence, we are still to reach Mahatma Gandhi's goal of Swarajya. We may have got independence from the British, but we still have a long way to go for Swarajya. The power in our country is still centered around a handful of people and we are still to decentralize power. Our villages are still to rejoice in Swarajya even after 50 years of Independence. More than 45 percent of our people are still languishing below the poverty line and there is no one to take care of them. All the time, we are crying ourselves hoarse about economic liberalization but not a single kilowatt of power has increased in our villages. Ice creams may be in plenty of our cities, but what about the needs of our brethren in the villages. We talk of having gained so much, but have we ever thought about the cost of all these things. At what cost is all this development that we keep referring to.

Madan Lal Khurana (Former Chief Minister of Delhi).

5

In Lahore….

16

The Partition, 1947

Sir Muhammad Zafrullah Khan

While at Delhi, I was sent for by Mr. Jinnah, who asked me to argue the Muslim League case when the Boundary Commission to delimit the boundary between West Punjab and India - at that time, between West Punjab and East Punjab - was set up. Without any hesitation I took on that duty.

So, back from London, I went straight to Lahore, where the Boundary Commission had in the meantime been constituted. During my stay in England it had been announced that Sir Cyril Radcliffe would be the umpire of the Punjab and Bengal Boundary Commissions. This meant that the boundary would be determined on a unanimous or a majority report of the commission concerned, but in case of tie the umpire's decision would prevail. In each case there was bound to be a tie as each of the commissions was composed of two Muslim and two non-Muslim members. The two Muslim members of the Punjab Boundary Commission were Mr. Justice Din Mohammad and Mr. Justice Mohammad Munir, while Mr. Justice Mehr Chand Mahajan and Mr. Justice Teja Singh represented the non-Muslim side. There was bound to be deadlock in a Commission composed on such a basis. So, in effect, it was boundary in each case.

I believe it was Monday evening when I reached Lahore. I was told that Sir Cyril Radcliffe was already in town and had summoned the parties to meet him at 11 o'clock, the next morning. So we appeared before him; he gave us directions and fixed noon of the following Friday as the time-limit for the parties to put in their written cases before the Commission. The following Monday arguments were going to start before the Commission. He said he himself would not sit with the Commission in order to hear arguments because he was not sure whether at all his function as umpire would come into play. It was only after the Commission had made its report that he would come to know whether he would be called upon to function at all. But he would follow with great interest whatever was being argued before the Commission, as a transcript of the proceedings would be sent to him daily.

The next evening Mr. Justice Din Mohammad came to see me. He was very agitated and said, "I have a strong suspicion that the boundary line has already been decided upon and all of us are going to be engaged in a farce". I asked him why he thought so. He said that after we had left the previous day Sir Cyril had mentioned that he would be going up the next morning for a flight to survey the area in dispute and to see how the land lay. Mr. Din Mohammad had asked him how the Commission would know what he had looked at and what impressions he had formed. They would be sitting in Lahore while he would have made a survey of which they would have no knowledge. This might prove awkward later on. Sir Cyril explained that the aircraft placed at his disposal was a small one but that two of them, one from each side, could go up with him. It was decided that Mr. Justice Munir and Mr. Justice Teja Singh would accompany him the next morning. So, the next morning all of them assembled at an early hour at Walton Airport but the flight was abandoned because of a dust storm. Just before leaving the airfield, Mr. Justice Munir

265

asked the pilot where they were to go. He put his hand in his pocket and brought out a slip of paper which he gave to Mr. Justice Munir saying those were the orders. Mr. Justice Munir brought that slip and gave it to Mr. Justice Din Mohammad. It carried directions to the pilot. He was to fly east as far as Pathankot where the Ravi emerges from the mountains and debouches into the plains of the Punjab and then he was to veer left towards Ferozepur.

Justice Din Mohammad was very sure that this was going to be the boundary. He could not see any other reason in going to a particular point and then following a definite course. It was not a flight over an area, it followed a definite line. Therefore, he decided to go to Delhi the same night and put the matter before Mr. Jinnah, suggesting that Munir and he should resign from the Commission on the ground that apparently the whole thing had been determined in advance. He thought that would result either in the appointment of a new commission or in the application of some other method to determine the boundary.

I told him I feared Mr. Jinnah might pooh-pooh the whole thing as he would not be easily persuaded unless the whole matter was put to him on some legal basis. He said "What do you mean by legal basis"? I answered, "I don't know whether you'll succeed with him even then but I suggest you to put to him this aspect of the case. We have accepted Sir Cyril Radcliffe as umpire in the case and we are bound to accept his decision as umpire. But, as umpire, it is his duty to base his decision on such material as is submitted to him by the Commission. As umpire, he is not entitled to receive *materil* from other sources or give any consideration to such a material. Decision can only he made on the basis of the material which the parties place before the Commission: that material along with the views of the Commission will he submitted to Sir Cyril Radcliffe and on that, together with the Prime Minister's announcement as providing the basis of the partition, he must make up his mind. Now, who suggested this trip to him? He knows nothing at all of the conditions here, he does not even know the parties' case. What is the meaning of this particular line that the flight was to follow? Mr. Jinnah should try to find out what lay behind this proposed trip which had to be abandoned and what the significance of the line is if he is satisfied that it had no significance at all, though it's difficult to believe that a definite line like that should have no significance, then matters may proceed. But if he is not satisfied, he should ask for an explanation. From which direction did this suggestion proceed? He can then make his point that the umpire is being influenced in a particular direction by people who are not directly concerned with this question and we have lost confidence in this procedure. That might perhaps go some distance with Mr. Jinnah, otherwise you may not entertain much hope merely because of this slip of paper."

He went to Delhi that night. Was there the next day, saw Mr. Jinnah, left Delhi in the evening, arrived back in Lahore on Friday morning and came straight from the railway station to see me. He was very crest fallen. Mr. Jinnah had told him to go ahead and to do his best and not to worry. Sir Cyril was a responsible man and would not let his mind be influenced by any outsider.

Curiously enough, when the award was announced the boundary followed the line described in the slip of paper except for one change, again, adverse to Pakistan. I shall come to that later.

On my return from England when I arrived at Lahore on Monday evening, I was received at the railway station by a large number of people including the Nawab of Mamdot. He told me that 11 o'clock the next morning we were going to see Sir Cyril Radcliffe and that later the same day I would he meeting some lawyers at 2.30 p.m. at his residence. I presumed that I would be meeting the lawyers who had been engaged in the prerparation of the case, for I had been assured by Mr. Jinnah that by the time I arrived at Lahore I would find the whole case ready and I would only have to take on its presentation on the basis of the brief prepared by the lawyers.

So, under that impression, at 2.30 I presented myself at Mamdot Villa, the residence of the Nawab of Mamdot. I found there a large number of lawyers most of whom I knew very well as personal friends and colleagues. Earlier, during our meeting with Sir Cyril in the morning he had fixed Friday noon as the deadline for filing written cases. So after the usual hand-shakes and greetings we sat down and I enquired which of them were working with me on the case. Khalifa Shuja-ud-Din, a senior lawyer, smiled and said, "Which case"? "The boundary case, of course. I was asked to meet the lawyers working on the boundary case this afternoon here". Khalifa Shuja-ud-Din replied that they knew nothing at all about the boundary case. He was at a loss to understand what I was talking about, the lawyers were there only to welcome me back to Lahore and to wish me success in the case.

To say the least, I was stunned not only to learn that nobody had been paying any attention to the case, much less preparing it, but at the alarm that within less than three days - it was already the afternoon of Tuesday - I would have to present a case in writing, on the partition of this part of the country. I did not know which way to turn for statistics or any other relevant materials to ascertain the principles on which the line should be drawn or on what ground to prepare the case.

Within a few minutes I said good bye to the assembled lawyers and asked the Nawab of Mamdot, whether the Muslim League Organization had prepared any

268

plan or collected any material or done anything in this direction. He uttered a laconic No.

Khawaja Abdur Rahim, who was then the Commissioner of Rawalpindi was staying at Lahore on a special duty in connection with the large influx of refugees that had already started pouring in from the other side. He had certain statistics on population prepared on his own. He came to see me the same afternoon and handed over the material to me. This was a piece of sheer good luck. I also found that four lawyers had come to Lahore from other towns, hoping that they might be of some use to me in the preparation of the case. Mr Nisar Ahmed and Sahibzada Nusrat Ali came from Montgomery; Syed Muhammad Shah from Pakpattan and Chaudhry Ali Akbar Khan(later Pakistan's Amhassador at Jiddah) from Hoshiarpur. There were also a couple of junior lawyers from Lahore; they would occasionally look in and were able to assist. not so much with the preparation of the case but on other odd matters requiring assistance. I am very grateful to all of them for their devoted help.

My anxiety now was to work day and night and get the case ready by Friday noon. Even now, looking back I cannot explain how it was possible for us to produce a case which we did by the Friday noon.

At that time, conditions in Lahore were topsy-turvy; the paramount anxiety was how to handle the refugee problem. Were it not for the people who rose to the occasion as a body, I am sure, the principal government would have proved absolutely unequal to the task and the administration would have foundered. It was the spirit of the people that carried us through. We also owe much to a few devoted officers and workers like Khawaja Abdur Rahim and his colleagues who were dealing with this influx of refugees. Train-loads came in, the dead and the wounded children with their eyes gouged out and hands cut off, women with their breasts chopped off - such savagery and inhumanity.

I imagine the same things happened on the other side too. The Punjab seemed to have become a howling wilderness of beasts rather than a land of human beings. All humanity had disappeared, all mercy and pity and human love and affection seemed to have evaporated. Altogether a dreadful business; I hate to recall it. Under such conditions, it was not surprising that everybody was at his wit's end and nothing could be arranged for certain.

Before leaving Mamdot Villa I had requested the Nawab to arrange that by 8 o'clock the next morning I should have two stenographers to work in relays at my lodging which was opposite to the Villa. I had also asked for the usual office equipment: pencils, paper, typewriters, etc. He had assured me that everything would be there by 7.30.

So I came back and started working on the available material and worked late into the night. I started again early in the morning, then I got ready, had my breakfast and at 7.30 I inquired whether the stenographer had arrived. There was nobody; eight o'clock, nobody. Not a pencil, not a sheet of paper, not a typewriter or a stenographer! Again, I had recourse to Khawaja Abdul ur Rahim, whose tent-office was just across the road. He was kind enough to send his two stenographers.

On Thursday night, when I had got the draft ready, I insisted that at least two of the Muslim League leaders Mian Mumtaz Daultana and Sirdar Shaukat Hayat Khan should come and read through it. I was submitting a case on behalf of the Muslim League and somebody on behalf of the League had to give me instructions. I dare not submit a case which might afterwards he repudiated. Sir Shaukat Hayat Khan could not come; he had high fever. Mian

270

Mumtaz Daultana very kindly came along. He said it was not necessary for him to read the draft as they had full confidence in me; however, I told him that it was not a matter of confidence but a matter of instructions and I had to have them from somebody. I insisted upon his reading through the draft and putting his imprimateur on it. He was kind enough to do it saying that he agreed entirely with it. The next morning, after putting some final touches to it, was able to deliver the document to the Commission.

Immediately afterwards I went to the Friday Service at a mosque where I was asked to take the service. I earnestly urged the congregation to be diligent in prayers as I feared that in certain parts of the Punjab Muslims would have to face the days in Spain under Isabella and Ferdinand. Unfortunately, that apprehension proved to be too well-founded.

The next Monday arguments started before the Commission. The case was argued very well on all sides. The Hindu case was put by Mr M.C.Setalvad, who was the Attorney-General of India. He had been asked to come from Bombay and was assisted by very competent lawyers including Bakhshi Tek Chand, who was a retired Judge of the Lahore High Court and had been for many years the ablest lawyer at the Lahore Bar. The Sikh case was put by a gentleman who became later the Advocate-General of East Punjab. It is not necessary to go into details about what was said, but the main contest centred round Gurdaspur District, Ferozepur District and parts of Jullundur District. The crux of the matter was how to interpret and apply the expression 'contiguous Muslim majority areas'.

We based our case on adopting tehsil or sub-district as the unit for the purpose of determining contiguous majority areas. One could take a village as a unit but that would have resulted in a completely crazy boundary line. It was not possible to determine by villages where the majority on one side ended and began on the other. Then, one could take a police station as a unit, but even that was too small to give us a workable boundary line. So, one could take a sub-district, as we did, or one could take a district as a unit. The choice was a difficult one.

If a district were taken as a unit the notional partition which had already been put into effect for the purpose of administration ad interim, would have to be confirmed and that would give the whole of the Gurdaspur District to Pakistan. But the risk was that if we confined our case to districts, it might he assumed that we were happy with the notional partition and our claim might be whittled down further to our serious prejudice. Adopting the tehsil as a unit would give us the Ferozerpur and Zira tehsils of Ferozepur District; the Jullundur and Nakodar tehsils of Hoshiarpur District. The line so drawn would also give us the state of Kapurthala (which had Muslim majority) and would enclose within Pakistan the whole of Amritsar District of which only one tehsil, Ajnala, had a Muslim majority. It would also give us Shakargarh, Batala and Gurdaspur tehsils of Gurdaspur District. One could also take as units what, in the Punjab, are known as doabs, that is to say, the areas between two rivers. If the boundary had gone by doabs, we could have got not only the sixteen districts which, under the notional partition, were later, given to us, but also Gurdasrpur District and Kangra District in the mountains.

Had any of these units been adopted the boundary line would have been more favourable than what it is now.

Everybody knew it already that there was going to be no unanimous or majority report. The non-Muslim Commissioners took one view while the Muslim Commissioners had just the opposite view. Consequently, the umpire had to give his award. After studying the record he held discussions with the members of the Commission at

Simla. We were told by the Muslim Commissioners that while Sir Cyril was not quite definite about Gurdaspur District, he was quite clear that the two sub-districts of Ferozepur District - the sub-district of Ferozepur itself and the sub-district of Zira - being Muslim majority areas and contiguous to the rest of the Muslim block would form part of Pakistan.

During the days when the award was expected Sir Evan Jenkins, the Governor of the West Punjab, received a communication on the phone from Mr. Abel, Lord Mountbatten's private secretary. This communication was based on two documents drawn up by Mr. Beaumont, a private secretary of Sir Cyril; one of them showed the boundary line on a map while the other described it from village to village. The Governor was told that this was the award and that it would be announced within forty-eight hours. He was asked to get into touch with his chief of police and take necessary measures to give effect to the award when it was announced. There is no doubt that a similar communication must have been sent to Mr Trivedi, the Governor of East Punjab. But no award was announced within forty-eight hours. As a matter of fact, the award was not announced for eight or ten days. By that time Sir Cyril Radcliffe had left the sub-continent.

The notes of the communication, taken down by Sir Evan Jenkins showed the two sub-districts of Ferozepur and Zira, as we had been expecting, formed part of the West Punjab and consequently of Pakistan. But eight or ten days later when the award came out these two sub-districts were put in India. No explanation for this change has ever been given. I have already hazarded one: I hazard it again for the purpose of this record. It appears to me that unless a clear and convincing explanation comes forth to displace this hypothesis, what 1 am going to say is the only thing that might have happened. We must remember that at that time there was no Pakistan and consequently, no Pakistan Government. There was only the Provisional Government of India headed by Pandit Jawahar Lal Nehru as its Prime Minister.

Mr. Trevidi, the Governor of the East Punjab, as an ICS officer, was under the authority of the Provisional Government; so was Sir Evan Jenkins, the Governor of the West Punjab. It stands to reason that on receiving the communication from Mr. Abel he conveyed its gist, probably through a personal visit, to the Prime Minister. The inclusion of Ferozepur sub-district in Pakistan meant the inclusion of the headworks of the Sutlej Valley canal system, situated just outside the town of Ferozepur. The whole of the water from these headworks went to Pakistan and Bikaner one of the Indian states; the division being on the proportion 83% and 17% respectively.

The states of Bikaner and Jaisalmer, both in Rajputana, being contiguous of both Pakistan and India, could accede to either of the countries. It was no secret that the rulers of both the states were inclined to accede to Pakistan as they expected a better deal from Pakistan rather than India.

The canal from Ferozepur Headworks to Bikaner, being the only irrigation system of the state, was almost its lifeline. So, coupled with the Maharaja's personal desire to accede to Pakistan the inclusion in Pakistan of the headworks controlling the canal would have been the decisive factor in the state's accession to Pakistan. In view of this contingency the inference that Mr. Nehru must have approached Lord Mountbatten to procure a modification of the award is almost irresistible. There is no other reason why the award was modified when it had been communicated to the Viceroy, to Mr. Abel, to Sir Evan Jenkins and to Mr. Trivedi and consequently the umpire had become functus officio, having no longer any authority to modify it. The whole thing did not come to the knowledge of the Pakistan authorities until months later, whereas, presumably, from the very outset, it was within Mr. Nehru's knowledge, through Mr. Trivedi. The Governor of the West Punjab owed no duty to anyone, except the Central Government of India headed by Mr. Nehru. Mr. Trivedi also owed no duty to anyone except Mr. Nehru. So it was quite right on the part of Mr. Trivedi to let Mr. Nehru know what was happening while the Governor of the West Punjab was under no such obligation to anyone on the Muslim League side since Pakistan had not yet come into existence and nobody on that side had any right to know in advance what the award was going to be.

The inclusion of Gurdaspur District in the East Punjab was a great blow to us; it fiacilitated the Indian intervention in Kashmir, as from the plains only Gurdaspur District could give the Indians an access to Kashmir. It had four sub-districts Shakargarh to the west of the Ravi was included in Pakistan while the three sub-districts, that is, Batala, Gurdspur and Pathankot being to the east of the Ravi were included in India, giving India an access to Kashmir, through the plains. In Gurdaspur District as a whole, Muslims were in majority. In the sub-districts taken separately they enjoyed majority in the tehsils of Shakargarh, Batala and Gurdaspur but in Pathankot, they were in minority. With Batala and Gurdaspur going to Pakistan, the Pathankot tehsil would have been isolated and blocked. To get access to Pathankot would have been possible for India through the Hoshiarpur District but it would have taken long to construct roads, bridges, communications, so necessary for military movements.

The modification of the award relating to the Ferozepur and Zira tehisils led directly to the Indus waters dispute. India, having obtained control of the headworks at Ferozepur, could easily turn off the waters and so it did

275

giving rise to the dispute. Thus ultimately the two disputes between India and Pakistan resulted from the two portions of the award, that could not be justified on any basis whatsoever.

As part of the machinery for sorting out things in connection with the Partition, a tribunal had been set up for the distribution of assets, under the chairmanship of the ex-Chief Justice of India, Sir Patrick Spens, now Lord Spens. The tribunal heard the parties, sorted out the assets assessed what was due from one side to the other, and gave its award. In making its assessment, it took into account the Indian claim that the irrigation system in the old, undivided province of the Punjab had been much better developed in the portion which had gone to Pakistan. This development having taken place at the expense of the whole of the province and the benefit of its major portion having gone to Pakistan, it was claimed that Pakistan must pay compensation for the excess share of the developed system now enjoyed by it. The tribunal took that into account in making its award and compensated India for obtaining a smaller share of the joint development that had been made at joint expense. Lord Spens stated publicly that the award of compensation to India was based on the assurance given to the tribunal by the Attorney-Generals of India and Pakistan that existing uses of the water from these rivers would not be interfered with.

The day after the tribunal had made its award India diverted the waters at the Ferozepur headworks asserting that Pakistan was no longer entitled to the waters of the Beas and Sutlej Rivers. So, at its very birth, Pakistan was threatened with extinction, as without these waters the greater part of West Pakistan would he turned into a desert.

On 4 May 1948, a provisional agreement was concluded between the governments of India and Pakistan. It provided that, leaving the legal position aside, India would not hinder the flow of waters into Pakistan for a period, but that it would have to be progressively reduced and Pakistan, in the meantime, should investigate alternative sources of substitution for these waters. This agreement was subject to the condition that Pakistan would pay into the State Bank of India or any other specified bank, a certain assessed amount in escrow and that India would take the amount as compensation for the use of the waters by Pakistan, if the final decision should be in favour of India. Later, India took up the position that Pakistan was not entitled to any part of these waters and India, as the upper riparian was entitled to divert the whole of the waters for its own benefit without any regard to the historical uses which had already been established.

Mr David Lilienthal who had been Chairman of the Tennessee Valley Authority was on a visit to the sub-continent and happened to fly over the Indus Valley. He wrote an article for the *Saturday Evening Post*, bringing about the possible consequences of the dispute. He drew particular attention to its impact on the economy of West Pakistan and suggested that the World Bank should offer its good offices to the parties in order to resolve this dispute on the basis of certain principles which should be accepted by both sides, namely that the established practice used should be respected, that if extra water was available from all these rivers, there should be an agreement on its use for the development of the whole of the Indus Basin (including both, the Indian and the Pakistani parts) and that was how the cost of such development should be apportioned.

Both the sides accepted the World Bank's good offices and there was a prolonged series of investigations and discussions. At long last an agreement was reached, was incorporated into a treaty and is now being worked out on the spot. One part of the agreement was that India should enjoy the waters of the eastern rivers and Pakistan should meet its needs from the western rivers by means of replacement works and channels: India paying the cost of the replacement. But when the cost was assessed, India said it could not afford to pay that much. Through the good offices of the World Bank it was arranged that it should pay as much as it could afford and the rest should be made up by friendly powers like the United States, the United Kingdom, Australia, etc. So far as projects for the future use as distinguished from the established use were concerned Pakistan was to bear the cost of its own works and India was to hear the cost of works on its own side.

I understand that some difficulty has since arisen. The basis on which the costs of replacement were calculated is completely changed because of the rising prices. I believe negotiations are going on with the bank in this direction.

(Excerpts from his autobiography *The Forgotten Years*)

17

In Lahore.....

JAHAN ARA SHAH NAWAZ

The exodus of Hindus and Sikhs from the Punjab had started, and caravan after caravan of them was leaving the cities and rural areas of West Pakistan. Suddenly, similar caravans of Muslims started arriving from the East Punjab and other places. The two Governments were to be installed, one in New Delhi and the other in Karachi, on the 14th August, 1947, and Lord Louis Mountbatten, the Viceroy, was to address the Constituent Assembly of Pakistan. Lord Radcliffe had been holding meetings and the cases of different parties had been placed before him with facts and figures by outstanding lawyers. People were anxiously awaiting the announcement of the Radcliffe Award.

Tazi and I left for Karachi on the 9th August, 1947, and we stayed at the Palace Hotel, where a number of other members of the Assembly were also putting up. Quaid-i-Azam was to take the oath as Governor-General of Pakistan on the 14th morning and on the 13th evening we were all having dinner at the same hotel when the names of the first Central Cabinet of Pakistan were announced. We, with Mr. Hassan Ispahani, Mr. Shaheed Suhrawardy, then Chief Minister of Bengal, and Mr. Altaf Hussain, Editor of *Dawn*, Karachi, were all dining at the same table. Seven ministers had been appointed and from Bengal Fazlur Rahman, a name which most of us had never heard and very few people seemed to know anything about, had been included. All the outstanding Bengal leaders had been left out. Nawab Muhammad Ismail Khan and the Raja of Mahmoodabad had not been encouraged to come to Pakistan, and some other members of the Muslim League Working Committee who could have handled a number of departments creditably were not included in the Cabinet. It was clear that only the Prime Minister's yes-men had been included. What a short-sighted policy, that in a Ministry none who could come up to the Prime Minister's ability had been included, and instead of having the best available talent in the country handling each department, some unknown persons had been selected! Moreover the appointment of only seven Ministers was inadequate. As soon as the Bengal leaders saw the list, Hassan left the table, Suhrawardy and Altaf Hussain were very depressed, and none of us knew what to say. This was not the case in the Centre only but in every province, whichever party came into power appointed their own stooges only, so that in some cases persons were given departments about which they knew nothing. In many places, staunch and able leaders who possessed administrative experience had been left out. Moreover, even during the elections to the Provincial Assemblies the Muslim League tickets for election to the Assemblies were given to the favourites of the men in power. What a tragedy for a young nation with a superhuman task before it, that during the crucial years of its development it should be placed in the hands of inexperienced people. Could there have been a greater blunder than this? The instable foundations were thus laid, and constant changes after that were inevitable.

It was at the reception to meet Lord Louis Mountbatten at the Governor-General's house that we learnt of the Radcliffe Award giving the Muslim majority district of

Gurdaspur, the roadway to Kashmir, to India, and about the division of the provinces of the Punjab and Bengal. The Radcliffe Award came as a bombshell to all Muslims, including those who had been working with him, because until that date they had been given to understand that the Muslim majority areas of Gurdaspur district would, ipso facto, be included in Pakistan. It was a great blow to all Muslims, even the Quaid-i-Azam. He had put his full trust in Radcliffe and no one could have imagined that, if not the whole district, at least the majority areas would not be given to Pakistan. Over and above this, the partition of both the major provinces and the lines of demarcation were not just and fair. During the opening session of the Constituent Assembly, one could see that the Quaid and Lord Louis Mountbatten were not cordial to each other. The reception had been arranged on Independence Day, but because of such depressing news a gloom hung over it and there was no jubilation at all.

Tazi and I returned from Karachi on the 18th August, 1947. News of the influx of lakhs of refugees, train-loads of Muslims and compartments full of blood or dead bodies, had been filling the air of Karachi, so we rushed to Lahore after spending only nine days there. My uncle, Mian Abdur Rashid, the Chief Justice of Pakistan, who had gone to administer the oath of office to the Quaid-i-Azam in Karachi, asked Tazi and myself to travel with him by the same plane. When we reached our house, we found that in the bungalows on both sides Hindu and Gurkha soldiers had been stationed.

An exodus of Muslims had begun from the East Punjab and people were pouring into Pakistan at Wagah, Khem Karan and other crossing places. A number of responsible citizens from Amritsar saw me and related incredible tales of happenings in Amritsar. Cart-loads of dead bodies were sent to Muslim houses and Muslim

281

women were made to march naked in the streets. We learnt that over a lakh of the Muslim population had gathered in Sharifpura, one of the Muslim majority suburbs in Amritsar, and that the Sikhs were going to attack them that very night, and were begged to move in the matter immediately. I rang up a few officials, but they all said that such rumours were being heard everywhere and one should take them with a grain of salt, but we knew that the news was correct. Tazi immediately devised a plan and she went and saw the representative of the *Herald Tribune* and two or three other reporters of well-known foreign papers and asked them to go and spend the night there, so that the Sikhs should think twice before attacking the poor, unarmed Muslims. They agreed to do so, but they had no conveyance to take them to Amritsar, so she gave them her own car and returned home in a taxi.

Killings started round about the city of Lahore and the Muslims in a Sikh village named Gunj, quite close to our village, Baghbanpura, were in danger of an attack. We came to know of this at about half-past eleven at night and the Nawab of Mamdot, the Leader, was informed, but he said that there was no one to go there at that time of the night. Would Tazi rest ? She went there with a few arms and Khan Muhammad Aslam Khan, Akbar's brother, at 11 a.m. and they arrived just in time to save the situation.

The Nawab of Mamdot rang me at 10 p.m. one evening and said that he had learnt from a reliable source that Batala city was to be attacked by the Sikhs that very night. The place was full of our tribesmen and the whole family of my aunt, Lady Rashid, was there, and he asked me to do whatever I could to save a huge massacre. Soon after the receipt of this message, Mian Ahmad Saeed, a cousin of Mian Sir Fazl-i-Hussain, rang up and gave me the same news and begged me to do something, as Batala was the seat of their family as well. I was very upset and I rang up Miss Maqueen, niece of Sir Francis Mudie, the Governor. She told me that the Governor had not been well and had gone to sleep, but I requested her to ask him to talk to me, as it was very urgent. He spoke to me on the telephone and I appealed to him to ring up the Governor-General of India, Lord Louis Mountbatten, and try to save Batala. I had sent my car to fetch Uncle Rashid and on his arrival I made him telephone Pundit Jawahar Lal Nehru, to ask him to prevent the massacre of the Muslims of Batala. Uncle talked to Punditji and he promised to do his best. My mother was in New Delhi at the time, staying with my brother, Mian Muhammad Rafi, Secretary of the Central Assembly. I telephoned her and asked her to see Punditji early next morning and requested him to help the Muslims in Batala. She saw Pundit Jawahar Lal Nehru, who respected her much, and he promised to help in the matter. Tazi and I could not sleep the whole night but, thank God, Batala was saved.

Early next morning, we were having our breakfast when we heard someone crying and shrieking. The servants came and told us that a gentleman named Chaudhri Shafqat Rasul, a very influential tribesman from the Ferozepur district, had arrived and was weeping like a child and asking for me. When I met him, I found him in such a terrible state of collapse that he could hardly relate his woes. Tea was sent for, but he did not touch anything, and with the greatest difficulty we persuaded him to drink some water. Slowly when he calmed down, he told us harrowing tales of what had happened in the Ferozepur district. He said that he had come in by a circuitous route and had, by the grace of God, reached Lahore somehow. Over seventy thousand Muslims, including his family with two young grown-up daughters, were taking refuge on a small island between the canals, Sikhs from Faridkot State were practically surrounding them, and they might all be massacred any moment. He said that he would rather see his family dead than have his daughters falling into the hands of the ferocious Sikhs. The tales received from different places were that they were killing the elder members of the families and taking the girls away. He was sobbing and beseeching me to save the honour of his family. For two days I tried to pull every string possible, but without any success. Shafqat Rasul was frantic and practically going mad with grief. On the third day, I decided to seek the help of Brigadier Muhammad Ayub Khan, who was Second-in-Command of the Boundary Force, a joint command appointed by the Boundary Commission to look after the interests of the communities on both sides of the border, as caravans were frequently being attacked in transit and had to be helped across. I rang up Ayub asking him to come to my house, and when he arrived Chaudhri Shafqat Rasul explained everything to him. Ayub thought over it a while and then said that the only help he could give was to send Shafqat Rasul in one of their weapon-carrier cars, and he advised me to send a letter to the British Brigadier in charge of the force in Ferozepur. When he gave me the name, I was glad to find that I knew him well and had come into contact with him during my work in the Defence Council. Shafqat was sent that very evening with an escort to Ferozepur and my letter to the Brigadier. Ayub was very helpful and sent a whole regiment of soldiers with Shafqat Rasul to the spot. They arrived just in time, when the main attack of Faridkot Sikhs had started and the lives of all the innocent besieged Muslims were saved.

Soon after my return from Karachi, Tazi started getting fever and she had to leave for Murree under doctor's orders. I learnt that a refugee camp had been set up at Walton, about seven miles from Lahore and I rushed to see it. I found that Nawabzada Ata Muhammad Khan Leghari, a senior C.S.P. officer, had been placed in charge of it. He was very glad to see me and asked me for all the help that I could possibly give him in organising the work and in looking after the women and children. Neither my sister nor Fatima Begum, President and Vice-President of the Muslim League Women's Committee, or Begum Tassaduq Hussain, the Secretary, were in Lahore, so I called a meeting of the Muslim League Women's Committee myself. Within a week, a number of women's sub-committees for collecting food, clothes and money, and for providing organised help were working. A corps of workers with badges was organised and hours of work allocated to the different sections. Begum Liaquat Ali Khan arrived in Lahore on 17th September, and a meeting of women was called by Miss Maqueen, the Governor's niece, at Government House. I learnt there that Begum Tassaduq Hussain had been nominated to represent Pakistan at the United Nations Assembly in New York. Miss Maqueen had suggested in her speech that a number of women's committees for relief work should be set up, and when I told her and Begum Liaquat Ali about the sub-committees that had been organised and were already working, they were rather surprised. At my suggestion, it was decided that a large meeting of women be held at Government House and a Women's Voluntary Service, on the lines of the British Women's Voluntary Service, should be organised. Rana Liaquat Ali was anxious that Tazi should take charge of it and a telegram was sent to Murree to ask her to return to Lahore. Tazi organized the voluntary service of women, which did inestimable good in the next few months. We asked Begum Liaquat Ali to get us a central building where an office could be set up and the house of Rai Bahadur Ram Saran Das at 11, Egerton Road was selected for the purpose. The keys were handed over to me and I asked a tehsildar to accompany us and have it opened. When I entered the house, I found that it was full of very costly articles of furniture, paintings, carpets, safes and other things. I had most of the expensive things packed and stored away in locked rooms and had them and the safes sealed. While we went home to have lunch, one of my clerks, whom I had stationed at the house, came rushing to inform me that the clerks of the revenue officers concerned had brought a truck and were filling it with valuables and taking them away. Tazi rushed to the spot with a cousin and they gave these people a piece of their mind, and stopped them from moving anything. Locks worth sixty rupees were purchased and the things carried into the house; even refrigerators and heavy things were moved and then locked in, and the place was sealed. About two or three months later, when Mr. Gopal Das, son of Rai Bahadur Ram Saran Das, came to Lahore to fetch his movable property and I helped him to have the things packed, a number of refugee women belonging to high families of the East Punjab, who were working in the office of the Pakistan W.V.S., came to see me and tried to stop me from doing it. They said that their houses in Jullundur, Ludhiana and elsewhere, full of costly things, had been looted and they had lost everything. Why should Hindu refugees be allowed to take their things away? I replied that it was our duty to show them what honesty and integrity meant, and that old and valued associations had not been broken in spite of Partition. When Mr. Gopal Das learned how their things had been taken care of he came to thank us personally

Refugee women and children were suffering a great deal in camps, especially the orphan children, and we decided to put them in a spacious evacuee building. I contacted the Minister in charge and asked him to give us the Ganga Ram Girls School building, situated on Jail Road. He told me that the building had been reserved by the Education Department and advised me to ask them to lend it to us for the time being. The Secretary of Education agreed, the Department concerned gave the keys to me to have the building opened, and an Indian Christian magistrate was asked to accompany me. The rooms were opened, and before handing it over to the lady in charge I asked the magistrate to prepare two lists of all the furniture and other things, one to be given to the Superintendent and one to be kept by him. Sitting down to write, he asked me what he should put down in the list. I asked him what he meant by it; a list of everything in the building was to be prepared. He smiled and said that I was only the second person he had come across out of all those he had to deal with who had told him to write down everything in a list of this type.

Begum Liaquat Ali and I were working together in the organisation of such things as the work in the camps. The Pakistan W.V.S. were doing excellent work and I was told by the officers in charge of certain sections of the camp that when persons died and cholera was suspected, it was the women volunteers who would unhesitatingly lift the dead bodies when men refused to do so. Lahore public was wonderfully kind and whenever an appeal for food was made on the radio, regardless of the time of the day, shopkeepers, house-wives and others would immediately send to the camps whatever they possibly could. This was apart from the food which was pouring into the camps regularly every day. One day, when Rana Liaquat Ali and I went there late in the evening and our car drove through three rows of dead bodies on each side of the road, we found that thousands of people were without food, as the train carrying fuel had not arrived from Changamanga. It was nearly half past nine and even a radio appeal could not have got us the amount of cooked food required to feed thousands of refugees. We did not know what to do, and on my return home, just as I was getting out of the car, I fainted. It was impossible to forget the little faces of the hungry children and the cries of young people clamouring for food. Begum Liaquat Ali called the Punjab Cabinet and she gave them hell. Nawabzada Liaquat Ali used to relate how, on his return after an important Cabinet meeting at 11

287

p.m., he found the Punjab Ministers sitting wordless while Rana Liaquat Ali scolded them like little children.

The women volunteers had lifted over twenty little babies from the rows of dead bodies where their mothers lay. To get the refugees out of trains full of blood; women out of the carriages without shoes or even *dopattas* (scarfs) and often with hardly any clothes on, crying for those gone or left behind; to see so many orphaned girls and boys--all this was indeed most painful. I advised Begum Liaquat Ali to organise a Women's National Guard, which she did, and the first meeting was held at my house.

A number of people I came across suddenly started talking against Brigadier Sardar Muhammad Ayub Khan, the Muslim representative on the Boundary Force, and attributing to him the wrong policies that were resulting in bloodshed and suffering for the Muslim refugees. I was upset, because we knew how much Ayub had been doing to lessen the hardships suffered by Muslims and how he had been helping destitute Muslims in the trains and by the wayside. A number of my own relations had been brought to Lahore from Simla, from the refugee camp in the Delhi Fort and from Batala by the Boundary Force, in trains and trucks under their protection, and most of them were full of the kind help given to them by Sardar Ayub and his officers. I tried to probe the matter and, to my surprise, I found that some unwise Punjab officials, whom the public had approached, had been saying that these policies were being framed by the British General in command of the Boundary Force and Hindu Generals, with the help and advice of Sardar Ayub. Tazi and I contradicted such rumours and presented the real facts to the representatives of the public. When we talked to Sardar Ayub Khan about it, he told us what his difficulties were and said that he would like the Quaid-iAzam to know about them. I rang up Quaid-i-Azam and while I was talking to him he wanted to know what Brigadier Ayub's advice would be: when I told him that he was there with me, Quaid said that he would like to talk to him. Sardar Ayub told the Quaid-iAzam that the Boundary Force was not serving the purpose for which it had been organised and he advised him that it should be dissolved and they could take care of the work on the Pakistan side of the border. The Quaid-i-Azam moved in the matter and the Force was dissolved.

I received a letter from the Chief Minister, the Nawab of Mamdot, asking me to take charge of the work of bringing refugee girls from the East Punjab. I wrote a reply the very next day, saying that it would not be possible for me to do so because of my legislative work in both the assemblies, especially of the Constituent Assembly. The letter was despatched and delivered, and the peon book was signed by his secretary. After twenty-eight days, Mr. Biscoe, Divisional Superintendent of the N.W.R., came to see me and told me that the Nawab of Mamdot had complained to him about my not having sent a reply to such an important letter and that was why the work for bringing the abducted girls to Pakistan had been delayed. I looked at him in surprise, called my clerk and showed him the peon book. On ringing up the Chief Minister, I learned that the letter had been Iying all that time with his secretary, Wali Muhammad. Fatima Begum was asked to take charge of the work which had been pending because of the secretary's mistake.

(Excerpt from her autobiography *Father And Daughter*)

18

MEMORIES OF PARTITION

BY MIAN AMIRUDDIN

The Shahalmi area within the walled city of Lahore was the stronghold of the Hindus. It was like an impregnable fortress. Countless weapons and ammunition were stored there, and the Hindus were sure that nothing could happen to Shahalmi. But when we launched our (Molotov) cocktails the Shahalmi fort could not withstand the attack. As the locality burned down, the Hindus lost heart and began to move towards Amritsar. At some distance from the rear of my house there was a big Hindu mansion which served as a stockpile of arms and petrol. It was consumed in the flames of its own petrol.

There were many Hindus and Sikhs who had personal relations with the Muslims and had sought refuge with them. I myself rescued many Hindu and Sikh friends from their vulnerable residences and conveyed them to safe places under a hail of bullets. Dozens were taken to the railway station by me and put into trains. At a number of places in East Punjab non-Muslims gave refuge to their Muslim friends. But that terrible catastrophe did not affect personal and family relations. It raged at the national level. The Hindus and Sikhs were one nation, the Muslims another. It was a clash between two nations.

One day as I was returning home and passing before the residence of the late Hakim Faqir Muhammad Chishti 1 saw a Muslim boy running and being chased by a military officer and a soldier. The boy said to me. "They want my metal helmet." I asked the two men what was up when the boy ran way and hid in the entrance of my house which was nearby. The two of them pointed their guns at me and asked, "Tell us, where is that boy hiding?" as if I was instrumental in letting him escape. God alone knows what prevented them from firing at me. Another day I was returning home a bit late from outside the city which came under curfew at about sunset. I was stopped by armed soldiers. I had to tell them that I was Mayor of Lahore and I too had some responsibility for maintaining the peace and for that I had to go out. They wouldn't let me go ahead. So, re-tracing my steps, I spent the night with Qureshi Muhammad Zakir.

In those days of rioting and killing, there was one phenomenon that deserves special attention. People set fire to houses, and in the process they killed some one too, but they never touched valuables like gold and silver, expensive clothes and other precious objects. Things worth millions of rupees lay in the empty houses of Hindus and Sikhs till the actual Partition. I think it was when responsible persons claiming to be leaders sullied their hands with this loot that the common people shed their inhibition and began to follow suit.

It was really marvellous the way the Muslims of Amritsar put up a fight against the Hindus, and especially the Sikhs. The city was a stronghold of the Sikhs, but they fared badly at the hands of the Muslims. However, after the announcement of 3 June, when it became obvious that Punjab was to be divided, the Muslims too began to look at things from a more realistic angle. Before the Partition a sort of subsidiary administration had been set up for those

291

parts of Punjab and Bengal where non-Muslims were in a majority. Under this arrangement Muslim and non-Muslim officers began to be transferred to places where their co-religionists were in strength. Thus by the end of July dozens, in fact hundreds, of families had moved from Amritsar to the safety of Lahore. And as the actual day of Partition approached, more and more Muslim families from Amritsar shifted to Lahore. Similarly, the non-Muslims of Lahore were gradually moving towards Delhi and Jullundhur.

The result of this was that the first to get the best houses and the best properties of non-Muslims were the Muslims of Amritsar. There were groups which occupied palatial mansions and didn't know how to put off an electric fan. Around Partition day, whole caravans began to stream into Lahore from other districts of East Punjab too. One night we were told that about a hundred thousand refugees had arrived all of a sudden. We appealed to the inhabitants of Lahore that everyone should cook as much bread, *rotis*, as they could and deposit them in the nearest police station. The result was that by the morning we had a stock of almost a million *rotis*. We went to greet the caravan. Many of them were in such a state of shock and physical deterioration that they could only take a few sips of tea, but even this heartened them.

We brought one family to our house. Mian Aslam? my brother, took over a baby girl whose mother was dumb. Later the girl was married off to a relation of Mian Aslam's wife and still lives in his house. Another girl was adopted by Brother Aminuddin. She too was married to a well-off young man working in Glaxo and is very happy. I assumed responsibility for two boys and a girl. These girls too were ultimately married off and settled, but the boy wouldn't study and works as a chauffeur with us.

The people of Lahore gave a right royal reception to the newcomers. Cauldrons of rice could be seen cooking all over the place for distribution among the refugees. I had a whole stockpile of rice left with me by some Hindus. People would come to take this rice from me and spend their money on getting it cooked. I think even the poorest of Lahoris did not lag behind in this service.

There was the problem of housing the refugees in the property left by the departing Hindus and Sikhs. I said to the Deputy Commissioner that not every one was going to tell the truth about their social and economic status in East Punjab. So it would be advisable to get members of the legislative assembly and municipal commissioners of every city and town in East Punjab to undertake the allotment of evacuee houses to the refugees, for only those officials could certify their background. Also, many Muslims in Lahore had been tenants of non-Muslims, and they should not be ignored in the distribution of residential accommodation. I am sorry to say my advice was ignored. Everyone who came for a house was asked to fill up a form stating that he belonged to such-and-such place and his word about his status was accepted. The result was a terrible kind of mal-distribution. Some decent people who had been well-to-do back home could not get a hut to live in while liars and unscrupulous persons became the owners of palatial mansions.

Many of the latter obtained the forms free and then sold them to their own friends and acquaintances. Some of the experiences were most painful. Lost sisters and killed mothers were forgotten in the process of grabbing houses, and nobody seemed to be bothered about the girls abducted in East Punjab and the insolence and cruelty gone through during the journey to Pakistan. I could never imagine that the memory of the sufferers could be so short, Refugees began to loot refugees, and the new game wiped out from their minds all images of what they had gone through, let alone any thought of seeking vengeance for the bloody deeds witnessed by them.

I had also advised the Deputy Commissioner that all shops should be sealed and whoever was given one worth a lakh of rupees should be asked to pay Rs 60,000 to the government at his convenience. The government was hard-pressed for funds, for it had no money. But no regulatory system could be devised. Soon there was such a mad rush for shops that one couldn't even imagine the likes of it. Officers who belonged to East Punjab began to show favours to refugees from their area. Those from IJP did not consider anyone else as a genuine refugee, and behaved as if all others had come to Lahore for sight-seeing. Officers from Jullundhur would only patronise Jullundhris, particularly the Pathans from that district broke all bounds and limits of equity in their favouritism and nepotism. Same was the case with officers and refugees from Ambala.

In the distribution, or rather, looting of movable property too justice and honesty were nowhere to be seen. Those with clout and influence set the ball rolling, and their corrupt example was followed by their underlings and by the general public. Take just one case. In the Lahore Fort goods worth lakhs were stored. In today's currency it would be worth crores. But they were auctioned away --- an article worth a hundred rupees went for ten rupees, and the official in charge of the auction took his cut. I live near the fort and I saw all this with my own eyes. The dishonesty and corruption were on a gargantuan scale.

There was an institution, the Lahore Poor House, near Badshahi Mosque. Located inside Masti Gate it was run by the Hindus as a welfare home and did very useful work. One day an inmate rang me up that the police wanted the keys to the food go down. I rushed to the place, stopped the police from going ahead and informed the Director of

Food, I.U.Khan. Only the *moong daal* lying there was valued at Rs 36,000. All the stocks were then shifted to the Food Department leaving two sacks of the *daal* for the use of the inmates.

There are so many memories connected with the days of Partition. Some of the incidents are still very clear in my mind. Once, a few days before actual independence day, when Muslims were being killed in East Punjab, I was told that sixty Muslim cadets from the Indian Military Academy in Dehra Dun were leaving by train to report back after a vacation. It was obvious that their lives would be in danger while travelling through East Punjab, but the boys were adamant that they must go for it was a matter of military discipline. They were all around 14 years of age. It was imperative that they should be stopped at once because their train was ready to leave after some time. Not knowing what to do I rushed to Nawab Mamdot so that he should take some steps. He pleaded his inability to help. In a panic I picked up the telephone directory and started ringing up various numbers on Lahore railway station. After getting many Hindu and Sikhs officials I at last connected a Muslim railway man, a Train Examiner. He was impressed by my story and promised to find fault with the brakes of the train. This he did, for the train could not start its journey without the Train Examiner's giving his OK to the brakes. In the meantime measures were adopted to detain the boys.

On another occasion too a Train Examiner came to our help. Someone informed me on telephone that a train fully loaded with military equipment was about to leave for India from the Cantonment railway station. I talked to Zafrul Ahsan, the Deputy Commissioner. He told me there was a telegram from the supreme commander that the train be allowed to move out. In desperation I rang up Ghulam Ahmed, the Cantonment Magistrate and asked him to do something to prevent the train from leaving Lahore. At the same time I made a mention of the powers of Train Examiners. Ghulam Ahmed immediately arranged with the relevant Train Examiner to prohibit the train's departure.

Again, one day when Qurban Ali Khan, Inspector General of Police, was sitting with me, we received telephonic information that a train with currency notes worth crores of rupees was to leave soon for India. The report had come from Mian Anwar Ali, DIG. He was directed to detain the train, but he expressed doubt whether he could do so without the approval of Mr. Liaquat Ali Khan, and it was too late in the night to contact him. This time too we adopted the stratagem of failed brakes and had the train stopped with the help of a Train Examiner. Soon afterwards we found that the currency notes were actually being sent to Karachi, not India, for they were torn and soiled and had to be destroyed. So we immediately made the train brakes workable!

The war in Kashmir had started and petrol was in short supply there. Some of us managed to collect 18,000 gallons of petrol but the question was how to convey it to the place where it was needed. Colonel Dara and other friends were perplexed. I suddenly had a brain wave and got the water tankers of the Lahore Corporation filled with the petrol. The convoy left for its destination under the command of Colonel Dara. So what if the roads of Lahore were not sprinkled with water for a couple of days! Thus I found that if the will is there a way can be found, but you also need guts. Actually this petrol was meant to be despatched to Jammu which had already been occupied by India, but some patriotic-minded person had detained it in Lahore. The only problem was how to send it to the Kashmir front, and this is where the Corporation's water tankers came in useful.

There was another incident that deserves mention. During the last days of 1947 or early 1948, Chaudhry

Ghulam Abbas and Sardar Muhammad Ibrahim had suggested that the extensive property of Majarajah Hari Singh in Lahore and its environs should be handed over to Azad Kashmir so that refugees from occupied Kashmir could be monetarily helped. They had met the Deputy Commissioner but he had disappointed them. Even Nawab Mamdot, Chief Minister of West Punjab, had turned down the request. As a last resort they came to me to find a way out.

I sent for Maharajah Hari Singh's Agent, a Kashmiri Muslim and put the proposal before him. He went away saying that he sympathized with our programme but was helpless. He was the Maharajah's personal servant and couldn't be disloyal to him. Chaudhry Ghulam Abbas was dejected and wanted to leave but I asked him to stay on till my return. I then briefed one of my servants, Badruddin by name, to show the Agent's residence to a group of young men who should go there and make a demonstration against him. He must make sure that the boys are equipped with bamboo staves. Then, when the demonstration was at its loudest he (Badruddin) should reach there and tell the boys that I was annoyed at this show of force and that they should not harass the Agent Sahib and disperse peacefully. This Badruddin did, with the result that the Agent was overtaken by panic and ran away from Lahore.

I directed the employees of his office to come to me with all the documents of the property. Then I sent a message to the main tenants of Landa Bazaar and Serai Sultan to come over and see me. I asked them, "Do you want to pay rent to Hindus or to Muslims?" They did not need much conviction, so new lease deeds were got signed from them. The same I did in the case of sixty squares of land at Jallo and asked the agricultural tenants whether they wanted to pay rent to the Hindu Maharajah or to Muslim Kashmir. In their case too new papers were drawn up and signed. A similar procedure was followed in regard to Haveli Dhyan Singh in the walled city and the Sunnyview Hotel. All these properties worth crores of rupees were transferred in the name of a committee. Later when Mr Mushtaq Ahmed Gurmani became Minister for Kashmir Affairs he praised the manner in which I had enriched the Azad Kashmir government. The income is still being received by that government.

(Excerpts translated from his autobiography *Yaad-i-Ayyam*)

CONTRIBUTORS

Gopal Mittal

Gopal Mittal, the noted Urdu writer and poet, was born in Malerkotla. After graduation in 1932, he moved to Ludhiana but soon left for Lahore, where he spent a major and significant part of his life. During 1932-47, he was intimately connected with the literary, journalistic and political events. During these years he played varied roles: editor, translator, journalist, political activist and trade union leader.

His famous autobiographical account *Lahore Ka Jo Zikr Kiya* is a blend of personal reminiscences and of momentous historical events in the Indo-Pak sub-continent. After partition, he made Delhi his home. He started monthly *Tehreek* a literary and socio-political journal. Besides editing *Tehreek*, he also wrote poetry. His most famous poetry collection, *"Sehra Mein Azan"* is the work of a mature mind.

Madan Lal Khurana

Madan Lal Khurana was born in Lyallpur (present Faisalabad, Pakistan) in 1936. He was only 11 years old when he left his native town for India. In India, he rose to the position of Chief Minister of Delhi.

Alys Faiz

Alys Faiz was born in London. She came to Amritsar, India in 1938 to visit her sister Christabel Taseer and her brother-in-law, Dr. M. D. Taseer. Dr. Taseer was then Principal of M.A.O College, Amritsar, where Faiz Ahmed Faiz was a lecturer in English.

In 1941, Dr. Taseer was invited to become Principal of S.P College, Srinagar. Faiz and Alys were married in Srinagar the same year. Their nikah was performed by Sheikh Abdullah of Kashmir.

Alys Faiz has been both teacher and journalist during the long years that she has lived in India and Pakistan. She taught in Simla, Amritsar, Karachi and Lahore. She edited the Women's and Children pages of *The Pakistan Time* from 1951 to 1962.

She has always been associated with a number of social welfare agencies, has worked with UNICEF in Islamabad and as Assistant Editor in *Viewpoint*, an English language weekly of Lahore.

She has two married daughters and four grand-children. She lives permanentlty in Lahore.

Satish Gujral

Satish Gujral was born in Jhelum, West Punjab, in December 1925. He studied at the Mayo School of Arts, Lahore, and later at the JJ School of Arts, Bombay. Following Partition, the family moved to the Indian half of the Punjab. Satish Gujral worked as a graphic artist with the Punjab government for two years. In 1952 he won a scholarship to study art in Mexico, where he apprenticed himself to David Alfaro Siqueiros and collaborated on murals with Diego Rivera. Since his return to India in 1954, he has lived in New Delhi.

Over the past five decades he has achieved world renown and critical acclaim for his work as painter, sculptor, muralist, graphic designer and architect. He is married to Kiran Ram Nath, an artist in her own right, who is deeply involved in crafts and interior design. They have a son and two daughters.

Satish Gujral has won numerous national and international awards. He is an honorary fellow of the Indian Institute of Architecture. He has been honoured by the states of Punjab and Delhi. His name is included in the International Dictionary of Arts and Artists published by Macmillan (UK).

Som Anand

Som Anand, born in Lahore, spent his childhood and youth in that city where his father, Faqir Chand Anand, was a respected banker. Som grew up totally free of religious bias, maybe because he always consorted with Muslims who shared his world-view. When partition took place, the Anands decided to stay on in Model Town, Lahore, and Som was a witness to the communal excesses which took place at the time. In this loving and sensitive memoir, which recalls a pre-partition Lahore of harmony and peace, Som seeks to restore his spiritual links with the great city of his childhood.

In Model Town, the suburban hide-out of the wealthy aristocracy, the Hindus and Muslims lived in social isolation from each other but were friendly. In Ichhra, a Lahore suburban village, Som moved about with the followers of Allama Mashriqi, founder of the Khaksar movement. In the walled city, he mixed with the Fakirs of Fakir Khana. He saw Ataullah Shah Bukhari calm down a crowed that had just broken the head of Zafar Ali Khan, the editor of *Zamindar*. He was friendly with the Bedis, and knew Englishwoman Freda Bedi who wrote her book about Punjabi women while she waited for her communist husband to be released from prison.

Som Anand was a columnist for *Imroze* Lahore, for five years until the paper and its sister publication, *The Pakistan Times*, were overtaken by the martial law regime of F M Ayub Khan. Eventually, Som left for India where he now works as a freelance journalist.

Sir Muhammad Zafrullah Khan

Sir Muhammad Zafrullah Khan, Pakistan's first foreign minister after independence, later rose to become President of the General Assembly of the United Nations and President of the International Court of Justice at The Hague.

His memoirs, edited by Ashiq Hussain Batalvi, shed fascinating light on the men and events that have shaped the post-second world war history of our times. The personality of Sir Zafrullah which emerges from the book is an engaging one, of a man who was gentle, unassertive and introverted. *Tehdith-i-Nemat* is his famous autobiography.

Khushwant Singh

Khushwant Singh, a distinguished writer and best-known columnist of India was born in 1915 in Hadali, now in Pakistan, and educated at Government College Lahore, King's College, and the Inner Temple in London. After he gave up his law practice he joined the

Indian Ministry of Foreign Affairs in 1947, and was sent on diplomatice postings to Canada and London, and later to Paris with UNESCO.

His journalistic career spans almost five decades, during which he was the editor of celebrated publications such as *Yojna* (1951-3), *The Illustrated Weekly of India* (1969-79), *National Herald* (1978-9), and *The Hindustan Times* (1980-3).

His first novel, *Train to Pakistan* won him the Grove Press Award for the best work of fiction in 1954. His other novels include *I Shall Not Hear the Nightingale* and *Delhi*. He has also published a two-volume scholarly history of the Sikhs, several translated works, and a non-fiction work on Delhi, its nature and current affairs.

Khushwant Singh was a Member of Parliament (1980-6), and received numerous awards in recognition of his literary attainments. In 1984 He returned the Padma Bhushan, awarded him in 1974, in the wake of the Golden Temple tragedy.

Prakash Tandon

Parkash Tandon was born in 1911 at the headworks of Balloki Dam on the river Ravi in Pakistani Punjab. His father was an irrigation engineer with the government and was posted frequently to various places in West and South Punjab, the family shifting with him to each new posting. Parkash Tandon took a degree in science from Government College, Lahore in 1929, and then went to England where he studied commerce at the University of Manchester and later qualified as a chartered accountant. Upon his return to India in 1937, he joined the Unilever subsidiary and eventually became its first Indian chairman. He left the company in 1968 to join the public sector, first as chairman of the State Trading Corporation of India for four years, and then of the Punjab National Bank for three years. He has served on the boards of several other institutions such as the Reserve Bank of India, the Food Corporation of India, Hindustan Steel and Hindustan Aeronautics and has been part of several committees formed by the states and the central government. He has taught at Berkeley, Boston, California, Chandigarh, Delhi and Ahmedabad. The three books that comprise his autobiography---*Punjabi Century, Beyond Punjab* and *Return to Punjab*---are regarded as modern classics and are published together in Penguin Books as *Punjabi Saga*.

Fikr Taunsvi

Fikr Taunsvi was born in 1918 in Taunsa Sharif (South Punjab, Pakistan). He began as a literary journalist in Lahore and served on the editorial staff of *'Savera'* and *'Adab-i-Lateef'*. He went away to India after Partition and wrote some excellent stories, *'Chhatta Darya'*(Lahore diary of 1947) and *'Satwan Asman'* being the most well-known, on the havoc caused by partition. A noted columnist, his *'Pyaz ke Chhike'* appeared in *'Naya Zamana'* and *'Milan'* with unfailing regularity for 25 years. From the time Awadh Punch was published in Lucknow, humour and satire occupied a prominent place in Urdu literature. Fikr Taunsvi enriched this tradition. He was a gifted writer with acute sensitivity to human tragedies. He died in 1987.

Pran Nevile

Pran Nevile was born and educated in Lahore. An M.A. in Economics from Government College, he began his career as a journalist in the Ministry of Information and Broadcasting. He was later inducted into the Indian Foreign Service which he left prematurely to join the United Nations Conference on Trade and Development (UNCTAD).

A freelance writer since his retirement, Nevile has contributed articles to leading newspapers and journals on a variety of subjects, besides economics. *'Lahore: A Sentimental Journey'* is his first full-length literary work.

B. C. Sanyal

B. C. Sanyal was born in Dibrugarh, Assam in 1902. He lost his father Charu Chandra Sanyal when he was only four years old. His first introduction to a work of art was an oleograph print of King Edward VII in his classroom which was later replaced by that of King George V. He joined Serampur College in 1920. And made frequent visits to Calcutta. The special Congress Session was a great attraction for him. At the same time, he attended lectures at the University Institute of Calcutta by eminent speakers like Sir Surendra Nath Banerjee, B. P. Pal, Annie Besant. He gave up general studies and joined the Government School of Art, Calcutta in 1923.

During his time in the Art School he received two awards in sculpture from the Calcutta Society of Fine Arts. However, the six years which he spent at the Art school left a sense of unfulfilment in him.

Sanyal left for Lahore in 1929. The purpose was to prepare a bust-portrait of Lala Lajpat Rai who had died due to police beating in Lahore. Almost at the same time as Bhagat Singh was executed by the British, Sanyal finished Lajpat Rai's portrait amidst political unrest. In early 1930's he joined the Mayo School of Art. He was given charge of the painting and modeling departments. He then decided to make Lahore his home.

He set up a studio at the Forman Christian College in mid 1930's. In 1936, he started a new studio-cum-teaching workshop in the Dayal Singh Building on the Mall. The inauguration of the studio took place with an exhibition of paintings, the first of its kind in Lahore.

During 1936-47, he took part in the discussions on Socialist Realism initiated by Indian poets, writers and other creative people. At about this time he met Snehlata his future wife. He attended the Kisan Conferences at Bhakna and Jhandiala villages in Punjab. When the Second World War broke out, he sent sketches of his anti-Japanese posters to Delhi.

After partition, he moved to Delhi. He still lives in Nizamuddin Delhi, a young and energetic artist of 99 of years.

Amrita Pritam

Amrita Pritam was born in August 1919 in Gujranwala. A poet, novelist and short story writer, she has more than seventy-five books to her credit. She is the first woman recipient of the Sahitya Akademi Award in 1956 which she won for *Sunehre* a collection of Poems. She received the *Padma Shree* from the President of India in 1969.

She received the Vaptsarov Award (International) from Bulgaria in 1980 and "Bhartiya Jnanpith" award in 1982 for a collection of poems *Kagaz Te Kanvas. She ib by far the most articulate and* uninhibited *among women writers of India.*
She has also been a Member of the Rajya Sabha..

Begam Jahanara Shah Nawaz

Jahanara Shah Nawaz, born in 1896, belonged to the Arain Muslim community. She was the daughter of Sir Muhammad Shafi. She was educated in Queen Mary's College, Lahore and married Mian Shah Nawaz, a leading criminal lawyer of Lahore.

Jahanara entered public life very early. She participated in All India Muslim League politics but was elected as a Unionist member of the Punjab Legislative Assembly in 1937, and relected in 1946. She was Parliamentary Secretary, Education and Public Health, during 1937-43.

She was elected as a member of the Constituent Assembly of Pakistan in 1947 and played an important part in Pakistani politics also.

Jahanara Shah Nawaz is author of *Father And Daughter* (an autobiography) and an Urdu novel *Husan Ara Bergum*

SELECT BIBLIOGRAPHY

A. Primary Sources

1. Fikr Taunsvi, Chhata Darya-Eik Diary, Naya Idara, Lahore, 1948.
2. Ibrahim Jalees, Doa Mulk, Eik Kahani, Naya Idara, n.d.
3. Gopal Mittal, Lahore Ka Jo Zikr Kiya, Maktaba-i-Urdu Adab, Lahore, n.d.
4. Mushirul Hasan (Ed.) India Partitioned, the other face of Freedom, 1947-1997, Jubilee Edition, Vols. 1&2, Revised and Enlarged edition, Roli Books, New Delhi, 1997.
5. Jahan Ara Shahnawaz, Father And Daughter, A Political Autobiography, Nigarishat, Lahore, 1971.
6. Anees Jillani (Ed.) Partition: Surgery Without Anesthesia, SPARC, Islamabad, 1998.
7. Common Heritage, Oxford University Press, Karachi, 1997.
8. Som Anand, Lahore-Portrait of a Lost city, Vanguard Books, Lahore, 1998.
9. A. H. Batalvi, The Forgotten years, Memoirs of Sir Muhammad Zafrullah Khan, Vanguard Books, Lahore, 1991.
10. Alys Faiz, Over my shoulder, The Frontier Post Publications, Lahore, 1993.
11. Satish Gujral, a brush with life, Viking, New Delhi, 1997.
12. Santo Datta (Ed.) The Vertical Woman, Reminiscences of B. C. Sanyal 1902-1947, National Gallory of Modern Art, New Delhi, 1998.
13. Parkash Tandon, Punjabi Saga 1857-1987, The Monumental Story of Five Generations. A Remarkable Punjabi Family, Penguin Books, New Delhi, 1988.
14. Amrita Pritam, The Revenue Stamp, an autobiography, Tarang Paperbacks Vikas Publishing House Pvt. Ltd, New Delhi, 1994.
15. Dev Bhardwaj, Gurdev Chauhan (Ed) Amrita Pritam-A Living Legend.

B. Further Readings.

1. Shauna Singh Baldwin, What The Body Remembers, Transworld Publishers, London, 1999.
2. Richard Symonds, In The Margins of Independence, A Relief Worker in India and Pakistan, 1942-1949, Oxford University Press, Karachi, 2001.
3. Sucheta Mahajan, Independence and Partition, Sage Publications, New Delhi, 2000.
4. Ranabir Samaddar, Vikas Publishing House Pvt. Ltd., New Delhi, 1997.
5. Stephen Alter, Amritsar to Lahore, crossing the Border Between India & Pakistan. Punjab Books India, New Delhi, 2000.
6. S. R. Chakravarty, Mazhar Hussain (Ed.), Partition of India, Literary Responses, Har-Anand Publications, New Delhi.
7. Ian Talbot and Gurharpal Singh (Ed.), Region & Partitions, Bengal, Punjab and the partition of the Sub continent, Oxford University Press, Karachi, 1999.
8. Mushirul Hasan (Ed.), Inventing Boundaries, Gender, Politics and the Partition of India, Oxford University Press, New Delhi, 2000.
9. Amrik Singh (Ed.), The Partition In Retrospect, Ananika Publishers & Distributors (P) Ltd., New Delhi, 2000.